Desire and Motivation in Indian Philosophy

Desireless action is typically cited as a criterion of the liberated person in classical Indian texts. Contemporary authors argue with near unanimity that since all action is motivated by desire, desireless action is a contradiction. They conclude that desireless action is action performed without certain desires; other desires are permissible.

In this book, the author surveys the contemporary literature on desireless action and argues that the arguments for the standard interpretation are unconvincing. He translates, interprets, and evaluates passages from a number of seminal classical Sanskrit texts, and argues that the doctrine of desireless action should indeed be taken literally, as the advice to act without any desire at all. The author argues that the theories of motivation advanced in these texts are not only consistent, but plausible.

This book is the first in-depth analysis of the doctrine of desireless action in Indian philosophy. It serves as a reference to both contemporary and classical literature on the topic.

Christopher G. Framarin is Assistant Professor in the Departments of Philosophy and Religious Studies at the University of Calgary, Canada. His areas of research are Indian philosophy, philosophy of religion, and ethics.

Routledge Hindu Studies Series
Series Editor: Gavin Flood, University of Stirling
Former Series Editor: Francis X. Clooney, SJ, Harvard University

The *Routledge Hindu Studies Series*, in association with the Oxford Centre for Hindu Studies, intends the publication of constructive Hindu theological, philosophical and ethical projects aimed at bringing Hindu traditions into dialogue with contemporary trends in scholarship and contemporary society. The series invites original, high-quality, research-level work on religion, culture and society of Hindus living in India and abroad. Proposals for annotated translations of important primary sources and studies in the history of the Hindu religious traditions will also be considered.

Epistemologies and the Limitations of Philosophical Inquiry
Doctrine in Mādhva Vedānta
Deepak Sarma

A Hindu Critique of Buddhist Epistemology
Kumārila on Perception
The "Determination of Perception" Chapter of Kumārila Bhaṭṭa's *Ślokarvārttika*
Translation and Commentary
John Taber

Samkara's Advaita Vedanta
A Way of Teaching
Jacqueline Hirst

Attending Kṛṣṇa's Image
Caitanya Vaiṣṇava Mūrti-sevā as Devotional Truth
Kenneth Russell Valpey

Advaita Vedānta and Vaiṣṇavvism
The Philosophy of Madhusūdana Sarasvatī
Sanjukta Gupta

Classical Sāṃkhya and Yoga
An Indian Metaphysics of Experience
Mikel Burley

Self-surrender (Prapatti) to God In Śrīvaiṣṇavvism
Tamil Cats and Sanskrit Monkeys
Srilata Raman

The Caitanya Vaiṣṇava Vedānta of Jīva Gosvāmī
When Knowledge Meets Devotion
Ravi M. Gupta

Gender and Narrative in the *Mahābhārata*
Edited by Simon Brodbeck and
Brian Black

Yoga in the Modern World
Contemporary Perspectives
Edited by Mark Singleton and
Jean Byrne

Consciousness in Indian Philosophy
The Advaita Doctrine of 'Awareness Only'
Sthaneshwar Timalsina

Desire and Motivation in Indian Philosophy
Christopher G. Framarin

Desire and Motivation in Indian Philosophy

Christopher G. Framarin

Routledge
Taylor & Francis Group
LONDON AND NEW YORK

First published 2009
by Routledge
2 Park Square, Milton Park, Abingdon, Oxon OX14 4RN

Simultaneously published in the USA and Canada
by Routledge
711 Third Avenue, New York, NY 10017

Routledge is an imprint of the Taylor & Francis Group, an informa business

First issued in paperback 2012

Typeset in Times New Roman by
RefineCatch Limited, Bungay, Suffolk

British Library Cataloguing in Publication Data
A catalogue record for this book is available from the British Library

Library of Congress Cataloging-in-Publication Data
Framarin, Christopher G.
Desire and Motivation in Indian Philosophy /
Christopher G. Framarin
p. cm.—(Routledge Hindu studies series ; 12)
Includes bibliographical references and index.
1. Desire (Philosophy) 2. Philosophy, Hindu. 3. Desire—Religious aspects—Hinduism. 4. Motivation (Psychology)—Religious aspects—Hinduism. 5. Hinduism—Doctrines. 6. Bhagavadgita—Criticism, interpretation, etc. I. Title.
B132.D48F73 2009
170.954—dc22

2008036785

ISBN13: 978–0–415–46194–8 (hbk)
ISBN13: 978–0–203–88367–9 (ebk)
ISBN13: 978–0–415–62757–3 (pbk)

Dedicated to Jennifer

Contents

Preface xii
Acknowledgments xiv
Foreword xvi

Introduction 1

Context and overview 1
Some notes on translation 3

1 **Four interpretations of desireless action** 4

The basic argument 5
Three interpretations 6
A fourth interpretation 15
A second justification for the Some Desires Interpretation 21

2 **Desireless action in the *Yogasūtra*** 23

The first condition of permissible desires 24
The second condition of permissible desires 29
An analysis of value 31
Permissible and impermissible desires in the Yogasūtra 34

3 **The desire for *Mokṣa*** 41

Three versions of the Some Desires Interpretation 42
The Mokṣa*-only Interpretation 44*
Four arguments for the Mokṣa*-only Interpretation 46*
A fifth argument for the Mokṣa*-only Interpretation 57*

4 **Unselfish desires** 60

Unselfishness 61

Three versions of the No Selfish Desires Interpretation 62
A fourth version of the No Selfish Desires Interpretation 74

5 Desireless action in the *Manusmṛti* 76

Motivation in the Manusmṛti 77
Two Humean objections 80
A reconsideration of the Bhagavadgītā 88
A reconsideration of the Yogasūtra 92

6 Desireless action in the *Nyāyasūtra* and *Brahmasiddhi* 93

The Basic Nyāya–Vedāntin debate 94
The standard interpretation 97
Objections to the standard account 100
The revised account 103
A reconsideration of the second argument for the Some Desires Interpretation 109

7 A defense of desireless action 110

The direction of fit argument: a preliminary formulation 111
An objection and reply 115
Additional objections 117

Conclusion 123

Adaptations of the Some Desires Interpretations 123
A final objection 126

Appendix i 127
Appendix ii 142
Appendix iii 155

Notes 172
References 189
Index 195

As soon as the will begins to cast a covetous eye on the outcome, the individual begins to become immoral.

Søren Keirkegaard
(Kierkegaard 1992: 35)

Preface

In the fall of 2000 I took a graduate seminar on the *Bhagavadgītā* at the University of Hawai'i from Arindam Chakrabarti. During the second or third week of the semester, we considered the problem of desireless action. The final two verses of the second chapter of the *Gītā* read:[1]

> The person who, having abandoned all desires (*sarvān karmān*), acts without desire (*niḥspṛhaḥ*), without a sense of mineness (*nirmama*), without a sense of self (*nirahaṅkāra*), that person attains peace.
>
> This is establishment in Brahman (*brāhmī sthitiḥ*), O Arjuna. Having attained this, one is not confused. Established [in this] even at the time of death, a person reaches cessation in *Brahman* (*brahmanirvāṇam*).
>
> (2.71–72, Sadhale 1985a: 242, line 9 and 243, lines 27–28)[2]

A friend of mine raised what might be a devastating objection: if one is perfectly desireless, then one cannot act. So desireless action is a contradiction. If desireless action is a condition of attaining liberation, then liberation is impossible.

Most of the other students in the class attempted to defend the *Gītā* from the charge of absurdity. Our replies to the objection, however, were much less successful than my friend's refutations of our replies. Someone said, "Arjuna fights for the sake of maintaining the order of the world (*lokasaṃgraha*)," and my friend replied, "then he desires the maintenance of the order of the world!" Another said, "he fights because it is his duty," and he replied, "then he desires to do his duty!" In the meanwhile, I had one nascent thought. "There has to be something more to this injunction to act desirelessly."

I know now that a nearly identical conversation occurs regularly among students of Indian philosophy. I have had the conversation many times since. A similar conversation also occurs among western philosophy students who study Aristotle, Hume, Kant, or contemporary philosophers who write on motivation. The same basic assumption invariably dominates these discussions: If an agent acts intentionally, it follows that they desire something.

In the fall of 2001, I began my PhD work at the University of New Mexico, and took an ethics seminar with my eventual supervisor, Fred Schueler. I read Schueler's *Desire: Its Role in Practical Reason and the Explanation of Action*, in which he claims that the word 'desire' is ambiguous. In one sense, it refers to the agent's purpose or reason for acting. In another sense, it refers more narrowly to a certain type of mental state that can be contrasted with beliefs, intentions, and so on. Schueler argues that desire in the first sense, but not the second, is entailed by action.[3]

Since then, I have come to agree that desire in the latter sense is not entailed by action, and that desireless action is not only coherent, but plausible. The more important point, however, is that even if it turns out that the so-called Humeans are correct, and there is an entailment between action and desire of this sort, the entailment is not obvious enough to serve as a constraint on the interpretation of Indian texts. Even if desire is entailed by action, it does not follow that we must assume that all Indian texts are consistent with this claim.

I have found, however, that most contemporary authors who write on desireless action in the Indian context do simply assume from the outset, with little or no explanation, that Kṛṣṇa's advice to act without desire cannot be taken literally. I began to wonder if the supposed problem of desireless action did not depend on confusing the two senses of 'desire' that Schueler distinguishes. This book is the result of the investigations that began in this way.

Among other things, I have learned that many of the mistakes that contemporary scholars make in analyzing desireless action – and probably any other topic in comparative philosophy – have as much, if not more, to do with misunderstanding our own western concepts and doctrines than with the obscurity of the Sanskrit texts themselves.

Acknowledgments

First, I want to thank my advisors, Fred Schueler and John Taber, at the University of New Mexico. Both guided me through my dissertation, in which I began to develop some of the ideas contained in this book. I worked extensively with John on previous drafts of the translations of the *Manusmṛti*, *Nyāyasūtra*, *Brahmasiddhi*, and their commentaries. Fred read a later draft of Chapter 7 and provided helpful feedback. John read a draft of Chapter 4 and helped me to improve it. I also thank Arindam Chakrabarti, my MA advisor and dissertation committee member, for encouraging and inspiring me to pursue both Indian and so-called analytic philosophy.

My thanks also to Richard Hayes, Brent Kalar, Kelly Becker, Jeremy Fantl, Terry Penelhum, Simon Brodbeck, Christian Wood, Kristian Simcox, Mark Migotti, Elizabeth Brake, Dennis McKerlie, Ann Levey, Morny Joy, Tinu Ruparell, Michael McGhee, Frank Clooney, Vincent Shen, Dan Lusthaus, Christina Yanko, and Hans Wiens for feedback on portions of this book and/or discussions about its content. And thanks to Walter H. Maurer, my first Sanskrit teacher.

I am also grateful to the University of New Mexico's Watumull fellowship, which supported my research during the 2004/2005 school year, and the Departments of Philosophy and Religious Studies at the University of Calgary, to whom I presented drafts of chapters 4 and 5. My thanks to Gavin Flood, Dorothea Schaefter, and Suzanne Chilestone at Routledge.

My deep appreciation to my family – Armand, Pam, Meg, Kyle, Olivia, Chiara, Jim, MaryAnn, Mara, Adam, Annalise, Aaron, and Rachael – for their support. And most of all, thanks to my wife Jennifer and my son Henry, for their support and sacrifice.

Portions of this book are based on previously published material. Chapter 4 is an edited version of "Unselfishness," published in *International Philosophical Quarterly*, vol. 48, 69–83 (© *International Philosophical Quarterly*). The first half of Chapter 5 is a revised version of "Motivation in the *Manusmṛti*," *Journal of Indian Philosophy*, vol. 34, 604–617 (© Springer). The first half of Chapter 6 is a revised version of the first half of "Motivation in the *Nyāyasūtra* and *Brahmasiddhi*," *Religious Studies*, vol. 44, 43–61 (© Cambridge University Press). Some of my arguments in Chapter 6 are based on arguments first presented in my paper, "The Desire You are Required to Get Rid of: A Functionalist Analysis of Desire in the *Bhagavadgītā*," *Philosophy East and West*, vol. 56, 604–617 (© *Philosophy East and West*). My thanks to each of these publishers for their consent to use this material.

Foreword

The Routledge Hindu Studies Series, published in collaboration with the Oxford Centre for Hindu Studies, intends primarily the publication of constructive Hindu theological, philosophical, and ethical projects. The focus is on issues and concerns of relevance to readers interested in Hindu traditions in particular, yet also in the context of a wider range of related religious concerns that matter in today's world. The Series seeks to promote excellent scholarship and, in relation to it, an open and critical conversation among scholars and the wider audience of interested readers. Though contemporary in its purpose, the Series recognizes the importance of retrieving the classic texts and ideas, beliefs and practices, of Hindu traditions, so that the great intellectuals of these traditions may as it were become conversation partners in the conversations of today.

Questions in the philosophy of action and philosophy of mind about the nature of action in relation to causation, ethics and purpose have long been debated in philosophy departments. This book is a welcome contribution to the study of action in an Indian philosophical context. The author examines the coherence of the idea of desireless action with particular reference to the *Bhagavad Gītā* and raises philosophical questions about ethics, grounding his arguments in Indian philosophy. The author argues from an examination of the texts as well as close reasoning, that the concept is not incoherent and, indeed, a central idea in notions of liberation and what the purposes of life are. The book is not simply a descriptive account of desireless action in the *Gītā* and Indian philosophical traditions but is also a philosophical account that argues for the coherence of the idea and its potential for human values. This is a thought-provoking and engaging book that makes us reconsider the idea of desireless action in the *Gītā* and makes us think about its philosophical value and coherence.

Introduction

Context and overview

In this book I am concerned with the well-known, if not well-understood, doctrine of desireless action. My analysis is limited to the so-called orthodox Indian traditions – those that accept the authority of the Vedas.[1]

There are many references to desire and desirelessness in the *Upaniṣads*.[2] The most famous formulation of desireless action, however, is in the second chapter of the *Bhagavadgītā*. The final two verses of the chapter read:

> The person who, having abandoned all desires (*sarvān karmān*), acts without desire (*nisspṛhaḥ*), without a sense of mineness (*nirmama*), without a sense of self (*nirahaṅkāra*), that person attains peace.
>
> This is establishment in Brahman (*brāhmī sthitiḥ*), O Arjuna. Having attained this, one is not confused. Established [in this] even at the time of death, a person reaches cessation in Brahman (*brahmanirvāṇam*).
>
> (2.71–72, Sadhale 1985a: 242, line 9 and 243, lines 27–28)[3]

In the *Gītā's* commentarial tradition, the injunction to act without desire is referred to as *niṣkāma karma* – literally, action (*karma*) without (*niṣ*) desire (*kāma*).[4] Since the phrase *niṣkāma karma* is well-known and often used, I will occasionally use it, particularly when discussing the *Bhagavadgītā*. Generally, however, I will use the phrase 'desireless action' instead. The primary reason for this is that all of the texts I consider – including the *Bhagavadgītā* – use a wide variety of words to refer to those discouraged states that are generally translated as 'desire' in English, such as *rāga*, *icchā*, *abhilāṣa*, and so on. *Niṣkāma karma*, therefore, is not always accurate shorthand.

Although I begin with a consideration of the *Gītā*, return to the *Gītā* throughout the book, and consider the objective of developing a plausible interpretation of the *Gītā's* doctrine of desireless action an important goal, I do not limit myself to the doctrine as it appears in the *Gītā*. Originally I wanted to look at other texts in order to understand the context of the claims made in the *Gītā*, and I think the other texts are helpful for that purpose. In its final version, however, this book offers a series of interrelated analyses of a range of seminal texts.

The standard interpretation of Kṛṣṇa's advice to act without desire goes as follows. Kṛṣṇa advises Arjuna to act without desire. Desire, however, is a necessary condition of action. Hence Kṛṣṇa's advice, if taken literally, is a contradiction. Hence Kṛṣṇa's advice should not be taken literally. Rather than advise the elimination of all desires, Kṛṣṇa advises the elimination of some desires. Others are permissible. I call this the 'Some Desires Interpretation'.

The argument for the Some Desires Interpretation is not as straightforward as it seems, however. In order to justify reverting to a less literal reading of the advice, the supposed inconsistency of Kṛṣṇa's advice must be so obvious that it is implausible to claim that the author of the *Gītā* failed to notice it. There is, however, a very lively debate among contemporary western philosophers over whether desire plays a necessary role in motivating action. It cannot be, then, that the claim that action entails desire is so obvious that it is implausible that the author of the *Gītā* denies it.

A second version of the argument for the Some Desires Interpretation avoids this problem. It states that the *Gītā* must be consistent with the claim that action entails desire, not because the claim is self-evident, but because the wider traditions of which the *Gītā* is a part widely accept the claim. If this is right, then a non-literal reading of the *Gītā* seems plausible.

With this background in mind, there are at least two questions that are central to the debate over how to interpret the doctrine of desireless action. First, if the Indian traditions widely claim that action entails desire, and the Some Desires Interpretation is correct, what distinguishes permissible desires from impermissible desires? Second, do the traditions widely claim that action entails desire?

As a means to answering the first question, I consider three seemingly plausible versions of the Some Desires Interpretation. According to the first – which I call the '*Mokṣa*-only Interpretation' – only a desire for *mokṣa* is permissible. All other desires are impermissible. According to the second – which I call the 'No Selfish Desires Interpretation' – only unselfish desires are permissible. Selfish desires are impermissible. According to the third – which I call the 'No Phenomenologically Salient Desires Interpretation' – only desires that lack phenomenological saliency are permissible. Desires that are phenomenologically salient are impermissible.

As a means to answering the second question, I analyze the theory of motivation in four additional seminal texts within the Indian traditions: the *Yogasūtra*, *Manusmṛti*, *Nyāyasūtra*, and *Brahmasiddhi*, along with their commentaries.

I argue for two central theses. First, even if the broader traditions of which the *Gītā* is a part widely accept the claim that desire entails action, the most common versions of the Some Desires Interpretation are implausible. Second, a number of seminal texts within the Indian traditions deny that desire is a necessary condition of action. Hence the arguments for adopting the Some Desires Interpretation in the first place are unconvincing. Kṛṣṇa's advice to act without desire, then, ought to be taken literally, as the advice to act without any desire whatever.

These conclusions naturally lead to a third question: Are the theories of motivation advanced in these texts plausible? I argue for a third thesis: the primary argument offered for the claim that desire is a necessary condition of action is unconvincing. Hence the theories of motivation advanced in the texts that I consider are plausible.

Some notes on translation

Throughout this book, I have translated the Sanskrit texts as literally as possible. I have intentionally used the standard prepositions and prepositional phrases to translate the Sanskrit cases whenever possible, even, at times, at the expense of fluidity. I expect this will make it easier for the interested Sanskrit student to follow my English translations in the Sanskrit.

Within the translations, I use brackets to indicate my own clarifications. I consider any clarification inserted into the translation itself to be non-speculative. My elaborations of the translations – which, obviously, are often speculative – follow the translations themselves. In the Appendices, my elaborations of the Sanskrit are indented. I use parentheses when giving the Sanskrit translation for an English word or vice versa.

I use single quotation marks when mentioning an English word, but not a Sanskrit word. Hence, "the word 'desire' is ambiguous," but "the word *ānanda* cannot mean bliss." I italicize all Sanskrit words, including *karma*.

My translations are consistent throughout the text and Appendices. I do not alter the translations depending on the context.

Finally, I translate Sanskrit words the first time that I use them. In many cases, I translate them again when they have not been used for a while, or when they are relatively obscure.

1 Four interpretations of desireless action

In this chapter I consider four interpretations of desireless action in the *Bhagavadgītā*. The first three interpretations begin with the basic inference that since all action is motivated by desire, the *Gītā's* doctrine of desireless action – if taken literally – is a contradiction. The three accounts diverge, however, in their further conclusions.

Some interpreters conclude that the advice to act without desire is simply nonsense, and ought to be disregarded. More charitable interpreters infer that the doctrine of desireless action should not be taken literally. Some argue that the kind of action that is advocated is not intentional action at all, and hence does not entail desire. Others draw a distinction between permissible and impermissible desires, and argue that desireless action is action devoid of only a certain kind of desire.

Initially I offer objections to the first two interpretations and argue that the third interpretation is the most plausible. I then introduce a distinction – which I adopt from G. F. Schueler (1995) – between two senses of the word 'desire'. In the first sense, 'desire' means reason, purpose, or goal. In the second sense, 'desire' refers to a narrower set of mental states that can be contrasted with beliefs, intentions, and so on. I argue that if the word 'desire' is understood in the second sense, the advice to act without any desire at all is straightforward and unproblematic, and a non-literal interpretation is not needed.

In order for the entailment[1] between action and desire to serve as a constraint on the interpretation of Indian texts – as almost all of the contemporary scholars who write on this topic claim – the entailment must be so obvious that it is implausible to deny that the authors of these texts fail to see it. The only entailment between action and desire that is obvious in this way, however, is the entailment between action and desire in the first sense – that is, the entailment between action and an agent's purpose or reason for acting. This implies that the advice to act without desire is not the advice to act without a purpose or reason.

There is no such entailment, however, between action and desire in the second sense. Even if desire of this kind is entailed by action – as most contemporary western philosophers and non-philosophers claim – the entailment is not obvious enough to serve as an interpretive constraint.

Hence there is no obvious reason to assume from the outset that the advice to act without desire cannot be taken literally, so long as 'desire' is taken to refer to the narrower class of states that can be contrasted with beliefs, intentions, and so on.

While the conflation of these two senses of the word 'desire' is central to the justification that most authors offer for taking the advice non-literally, some authors offer a justification that avoids the objection. They claim that the entailment between action and desire serves as an interpretive constraint because the entailment is widely accepted by the Indian tradition more broadly.

The basic argument

Most contemporary commentators on desireless action focus exclusively on the *Bhagavadgītā*. Since one of my primary goals in this chapter and the chapters that follow is to assess some of these commentators' interpretations, for now I limit myself to a consideration of desireless action in the *Gītā* in particular, and postpone any detailed consideration of other texts until later chapters.

It is worth noting, however, that many of these commentators' arguments are generalizable to some of the broader traditions. If it is a contradiction, for example, to advise acting without desire in the *Gītā*, then presumably it is a contradiction to advise desireless action in other contexts. If the most plausible solution to the interpretive problem in the *Gītā* is to draw a distinction between permissible and impermissible desires, then presumably this is a promising solution to the problem in other texts as well. Additionally, some contemporary authors draw evidence directly from other texts in the traditions. This implies that they take there to be some general consistency or continuity between the *Gītā* and the other text or texts cited. If this is right, and I think it is, then an analysis of the *Gītā* may have implications for the analyses of other texts within the traditions (and vice versa).

I want to begin by stating the supposed problem of desireless action as clearly as possible. Most contemporary commentators either begin their discussions with the following argument, or simply take its conclusion as an unproblematic assumption. In analyzing the *Gītā* in particular, they offer what I will call 'the basic argument':

> (BA)
>
> Premise One: Kṛṣṇa advises Arjuna to act without desire.
> Premise Two: Desire is a necessary condition of action.
> Conclusion: Hence Kṛṣṇa's advice is a contradiction – at least prima facie.

Since all action is motivated by desire, action not motivated by desire is impossible. Since Kṛṣṇa seems to advise desireless action, his advice seems to be inconsistent.

Most authors begin from the conclusion that a literal reading of the advice is a contradiction, but do not explicitly state the full argument. Others review the entire argument. Rajendra Prasad, for example, argues as follows:

> As per common experience, an intentional action X is possible without any desire for doing X, if there is another desire for doing something else. I drink intentionally, though I do not want, or desire, to drink, because I want, or desire, to please my boss who has himself offered me the glass to drink.
>
> (Prasad 1999: 59–60)

Even if someone denies that they desire to do what they are doing – "I really don't want to go to this meeting" – it must be that they desire some perceived consequence or aspect of what they are doing – "but I do want to keep my job, and attending this meeting will ensure that I do that." Otherwise motivation would not arise. The advice to act without desire seems inconsistent with this apparent fact.

Jagat Pal mentions the same line of argument. Since *niṣkāmakarma* (desireless action) is done intentionally, "and the act of intending is just not possible without desiring . . . because the notion of the act of intending always conceptually involves in its meaning a reference to the notion of desiring," desireless action is impossible (Pal 2004: 53). A number of other contemporary authors cite this argument as well.[2]

Indeed, the argument has its origin in classical Indian texts themselves. *Manusmṛti* 2.2, for example, reads: "Desirefulness (*kāmātmatā*) is not praiseworthy, but never does desirelessness (*akāmatā*) exist here on Earth, since the study of the Veda and the performance of Vedic actions are to be desired (*kāmya*)" (Dave 1972–1985: 154, lines 26–27).[3] Perhaps desire is not a good thing, but without it, nothing can be done.[4]

Three interpretations

There are at least three different responses to the supposed contradiction just mentioned.

The Absurdity Interpretation

The first response is to accept the conclusion that desireless action is impossible, and dismiss the advice as nonsensical. Rajendra Prasad is the best-known proponent of this view. He takes the contradiction literally, and concludes that the advice should be disregarded.

> [t]o do an intentional action . . . I must have at least some desire for

> something, or for doing something. But if I have no desire at all, if I am completely desireless, I cannot do any intentional action. Therefore, if Arjuna gives up all desires, he cannot do any intentional action, and then all of Kṛṣṇa's exhortations to him for doing actions without any desire . . . would become infructuous.
>
> (Prasad 1999: 60)

The final conclusion of this quotation should not be read in the optative tense, as it appears. According to Prasad, Kṛṣṇa's exhortations are in fact infructuous (that is, useless). He offers a number of objections to Kṛṣṇa's advice, most of which conclude that Kṛṣṇa's advice cannot be followed. If this conclusion is justified, then desireless action is a straightforward contradiction not only in the *Gītā*, but throughout the Indian traditions.

Prasad is not the only author to take this position, but it has relatively few proponents. Robert N. Minor mentions S. A. Desai as another example. "One critic to whom [S.] Radhakrishnan responded is S. A. Desai of the Brahmo Samaj, who in lectures to the Samaj argued that . . . the motiveless action which [the *Gītā*] preaches is an impossibility" (Minor 1986: 149).[5] Both Desai and Prasad ascribe the seemingly obvious contradiction to the *Gītā* and consequently dismiss the doctrine of desireless action as impossible. Their argument can be schematized in the following way:

(AI)

Premise One: Kṛṣṇa advises Arjuna to act without desire.
Premise Two: Desire is a necessary condition of action.
Conclusion One: Hence Kṛṣṇa's advice is a contradiction – at least prima facie.
Conclusion Two: Hence Kṛṣṇa's advice is nonsense, and should be disregarded.

Here the two premises and first conclusion constitute the basic argument from which most interpreters begin. The second conclusion is unique to what I will call the 'Absurdity Interpretation'. The interpretation's conclusion about the doctrine of desireless action is that it is absurd.

The fundamental problem with this interpretation is that it violates the principle of charity, which requires that the interpreter or translator attempt to avoid ascribing obviously false, or obviously contradictory claims to a text (or speaker). As W. V. O. Quine says, "one's interlocutor's silliness, beyond a certain point, is less likely than bad translation" (Quine 1960: 59). If I take my Spanish-speaking friend to be ordering soap at a fancy restaurant, I ought to wonder whether 'sopa' might not mean something else.

The Indian tradition relies heavily on a similar exegetical principle. If the primary meaning of a word leads to an obvious falsehood or contradiction, the word's secondary meaning – its *lakṣaṇā* – must be adopted.[6] As

Vācaspati says in his commentary to *Nyāyasūtra* 1.1.22, "if the primary (*mukhya*) [meaning] is inconsistent, the secondary (*gauṇa*) [meaning] is [legitimately] reverted to" (Thakur 1967: 459, line 14).[7] The principle requires – at least preliminarily – that the interpreter avoid ascribing an obvious falsehood or an obvious contradiction to a text, all other things being equal.[8] There are some examples of this interpretive technique from Śaṅkara and Rāmānuja later in this chapter.

In the present case, the principle of charity seems to require that we at least consider less literal readings of the text. It may be, for example, that the contradiction is merely apparent, and can be reconciled on a subtler reading. Most authors take the seemingly obvious contradiction in Conclusion One as evidence that one of the premises that seem to support it is false. Perhaps Kṛṣṇa does not really advise desireless action, or perhaps desire is not really required for action.

Radhakrishnan, for example, considers the basic argument, and takes the conclusion that a literal reading is a contradiction as reason to interpret it non-literally. "We are not asked to uproot all desires; for that would imply the cessation of all activity" (Radhakrishnan 1911: 475).[9] That is, since desireless action, taken literally, precludes all action, and is therefore a contradiction, this cannot be Kṛṣṇa's advice. Jagat Pal makes the same point. He considers the basic argument and concludes that "[i]f this be the case, then we will have to admit that the concept of *niṣkāma karma* does not exclude from its meaning an element of desire for the doing of action" (Pal 2004: 53). That is, if desireless action leads to a contradiction, it must be that Kṛṣṇa permits certain desires, and that these desires motivate the enjoined actions.

Since Prasad seems to ignore the principle of charity, and ascribes an obvious contradiction to the *Bhagavadgītā* without considering alternative interpretations, his interpretation is at least initially implausible. Ultimately, it will be defensible only if additional, and sufficient textual evidence is offered in its support, or if alternative interpretations are at least equally problematic. This remains to be seen.

The No Action Interpretation

According to the second interpretation of desireless action, the word 'action' should not be taken literally. Simon Brodbeck, for example, reviews the basic argument and concludes that Kṛṣṇa advises Arjuna to eliminate all desires, and hence to cease acting intentionally. According to Brodbeck, Kṛṣṇa's "technique . . . is a comprehensive deconstructive philosophy of deliberate behaviours" (Brodbeck 2004: 84).

George Teschner defends a similar position. He claims that "the *Gītā* is advocating a more radical and unfamiliar conception of action . . . a conception of human action that is non-teleological" (Teschner 1992: 61). Hence Brodbeck and Teschner avoid the contradiction cited in the basic argument by denying that the desireless agent continues to act in any ordinary sense.

I want to make a terminological distinction at this point. Both Teschner and Brodbeck draw a distinction between intentional and non-intentional action. It is typical in both western philosophy and ordinary English to use the word 'action' to refer exclusively to human behavior performed intentionally, and exclude any behavior not performed intentionally. My behavior of playing volleyball is an action, but my behavior of digesting lunch is not, because I play volleyball motivated by the intention, or purpose, of getting some exercise, winning, or whatever, whereas I do not digest lunch for a reason. In what follows, I will use the word 'action' to refer to intentional actions, and refer to what Teschner and Brodbeck call 'non-intentional actions' simply as 'behaviors'.

My argument does not depend on this distinction, but besides following convention, the distinction helps to clarify a basic point about the view under consideration. The solution to the apparent problem of desireless action that both Teschner and Brodbeck advance amounts to denying that desireless action is actually action. The initial problem is that action entails desire. This is only true of intentional action, however, not mere human behavior. The argument can be schematized in the following way:

(NAI)

Premise One: Kṛṣṇa advises Arjuna to act without desire.
Premise Two: Desire is a necessary condition of action.
Conclusion One: Hence Kṛṣṇa's advice is a contradiction – at least prima facie.
Conclusion Two: So this cannot be Kṛṣṇa's advice.
Conclusion Three: Kṛṣṇa advises Arjuna against acting.

Here, again, the first two premises and the first conclusion constitute the basic argument from which most interpreters begin. The second conclusion is common to all non-literal interpretations. It denies that the apparent contradiction is an actual contradiction. The third conclusion is unique to what I will call the 'No Action Interpretation'. It should be kept in mind that according to Teschner and Brodbeck, this final conclusion is consistent with Arjuna continuing to behave, and even exhibit complex behaviors like fighting in the battle as Kṛṣṇa advises – so long as it is not done intentionally.

Both Teschner and Brodbeck offer the same basic argument for their positions. The *Gītā* analyzes human behavior in terms of the interaction of the *guṇas* (qualities or strings that constitute the entire material universe, including the agent and their mental states), which are material, and governed by physical laws of cause and effect. Hence human behavior is explained causally, in terms of the interaction of the *guṇas*. If human behavior is explained causally, then it is not explained teleologically, in terms of the agent's desires and intentions.[10] Hence human behavior is not intentional. According to Teschner, "the *Gītā* is claiming that what is taken as rational conscious action is in fact non-intentional" (Teschner 1992: 61). Brodbeck agrees: "Kṛṣṇa insists that there are no desires, intentions or fruits at play" in an agent's motivation (Brodbeck 2004: 86).

Teschner offers an analogy. It is natural to speak of a flower "turning towards the sun" as if it has some purpose in doing so. In reality, however, the flower's behavior can be explained in terms of cause and effect. "The sun causes faster growth on one side of the plant than on the other, resulting in turning the face of the flower" (Teschner 1992: 65).[11] It is simply false, then, that a flower turns towards the sun in order to take in sunlight, or because it desires to grow. The flower does not intend or desire anything. Its behavior is explained causally, without reference to beliefs, desires or intentions.

Since, according to the *Gītā's* proto-Sāṃkhyan metaphysics,[12] human behavior is also explained in terms of cause and effect, human behavior can also be explained without reference to beliefs, desires and intentions. Human behavior is no more intentional, then, than the behavior of a flower. As Brodbeck says, "the non-attached actor's behaviour is motivated in the same sense as blinking, sleepwalking or digestive processes are motivated" (Brodbeck 2004: 93).

There are a number of problems with this account. The first problem is that according to Teschner and Brodbeck, Kṛṣṇa advises Arjuna to eliminate intentions and desires. Teschner translates *Gītā* 2.47 to read: "Never should consequences, results, purposes, etc. be your motive to act" (Teschner 1992: 63). This suggests that purposes might motivate an action, and that this should be avoided. Brodbeck asks:

> So what are we to make of the things we do that seem to follow causally from our intentions? According to Kṛṣṇa's analysis such activities are perilous, since even if we manage to sustain the intention to the extent of performing the intended action, the intention implies an envisaged future which is unlikely to match the actual one, and suffering will result. Hence actions requiring a corresponding antecedent intention are to be avoided.
> (Brodbeck 2004: 93)

This too suggests that some actions are motivated by intentions, and that Kṛṣṇa means to advise Arjuna against acting from intentions. If all human behavior is non-intentional, however, then the advice is useless – all human beings are already desireless!

This inconsistency can be avoided, however. Both Teschner and Brodbeck use the word 'intention' ambiguously. In one sense, they use the word to refer to the agent's reason or purpose – the mental state that distinguishes action from mere behavior. Both claim that the *Gītā* denies that human beings have intentions of this sort when they claim that the *Gītā* denies the teleological explanation of action.

In a second sense, they use the word 'intention' to refer to beliefs about action, agency, and the consequences of action. Teschner claims that

> [t]he injunction of Karma Yoga [which entails desireless action] interpreted in this light is a method of engaging in action without representing action as intentional. To engage in action without concern for fruits of action is to act without depicting the action in thought and speech as having its reason for being in a projected goal.
>
> (Teschner 1992: 66)

Here Teschner uses the word 'intention' to refer to a certain belief about human agency, presumably the belief that a person can act for some purpose (which on his interpretation of the *Gītā* is false). It is only in this sense that intentions do indeed exist, but ought to be eliminated. Hence Teschner's view is that since there are no intentions – in the sense of purposes – the agent should eliminate intentions – in the sense of false beliefs about actions being motivated by purposes.

Brodbeck uses the term 'intention' to refer to both purposes and beliefs about what one will do in the future. "Human beings are not able to predict exactly what they are going to do, and so such predictions as are made, in the form of intentions, are liable to be incorrect" (Brodbeck 2004: 92). It is in this sense that intentions do indeed exist, but ought to be eliminated. Hence Brodbeck's position is that there are no intentions – in the sense of purposes – and the agent should eliminate intentions – in the sense of false, or at least possibly false beliefs about the consequences of their behavior.[13]

These clarifications leave room for both Teschner and Brodbeck to adjust their positions accordingly. On Brodbeck's view, the *Gītā* denies intentions, but admits predictions about what one will do. When agents predict their actions, they are disposed towards disappointment, since the predictions can be false. Hence the agent should abandon predictions, as a means of avoiding this form of suffering.

Teschner can say that the *Gītā* denies intentions, but admits beliefs about human agency, such as "I am the doer" (*Gītā* 3.27, see below), and so on. Since these beliefs are false, and since they lead to fear, anxiety, and so on, they should be eliminated. My sense is that this is the most charitable way to read the two accounts.

The problem with the revised versions of these accounts is that they claim that Kṛṣṇa's advice to act without desire is advice about what to believe or think, rather than what to desire or do. Hence both authors resort to a radically non-literal interpretation of the advice to act without desire. Because of the ambiguities just mentioned, this fact is easily missed. It is their apparent talk of intentions that makes it seem as if they are talking about something related to desireless action in the first place. Once it is clear that the No Action Interpretation denies that the advice to act without desire is advice about desire at all, the view seems implausible.

Both Teschner and Brodbeck cite a range of *Gītā* verses that seem to deny human agency, and the evidence – taken by itself – is quite strong. First, there are a number of verses in which Kṛṣṇa seems to advise Arjuna to act without purpose. Teschner admits, however, that the words that must be translated as 'purpose' in order to support the position are ambiguous, and can also mean "selfless purpose" (Teschner 1992: 64).[14]

Second, a range of verses describe the agent as a mere observer of the *guṇas*, which carry out action independently. Brodbeck cites verses 3.27–28, for example, and translates them as follows:

> Actions are being done wholly by the qualities (*guṇas*) of material nature (*prakṛti*). The one who is bewildered by ego (*ahaṃkāra*) thinks 'I am the doer'. The knower of the truth of the distributions of actions and of *guṇas*, thinking 'the *guṇas* are moving amongst the *guṇas*', does not attach themselves.
>
> (Brodbeck 2004: 89)[15]

If it is a mistake to think 'I am the doer', then I am not the doer. If I am not the doer, then the behaviors that my body exhibits are not intentional. If they were, then I would be the doer. If I am not acting, intending or desiring, then the advice to act without desire is not about acting, intending or desiring. Additionally, the second verse – "The one who is bewildered by ego (*ahaṃkāra*) thinks 'I am the doer' " – can be taken to equate the elimination of the false belief about agency and the elimination of attachment – that is, desire.[16] This suggests that believing that I am not the doer is just being desireless.[17]

There are two problems with this analysis of these passages. The first problem is that the most influential classical commentators on the *Gītā* carefully avoid the conclusion that the claim that action is carried out by *prakṛti* (matter) entails a denial of free action. Śaṅkara considers the objection explicitly in his commentary to *Gītā* 3.34: "If all beings act only according to their own *prakṛti*, and there is never an absence of *prakṛti*, then . . . scripture becomes irrelevant, due to the absence of a sphere for human effort" (Sadhale 1985a: 333, lines 12–13).[18] That is, if all actions are determined by the *guṇas*, the scriptural injunctions are inexplicable.

He responds that when a person controls *rāga* and *dveṣa* (desire and aversion), they cease to be led by *prakṛti*. This, according to Śaṅkara, is what the *Gītā* means to advise. It is not asserting fatalism or determinism. Rāmānuja makes the same point in his commentary to this verse. He considers the objection that if *prakṛti* causes action, there is an inconsistency with injunctions of *śāstra* (scripture). He replies that desire and aversion cause action, but can be resisted (Sadhale 1985a: 333, lines 33–34).[19]

Hence some of the evidence that Teschner and Brodbeck cite supports their reading only if the warnings of Śaṅkara and Rāmānuja are ignored. Otherwise, these commentaries support the opposite view: the injunction to act without desire is an injunction to resist the influence of desire, which, when left unchecked, robs one of free will. Additionally, part of the rationale for discouraging desire becomes apparent in this context – desire determines action, and so long as one's actions are determined, one is not free.

Notice the use of the principle of charity in these arguments. Both Śaṅkara and Rāmānuja point out that if the *Gītā* asserts determinism, then it both enjoins certain actions, which implies freedom, and denies freedom. Both take this as sufficient reason to abandon the literal interpretation – all action is determined – and revert to a less literal interpretation – action is determined when the agent allows desire and aversion to motivate action.

The second problem with this analysis is that according to the proto-Sāṃkhyan metaphysics of the *Gītā*, intentions are part of the explanation of action. Teschner claims that

> Clearly according to the *Saṁkhya Kārikā* . . . [a]ll action is performed by the activity of something that is fundamentally inert and unconscious and which must be discriminated from consciousness as such . . . Not only is the *Gītā* claiming that there is no egoistic intention in action, but that there is nothing intentional at all. The *Gītā* is repudiating the intentionality and teleology of human action. The principle of intentionality resides within what the *Saṁkhya Kārikā* calls *puruṣa* that does not act, where that which acts, the insentient *prakṛti* [*sic*], is devoid of intentionality.
>
> (Teschner 1992: 69)

This is simply not accurate of the *Gītā* or the Sāṃkhyan system with which Teschner compares it, however. The distinction between *prakṛti* and *puruṣa* is often explained as a distinction between that which is or can be the object of consciousness, and consciousness itself, respectively. *Prakṛti* includes the entire psyche of the agent, including mental states like beliefs, desires and intentions.[20] Intentions play a crucial role in the causality that produces action. Hence in the proto-Sāṃkhyan context of the *Gītā*, Teschner's inference from the claim that human behavior is caused to the claim that human behavior is not teleological is unjustified, because intentions are part of the causal chain that produces action.[21]

Teschner might reply that since intentions are part of a causal network, human beings do not control them. If intentions are outside of human control, it cannot be that the *Gītā* advises adopting certain intentions, and abandoning others. The same objection can be leveled against Teschner's account, however. On the Sāṃkhyan view, one's beliefs are also *prakṛti*.[22] If the fact that something consists of *prakṛti* entails that it is determined, then an agent's beliefs are outside of the agent's control as well. If the epistemological remedy for which Teschner and Brodbeck argue can be prescribed in any meaningful way, then it must be that the agent can have some effect on what they believe. If this is admitted, however, then the agent can have some effect on what purposes they adopt as well. Indeed, in order to change beliefs on purpose, the agent must adopt the purpose to do so! If the agent can have some effect on what purposes they adopt, then they can have some effect on what they desire and do.

Brodbeck offers the same basic objection to Teschner's account. "[I]f *prakṛti* governs the actions that Arjuna will do, then it must also govern whether or not he will do those actions without attachment" (Brodbeck 2004: 98). Brodbeck argues that since the behaviors of human beings are determined by the *guṇas*, and the *guṇas*, in turn, are determined by previous behaviors, and so on, it is not in the control of the agent to perform any particular action at a given time or adopt or abandon any belief at a given time. Ultimately the attainment of *mokṣa* (liberation) occurs by chance, much like being struck by lightning, even if it can be explained in terms of the *guṇas* and the history of a particular self (ibid.).

This consequence does not square well, however, with a text and traditions that emphasize ethics to the extent that the Indian traditions do. On this interpretation, injunctions do not effectively motivate agents to act – where action entails not only purpose, but free will – and no agent is responsible in any ordinary sense for what they do.[23]

Brodbeck responds to this kind of concern by claiming that the positing of seemingly moral goals, like the goal of *lokasaṃgraha* (the holding together of the world), must be a "red herring, featuring in the text to ensure the continuity of the brāhmaṇical ritual tradition with its conventional analysis of the causes of action" (Brodbeck 2004: 89). He admits that there is a tension within Kṛṣṇa's teaching. Kṛṣṇa seems to both advise certain actions and deny that action is possible. He both emphasizes moral responsibility and refutes it. "[I]t is clear," Brodbeck says, "that we cannot make philosophical progress without ignoring some of what Kṛṣṇa says" (ibid).

It is important, however, to see the choice about which passages to ignore – or at least take less literally – as clearly as possible here. An interpreter must either deny the importance of those passages in which Kṛṣṇa advises certain actions, and thereby deny the moral relevance of the *Gītā*, or adopt a less literal reading of the seemingly deterministic passages. Since classical commentators set the precedent of taking the deterministic passages less literally, the evidence seems to weigh in favor of preserving free will and the possibility of moral action over preserving determinism.[24]

The Some Desires Interpretation

A third response to the conclusion that a literal reading of desireless action is a contradiction is to take the word 'desire' non-literally, to refer to a subset of desires. On this interpretation, the injunction to act without desire is an injunction to act without a certain kind of desire.[25] This leaves another subset of desires available for motivating action. The argument is schematized as follows:

(SDI)

Premise One: Kṛṣṇa advises Arjuna to act without desire.

Premise Two: Desire is a necessary condition of action.
Conclusion One: Hence Kṛṣṇa's advice is a contradiction.
Conclusion Two: So this cannot be Kṛṣṇa's advice.
Conclusion Three: Kṛṣṇa advises Arjuna to act without some desires. He permits others.

Here again, the first two premises and the first conclusion constitute the basic argument from which most interpreters begin. The second conclusion is common to all non-literal interpretations. The third conclusion is unique to what I will call the 'Some Desires Interpretation'.

The Some Desires Interpretation is by far the most common contemporary interpretation of desireless action. It is accepted almost without exception. Various proponents of the Some Desires Interpretation offer a variety of interpretations – that only the desire for *mokṣa* is permitted, that only unselfish desires are permitted, and so on. The basic structure of their arguments, however, is the same.

In subsequent chapters, I consider some of the most plausible versions of the Some Desires Interpretation in detail. For now, however, I want to evaluate the cogency of the generic argument for the Some Desires Interpretation outlined above. At first glance it seems that the Some Desires Interpretation is the most plausible of the three under consideration. Taking the advice literally is implausible, because it violates the principle of charity. Hence the advice should not be taken literally. There are only two obvious non-literal interpretations of desireless action: either it is not really action, or it is not really desireless. The first of these interpretations is implausible for the reasons just mentioned. The second of these interpretations seems to be the only one left.

Additionally, there are no obvious problems with the third interpretation, so long as the initial argument is sound (through Conclusion Three), and a literal interpretation of the advice is a contradiction. And since this inference is accepted by almost every contemporary interpreter, it is, one might think, unassailable.

A fourth interpretation

The case for the third interpretation is not as simple as this, however. Remember that the argument for either non-literal interpretation – that is, the No Action Interpretation or the Some Desires Interpretation – goes as follows:

(BA)

Premise One: Kṛṣṇa advises Arjuna to act without desire.
Premise Two: Desire is a necessary condition of action.
Conclusion One: Hence Kṛṣṇa's advice is a contradiction – if it is taken literally.
Conclusion Two: So this cannot be Kṛṣṇa's advice.

I mentioned above that in drawing the second conclusion, the non-literal interpretations invoke the principle of charity. Since it is implausible that Kṛṣṇa's advice is obviously inconsistent, the advice must be taken non-literally, so that the contradiction is avoided.

I also mentioned that inconsistency by itself does not justify reverting to a less literal interpretation. Additionally, the inconsistency must be sufficiently obvious. It is not clear, however, that the contradiction in Kṛṣṇa's advice is sufficiently obvious. More specifically, it is not clear that the claim that desire is a necessary condition of action (Premise Two) is obviously true.

After all, there is a very lively debate in both modern and contemporary western philosophy between so-called Humeans and anti-Humeans, over whether or not desire is a necessary condition of action, respectively. David Hume begins his discussion of the topic by admitting that his view, according to which desire is entailed by action, is inconsistent with the traditional view, according to which reason alone can (and should) motivate action.

> Nothing is more usual in philosophy, and even in common life, than to talk of the combat of passion and reason, to give the preference to reason, and to assert that men are only so far virtuous as they conform to its dictates. Every rational creature, 'tis said, is oblig'd to regulate his actions by reason; and if any other motive or principle challenge the direction of his conduct, he ought to oppose it, 'till it be entirely subdu'd, or at least brought to a conformity with that superior principle. On this method of thinking the greatest part of moral philosophy, ancient and modern, seems to be founded . . . In order to shew the fallacy of all this philosophy, I shall endeavour to prove *first*, that reason alone can never be a motive to any action of the will; and *secondly*, that it can never oppose passion in the direction of the will.
>
> (Hume 1992: 413)

His point is that only desire motivates action, even though most of the philosophers and non-philosophers deny this, and wrongfully claim that reason can motivate action without the help of desire. In other words, Hume cites the view that desireless action is possible as a philosophical dogma of his day.[26]

Immanuel Kant is normally taken to assert this position when he claims that "an act from duty wholly excludes the influence of inclination and therewith every object of the will" (Kant 1995: 16). That is, an agent's action might be entirely independent of the desires of the agent; the agent can act from duty alone.

In light of this debate and its recent resurgence,[27] it seems implausible that the principle of charity requires interpreters to assume that the *Bhagavadgītā* accepts the Humean theory of motivation. If Kant can deny that all action is motivated by desire, then surely Kṛṣṇa can as well.[28] So it seems strange that contemporary interpreters take the entailment between action and desire to be so obvious that it cannot be that Kṛṣṇa fails to see it.

Most authors offer little explanation for this assumption. Among those I have mentioned, Pal explains that "the concept of action conceptually involves in its meaning the notion of an element of desire" (Pal 2004: 53). This suggests that he takes the claim that action is motivated by desire to be an analytic truth, much like the claim that a bachelor is an unmarried man.

One typical way to determine if a claim is analytically true, however, is to consider whether someone who fully understands the subject can consistently deny the predicate. If the predicate cannot be consistently denied, then the claim is analytically true. In the case of the term 'bachelor', it is not possible to consistently deny that a bachelor is unmarried, because the speaker already accepts that the bachelor is unmarried, in virtue of fully grasping the concept bachelor. If the speaker then claims that the bachelor is married, then one of two things must be true. Either the speaker does not fully grasp the meaning of the term 'bachelor', or the speaker has inconsistent beliefs about what a bachelor is.

This is not true of the claim that action entails desire, however. Hume's argument for the claim that action entails desire is somewhat obscure, but it is at least clear that he offers an argument. He does not simply point out that his opponents fail to fully grasp the concept of action or desire – as we should expect if the dispute is semantic. Hence desire – at least in the sense that Hume has in mind – is not analytically entailed by action.[29]

Another possibility is that contemporary interpreters of the *Gītā* take the claim that action entails desire to be obviously true, even if it is not analytically true, perhaps because they take the arguments in favor of the position to be so obviously convincing. This seems to be the sense of Prasad's claim in the quotation above that "common experience" testifies to the entailment. If common experience is needed to testify to the entailment, it is probably not an analytic truth.[30]

It is typical for western philosophers to count the Humean view as the default position, and put the onus on the opponent of this kind of view to produce an argument for abandoning it. Donald C. Hubin, for example, claims that "Humeanism, it is fair to say, is the theory to beat; perhaps it is even accurate to think of it as the default position" (Hubin 1999: 30). If the Humean view is the default position, perhaps we should assume that the authors of Indian texts accept it, at least absent any countervailing evidence.

Even if the Humean theory of motivation is prevalent to this extent, however, it does not follow that all texts must be interpreted in a way that is consistent with it. Remember that just the reverse is true in Hume's time – the claim that action might be motivated without the help of desire is the default view.

A third possibility is that the argument for a non-literal interpretation depends on an equivocation. G. F. Schueler points out that the word 'desire' is ambiguous. In one sense it means the agent's reason or purpose. Only desire in this sense is entailed by action. As I mentioned above, the word 'action' typically refers to intentional action – action done for some reason.

In a second sense, however, 'desire' refers more narrowly to a class of mental states that can be contrasted with beliefs, intentions, wishes, and so on. Schueler calls these 'desires proper' (Schueler 1995: 29).[31] This is the sense of desire that Hume has in mind when he argues that beliefs cannot motivate action without the help of the passions.

The basic argument with which most interpreters of the *Gītā* begin is convincing only if the word 'desire' is taken in the first sense, to mean purpose. Understood this way, the argument reads:

(BA′)

Premise One: Kṛṣṇa advises Arjuna to act without purpose.
Premise Two: Purpose is a necessary condition of action.
Conclusion One: Hence Kṛṣṇa's advice is a contradiction – at least prima facie.
Conclusion Two: So this cannot be Kṛṣṇa's advice.

On this reading, Premise Two is indeed an analytic truth, as Pal seems to say. The principle of charity seems to require that the basic argument be read in this way. If instead the word 'desire' in the basic argument refers to desires proper, the argument is not convincing – at least in the absence of an additional argument.[32]

If 'desire' means purpose in the basic argument, however, then it leaves open the possibility that all desires proper are discouraged. The most obvious inference to draw from the basic argument above is: Conclusion Three: So Kṛṣṇa advises eliminating all desires (proper).

(ND)

Premise One: Kṛṣṇa advises Arjuna to act without purpose.
Premise Two: Purpose is a necessary condition of action.
Conclusion One: Hence Kṛṣṇa's advice is a contradiction.
Conclusion Two: So this cannot be Kṛṣṇa's advice.
Conclusion Three: So Kṛṣṇa advises eliminating all desires (proper).[33]

I call this interpretation the 'No Desires Interpretation'.

After all, the textual evidence favors the broadest possible interpretation of the class of desires that are discouraged. The *Gītā* uses the word *sarva* – all – to qualify the desires that are to be abandoned in a number of places. Kṛṣṇa defines the sage as a person who has abandoned "all desires" (*kāmān sarvān*) at 2.55 (Sadhale 1985a: 214, line 2). At 2.71 he claims that the wise is the one "who, having abandoned all desires, acts without desire" (*vihāya kāmān yaḥ sarvān pumāṃścarati niḥspṛhaḥ*) (Sadhale 1985a: 242, line 8). At 6.18, he describes the yogic mind as "free from attachment to all desires" (*nisspṛhaḥ sarvakāmebhyo yukta ity ucyate . . .*) (Sadhale 1985a: 552, line 39).[34] And at 6.24, Kṛṣṇa specifies that one should abandon "all desires without exception (*sarvānaśeṣatas*)" (Sadhale 1985a: 555, line 10).[35]

In his commentary to *Yogasūtra* 1.2, Vyāsa comments on the use of the adjective *sarva*. The verse reads, "Yoga is the cessation of mental activity" (Sārvabhauma and Nyāyaratna 1970: 1, line 2).[36] Vyāsa explains that since the word *sarva* is absent – that is, since the verse does not read, "Yoga is the cessation of all mental activity" – the verse does not exclude all mental activity. "Since there is the non-mentioning of the word *sarva*, *saṃprajñāta* [*samādhi*] (concentration on an object, mediated by mental activity) is also to be considered Yoga" (Sārvabhauma and Nyāyaratna 1970: 12, lines 1–2).[37] This suggests that the word *sarva* is typically used to explicitly deny exceptions. If this is the case in the *Bhagavadgītā*, the advice to eliminate desire is the advice to eliminate desire without exception. Since this cannot mean that all purposes are to be eliminated without exception, it should be taken to cover the next broadest possible interpretation – namely that all desires are to be eliminated without exception.

Kṛṣṇa also uses a wide range of words that might be translated as 'desire' in English, and advises their elimination. The two most common terms are *kāma* (2.62, 3.37, 3.39, 4.19, 6.18, 6.24, 7.11, 7.20, 10.1, 15.5, 16.10, 16.11, 16.12, 16.16, 16.21, 16.23, 17.5, 18.2, 18.24, 18.53) and *saṅga* (2.62, 4.20, 5.10, 5.11, 11.55, 12.18, 14.6, 14.7, 14.15, 15.5, 18.6),[38] but the *Gītā* also uses the words *icchā* (7.27, 11.7, 13.6, 11.3, 18.60, 18.63), *rāga* (2.56, 2.64, 3.34, 4.10, 14.7, 17.5, 18.23, 18.51), *dveṣa* (2.64, 3.34, 5.3, 14.22, 7.27, 18.23, 18.51), *spṛha* (2.56, 4.14, 14.12, 18.49), *āśī* (3.30, 4.21, 6.10), and verb forms derived from the root √ *kāṅkṣ* (12.17, 14.22), among others.[39]

Kṛṣṇa describes either himself or the wise person as having abandoned *kāma* (2.55, 4.14, 4.19, 6.24, 16.21, 18.53), *rāga* (2.56, 3.34, 8.11, 18.23, 18.51, 18.52), *dveṣa* (3.34, 5.3, 14.22, 18.23, 18.51), *sakta* (3.7, 3.19, 9.9, 18.49), *saṅga* (4.20, 4.23, 5.10 5.11, 11.55, 15.5), *āśī* (4.21, 6.10, 12.16), and *spṛha* (18.49).

Even if there is a case to be made for translating each of these terms more narrowly, as desires of a certain sort, it is less obvious that all of these terms taken together refer narrowly as well. Even if the case might be made that all of these terms taken together refer to only a subset of desires, contemporary commentators do not make the case. This suggests that it is not part of their justification for their positions. They simply assume that since not all purposes can be eliminated, not all desires can be eliminated.

Teschner, for example, limits his analysis of *niṣkāmakarma* to two possible candidates from the outset, with no explanation.

> Either the *Gītā* is recommending the familiar conception of selfless moral action, i.e. action that is unmotivated by a concern for personal and selfish gain, or the *Gītā* is advocating a more radical and unfamiliar conception of action that is without any consciousness of consequence

> or purpose. The latter is a conception of human action that is non-teleological.
>
> (Teschner 1992: 61)

He ignores the possibility that desireless action is indeed action – done intentionally – without any desire whatever. Yet this should, at the very least, be a third possible interpretation, deserving careful consideration. The most plausible explanation for this omission is that Teschner conflates desire and purpose, and assumes that if not all purposes are to be eliminated, then not all desires are to be eliminated.

In a related context, Daya Krishna seems to make the same mistake. He considers the relationship among the four *puruṣārtha's* (goals of human beings), and argues that *mokṣa*, understood as the "desire for release from desire itself . . . negates the *artha* [purpose] in the *puruṣārtha* [goals of human beings] in a radical manner" (Krishna 2007: 108). If the desire for *mokṣa* is a desire to eliminate all desires, then the desire for *mokṣa* negates all purposes. This is only true, however, if the elimination of desire entails the elimination of purposes. Krishna offers no argument for this claim, however.

So contemporary interpreters face a dilemma. If they take the word 'desire' to mean reason or purpose, then the final conclusion of the argument – the conclusion that only some desires are to be eliminated – is not justified, because they offer no argument against the conclusion that all desires are discouraged. If, on the other hand, they take the word 'desire' to mean desire, then Conclusion Two – that Kṛṣṇa cannot advise Arjuna to act without desire – is not justified, because Premise Two – the claim that action entails desire – is not obvious enough to justify invoking the principle of charity.

In order to make this crucial point as clearly as possible, consider an analogy. Suppose there is a rule within the Federal Aviation Administration that an armed marshal must be aboard every flight. On their first day on the job, two security screeners are reviewing the objectives of their position and come across the rule that no firearms are allowed beyond the security checkpoint. The first screener says, "Wait a minute, there is an armed marshal aboard every flight, so this rule cannot be taken literally. Some people with firearms are permitted beyond the security checkpoint, and others are prohibited." The second screener adds, "Well, convicted felons are not allowed to carry guns, so the prohibited class must be convicted felons, and the permitted class must be those who are not convicted felons. Hence those who are not convicted felons can carry guns on the plane."

Of course this reasoning is not convincing, because the fact that an armed marshal is required on every plane does not entail that some ordinary passengers must be allowed to carry guns as well. Likewise, however, the fact that a purpose is required to act (the analogue of the marshal) does not entail that some desires (the analogue of the passengers with guns) are permitted.

A second justification for the Some Desires Interpretation

There is another closely related, yet importantly different, justification that is sometimes offered for adopting this non-literal reading, which avoids the objection just mentioned. The argument can be schematized as follows.

(SDI2)

Premise One: Kṛṣṇa advises Arjuna to act without desire.
Premise Two: Desire is a necessary condition of action in the Indian traditions more generally.
Conclusion One: Hence desire is a necessary condition of action in the *Gītā*.
Conclusion Two: Hence Kṛṣṇa's advice is a contradiction – at least prima facie.
Conclusion Three: So this cannot be Kṛṣṇa's advice.
Conclusion Four: Kṛṣṇa advises Arjuna to act without some desires. He permits others.

Since desire is a necessary condition of action in the Indian philosophical traditions more generally, we should assume that the advice to act without desire in the *Gītā* amounts to the advice to act without a particular kind of desire. While the conclusion is the same, this second argument avoids the questions of whether desire is actually entailed by action, whether the entailment is sufficiently obvious, and so on.

Roy Perrett, for example, claims that it is "a commonplace of classical Indian action theory that desire is a necessary causal condition of an action," and concludes, "it must be action free of a particular kind of desire that is the renunciatory goal" (Perrett 1998: 23). Tara Chatterjea makes the same point: "Desire is the basis of all action . . . This is more or less accepted by all [of the orthodox systems]" (Chatterjea 2002: 125).

In a recent article on Indian action theory, J. N. Mohanty claims that

> the common structure regarding 'incitement to action' – a structure that is accepted by all thinkers in the Indian tradition – may be represented thus:
>
> knowledge ——desire ——will to do ——motor effect ——the action[40]
> (*jñāna*) (*cikīrṣā*) (*pravṛtti*) (*ceṣṭā*) (*kārya*)
> (Mohanty 2007: 60; cf. Mohanty 1997: 290)[41]

B. K. Matilal also adopts this basic model of motivation as an assumption in his analysis of *niṣkāmakarma*. He claims that "the simplest connection between beliefs, desires and action is this. Beliefs generate desire and desire generates action to obtain results" (Matilal 2002: 123). This suggests that desire is an essential element in Indian accounts of how action arises. If this is right, then there is reason to assume that the endorsement of desireless action in any text should not be taken literally.

One might think that this second justification for the adoption of a non-literal reading of desireless action is circular. If, in order to determine whether one text accepts that action entails desire, I must first determine whether a range of other texts accept that action entails desire, I end up in a regress. This regress can be avoided, however, if we first look at texts that deal with the relation between action and desire explicitly, and then use the conclusions drawn from those contexts in analyzing texts that do not deal explicitly with the relation.

The *Bhagavadgītā*, for example, does not deal with this relation explicitly,[42] but other texts do. Perrett, for example, mentions the *Bhāṣā-Pariccheda* in particular, which seems to claim that desire (*cikīrṣā*) is the source of all actions (Perrett 1998: 23, fn. 13). A good strategy, it seems, is to analyze the role of desire in action in the context of other texts, and to draw some more general conclusions about its role in texts that are less explicit.

Eventually I will argue that both the first and second justifications for reverting to a non-literal interpretation of the injunction to act without desire are unconvincing. In order to disprove the second justification, however, a great deal of work needs to be done. This work occupies many of the subsequent chapters. For now I want to leave open the question of whether or not the tradition of which the *Bhagavadgītā* is a part accepts that action entails desire. Hence I want to leave open the possibility that this interpretation of the *Bhagavadgītā* is plausible. Indeed, in the following chapters, I will assume that it is true, since there are a lot of questions other than this central one that need to be answered as well.

2 Desireless action in the *Yogasūtra*

In the last chapter I argued that at least one of the standard arguments for a non-literal interpretation of the *Bhagavadgītā's* advice to act without desire is not convincing. The truth of the claim that action entails desire – if it is indeed true – is not obvious enough to justify the assumption that the *Gītā* must be consistent with it. Hence any argument that claims that Kṛṣṇa's advice should not be taken literally because it is an obvious contradiction is unconvincing.

I also considered a second argument for a non-literal interpretation of the *Gītā* that avoids this problem. According to the second argument, the *Gītā* must be consistent with the claim that action entails desire because the rest of the tradition widely accepts this claim. In later chapters I evaluate this argument by considering the theories of motivation advanced in other seminal texts. For now, however, I assume that this argument is convincing, and therefore that the *Bhagavadgītā's* injunction to act without desire should not be taken literally.

In what follows, I assume that the Some Desires Interpretation – according to which the injunction to act without desire is an injunction to eliminate only some desires – is correct. Since the additional arguments that I offered against the Absurdity Interpretation and the No Action Interpretation in Chapter 1 are not avoided by the second argument for a non-literal reading, I continue to assume that these interpretations are implausible.

Any version of the Some Desires Interpretation draws a distinction between permissible and impermissible desires. In this chapter I argue that if some desires are permissible because desire plays a necessary role in motivating action – as the Some Desires Interpretation claims – presumably the permissible desires are those that play a necessary role in motivating the right action. This is the first condition of a permissible desire.

I then offer an overview of the role that desire is normally taken to play in motivating action. Both western and Indian philosophers draw the distinction between a desire for an end and a desire for a means. Under the right circumstances, both desires for ends and desires for means might play necessary roles in motivating action. Hence desires for ends and desires for means might meet this first condition of a permissible desire.

Not all desires that motivate the right action are permissible, however. In addition to playing a necessary role in motivating the right action, a permissible desire must take as its object the most valuable state of affairs appropriate for its desire type available to the agent. A desire for a means must take as its object the most valuable means available to the agent, and a desire for an end must take as its object the most valuable end available to the agent.

Following a number of contemporary western philosophers, I analyze value in terms of those states of affairs that a fully knowledgeable agent would desire. I argue that in the present context, this analysis must be modified. A fully knowledgeable agent has only those desires that both play a necessary role in motivating the right action and take as their objects the most valuable state of affairs appropriate for their desire type available to the agent. So, in the present context, a desire is permissible if and only if a fully knowledgeable agent would have it. In order to non-accidentally pursue the most valuable ends and means, an agent must know what is most valuable, and know how to bring about what is most valuable.

Finally, I argue that the distinction between permissible and impermissible desires in the *Yogasūtra* is a distinction between desires that a fully knowledgeable agent would have and desires that a fully knowledgeable agent would not have. Hence, according to the *Yogasūtra*, in order to act without desire, an agent must eliminate all desires that a fully knowledgeable agent would not have, and act motivated by desires that a fully knowledgeable agent would have – at least so long as the Some Desires Interpretation is correct. I argue that any version of the Some Desires Interpretation must be consistent with this conclusion.

The first condition of permissible desires

Any version of the Some Desires Interpretation claims that some desires are to be eliminated, and others are not to be eliminated. The desires that are to be eliminated are impermissible. The desires that are not to be eliminated are permissible. Hence any version of the Some Desires Interpretation draws the distinction between desires that are permissible and desires that are impermissible.

Since the argument for the Some Desires Interpretation claims that some desires are permissible because some desires play a necessary role in motivating action, presumably the desires that are permissible are those that play a necessary role in motivating action.[1] A modified version of the air marshal example from Chapter 1 is helpful here. If firearms must be allowed on planes because an armed air marshal must be aboard every flight, it does not follow that passengers other than the air marshal are permitted to carry firearms. Likewise, if desires are permissible because every action must be motivated by a desire, it does not follow that desires that do not motivate action are permissible. If they are, the proponent of the Some Desires Interpretation must offer an additional argument to this effect. Hence in order to be permissible, a desire must play a necessary role in motivating action.

Presumably not all desires that play a necessary role in motivating action are permissible, however. If this were the case, then the only objection that Kṛṣṇa could raise against Arjuna's desire to become a mendicant rather than fight in the battle (2.5) would be that Arjuna's desire to become a mendicant has not yet motivated him to do so. One way to avoid this kind of problem is to stipulate that the action that the permissible desire motivates must be the right action. Whatever desire is permissible in Arjuna's circumstances plays a necessary role in motivating the right action of fighting in the battle. Hence the first condition of a permissible desire is that it plays a necessary role in motivating the right action.

With this first condition in mind, it is worth clarifying the role that desire is typically taken to play in motivating action. As I said in Chapter 1, the predominant theory among western philosophers is the Humean view, according to which an action is produced by a combination of desire and belief.

More specifically, action is produced by a combination of a desire for some end and a means–end belief about how to bring about the desired end. It might be, for example, that my action of going to the café is motivated by my desire for a coffee and my belief that going to the café is a means to having a coffee. In this case, having a coffee is my end, and going to the café is the means to it. Hence in the simplest cases, action is motivated in the following way:

(HTM1)

desire
(for end)
+
belief
(about means to end) ⇨ action

In more complex cases, the desire that combines with belief to motivate action is itself the result of a desire and belief. It might be, for example, that my desire to drink coffee is produced by my desire to finish this chapter tonight, and my belief that drinking coffee is a means to this desired end. In this case, finishing the chapter is my end, and both drinking coffee and going to the café are means to it. These more complex cases may be diagrammed as follows:

(HTM2)

desire (for end) + belief (about means to end)	⇨	desire (for means) + belief (about means to means)	⇨	action

As Hume points out, this chain of means and ends can continue indefinitely. "Ask a man *why he uses exercise*; he will answer, *because he desires to keep his health*. If you then enquire, *why he desires health*, he will readily reply, *because sickness is painful*" (Hume 1951: 293). The desire to avoid pain, combined with the belief that sickness is painful, might produce the desire to avoid sickness. The desire to avoid sickness, combined with the belief that health is a means to avoiding sickness, might produce the desire for health. The desire for health, combined with the belief that exercise is a means to health, might produce the action of exercising.

No matter how long the chain of reasons, however, the explanation of action always ends with some state of affairs that the agent desires for its own sake. Hume continues,

> If you push your enquiries farther, and desire a reason *why he hates pain*, it is impossible he can ever give any. This is an ultimate end, and is never referred to any other object . . . It is impossible there can be a progress *in infinitum*; and that one thing can always be a reason why another is desired. Something must be desirable on its own account, and because of its immediate accord or agreement with human sentiment and affection.
> (Ibid.)

All actions have their origin in a desire for some ultimate end – a state of affairs that the agent does not desire as a means to something else.

In ordinary language, the word 'end' is ambiguous. In one sense, it refers to the agent's ultimate end – that state of affairs that an agent desires for its own sake. In a second sense, however, the word 'end' refers to whatever state of affairs an agent consciously represents as their immediate goal. There is a joke I remember from a movie I once saw. The first character asks, "Why are you here?" The second answers, " 'Why am I here?' Ah, the eternal question." The joke depends on this ambiguity. The first character asks, "What end do you have in mind as your immediate goal in coming here?" The second character answers the question: "What is your ultimate purpose in life?"

In what follows, I will use the word 'end' to refer to an ultimate end. I will refer to any non-ultimate end simply as a means.[2] This convention has at least one odd consequence: in many cases the state of affairs that the agent consciously represents as their immediate goal is not their end. If I ask someone in an awkward, overly philosophical way, "What is your end in riding the bus?" they are more likely to answer "getting to work" than "my family's prosperity," because getting to work is the goal they have in mind, even though on reflection they will admit that they do not go to work for its own sake. According to the distinction as I have drawn it, however, getting to work is not the agent's end, unless they desire to get to work for its own sake, and not as a means to something else.

On the other hand, if every state of affairs that an agent might cite in answer to an inquiry of this kind must be categorized as a desire for an end, then the category of desires for means is unnecessary. Even the desire to board the bus, the desire to pay the fare, and so on might be cited by the agent as their end, so long as my question is formulated as "Why are you standing up from the bench right now?", "why are you rooting through your pockets?," and so on. Yet it certainly seems accurate in the more complicated coffee case to say that my desire for a coffee is a desire for a means to an end, rather than a desire for an end. So in what follows, I simply refer to any state of affairs that an agent desires as a means to some further end as a desire for a means, and reserve the word 'end' for those states of affairs that an agent desires for their own sake.

This is not to say that the only states of affairs that might be the objects of desires for ends are states of affairs that an agent could not possibly desire for further reasons. Hume's example of the desire to avoid pain seems to be an example of this kind,[3] but even the desire for coffee with which I began might be a desire for an end, so long as I simply desire coffee for its own sake. Even if it is true that drinking coffee is a means to finishing the book, it need not be that I desire to drink coffee for this reason. So, while it may seem that I am defining the word 'end' rather narrowly, I mean to allow for any state of affairs that the agent desires for its own sake, no matter how seemingly trivial it is, to be the object of a desire for an end.

Indian texts commonly draw the distinction between a desire for a means and a desire for an end as well. One way in which these texts diverge from the Humean view is that they typically cite the desire to do what one is doing as an additional condition of action.[4] In his commentary to *Manusmṛti* 2.3, Kullūkabhaṭṭa explains the production of action in the following way:

> a *saṅkalpa* is a cognition, whose content (*viṣaya*) is: 'by this action, this desired result (*iṣṭhaṃphalaṃ*) is achieved'. Following that [*saṅkalpa*], it having been understood [that] by this means, the desired [purpose] [is attained], an *icchā* (desire) towards that [action] arises.
>
> (Dave 1972–1985: 158, lines 9–10)[5]

Thinking "this action is a means to this desired end," an agent comes to desire to perform the action that is a means to the desired end.

This same basic model is also endorsed by Viśvanātha Nyāya-Pañcānana in the *Bhāṣā-Pariccheda*. He explains that

> The desire to do (*cikīrṣā*) is that desire (*icchā*) characterized by feasibility by one's effort (*kṛti*). The cause of that [*cikīrṣā*] is the belief in the feasibility by one's effort and [the belief in the effort's] instrumentality to what is desired.
>
> (Viśvanātha Nyāya-Pañcānana 1954: 241)[6]

Again, a desired end, when accompanied by the belief that an action of the agent is a means to that end, produces the desire to perform the action believed to be a means to the agent's end.[7] The desire to do what one does is a desire for the means to one's end.

In order to represent each of these possibilities, (HTM2) can be revised to read:

(HTM3)

desire						
(for end)						
+	⇨	desire				
belief		(for means)				
(about means		+	⇨	desire	⇨	action
to end)		belief		(for means)		
		(about means				
		to means)				

It seems that under the right circumstances, both desires for ends and desires for means – of both sorts – might play a necessary role in motivating action. In the original, more complex example in which I go to the café in order to finish this chapter, if I do not desire to finish this chapter, I do not go to the café. Likewise, if I do not desire to drink coffee as a means to finishing this chapter, I do not go to the café. It might even be that if I do not desire to go to the café, I do not go to the café. We can imagine someone who desires a coffee, and knows that they must go to the café in order to get it, for example, who explains the fact that they do not walk to the café by saying, "I just don't want to go to the café." Hence desires for ends and desires for means (of both sorts) might play a necessary role in motivating action.

If both desires for ends and desires for means might play a necessary role in motivating action, then both desires for ends and desires for means might play a necessary role in motivating the right action – at least absent any argument to the contrary.[8] Hence both desires for ends and desires for means might meet the first condition of a permissible desire.

While Hume is certainly correct to point out that some actions are explained by a series of desires for means that are longer than that represented in (HTM3), for the sake of simplicity in what follows, I will focus on actions that fit within this model. This strategy has the advantage of avoiding redundancy, while at the same time analyzing desires of seemingly every sort.

The second condition of permissible desires

As I argued above, not all desires that play a necessary role in motivating action are permissible. In order to be permissible, a desire must play a necessary role in motivating the right action. Likewise, however, not all desires that play a necessary role in motivating the right action are permissible. In the context of the *Gītā*, Kṛṣṇa is careful to convince Arjuna not only to fight in the battle, and thereby perform the right action, but also to fight in the battle for the right reasons.

At the outset of the *Gītā*, Kṛṣṇa tells Arjuna that if he fights in the battle, he will benefit, regardless of whether his side wins or loses. If they win, Arjuna will attain sovereignty over the earth (2.37). If they lose, Arjuna will attain heaven as a result of participating in a righteous war (2.31 and 2.37). It is clear in both what precedes and what follows this passage, however, that Kṛṣṇa does not advise Arjuna to be motivated by desires for these things. These passages are widely taken as an appeal to Arjuna's lower nature.[9] Even if these desires play a necessary role in motivating the right action of fighting in the battle, they are nonetheless impermissible.

At this point I do not want to say too much about which desires Kṛṣṇa does endorse, since this is one of the central disputes under consideration in this book. In order to avoid this issue for the time being, let us assume that Kṛṣṇa's advice to act for the sake of *lokasaṃgraha* (the holding together of the world) in Chapter 3 (3.20) should be taken at face value, as the advice to act motivated by the desire for the end of *lokasaṃgraha*.

If Kṛṣṇa advises Arjuna to act motivated by a desire for the end of *lokasaṃgraha*, rather than a desire for heaven or sovereignty over the earth, then presumably he takes *lokasaṃgraha* to be a more valuable end than heaven or sovereignty over the earth. Indeed, if Kṛṣṇa advises Arjuna to act motivated by a desire for the end of *lokasaṃgraha*, presumably he takes *lokasaṃgraha* to be the most valuable end available by means of Arjuna's actions. Otherwise he would advise Arjuna to desire, and perhaps do, something else.[10]

This implies that a permissible desire for an end must meet a second condition. A desire for an end is permissible only if the state of affairs that it takes as its object is the most valuable end available to the agent. I qualify the condition with the phrase 'available to the agent' in order to avoid cases in which the agent has no way to contribute to the most valuable state of affairs. If we assume, for example, that the reversal of global warming is the most valuable state of affairs, it still might be that I can do little, if anything, to bring this about. If I can do nothing to bring this about, then I should not desire it – at least in the present context – because I should not act on it, and only desires that motivate action are permissible (as Condition One states).

If Kṛṣṇa advises Arjuna to fight in the battle as a means to the end of *lokasaṃgraha*, presumably he takes fighting in the battle to be the best means available by means of Arjuna's actions to the end of *lokasaṃgraha*.

Otherwise he would advise Arjuna to do otherwise. As I said in the last section, it might be that under certain circumstances, both a desire for an end and a desire for a means play necessary roles in motivating action. In order to understand cases like this, let us assume that in Arjuna's circumstances, both a desire for an end and a desire for a means play necessary roles in motivating his action of fighting in the battle, and that the desire for a means that Kṛṣṇa advises is the desire to fight in the battle.

If this is right, then a permissible desire for a means must also meet a second criterion. A desire for a means is permissible only if the state of affairs that it takes as its object is the best means available by means of some action of the agent to the most valuable end available by means of some action of the agent. This is a complicated way of putting the requirement, but it will have to do for now.

Like permissible desires for ends, permissible desires for means can also be analyzed in terms of value. If some state of affairs is a means to a valuable end, then it is also valuable, at least instrumentally. If some state of affairs is the best means to the most valuable end, then it is the most valuable means to the most valuable end.[11] Hence a desire for a means is permissible only if the state of affairs that it takes as its object is the most valuable means available by means of some action of the agent to the most valuable end available by means of some action of the agent.

Again, this is a complicated way of putting the requirement. In order to simplify it, I will use the phrase 'most valuable means available to the agent' to refer to the most valuable means available by means of some action of the agent to the most valuable end available by means of some action of the agent. Hence the second condition for a permissible desire for a means states: A desire for a means is permissible only if the state of affairs that it takes as its object is the most valuable means available to the agent. Put this way, the second condition for a permissible desire for a means parallels the second condition for a permissible desire for an end.

At this point, there are two versions of the second condition, one for each type of desire. A desire for an end is permissible only if the state of affairs that it takes as its object is the most valuable end available to the agent, and a desire for a means is permissible only if the state of affairs that it takes as its object is the most valuable means available to the agent. The two versions of Condition Two may be combined to read: A desire is permissible only if it takes as its object the most valuable state of affairs available by means of some action of the agent appropriate to the desire type.

Let me explain this further. In the example as I have described it, both the desire for the end of *lokasaṃgraha* and the desire for the means of fighting in the battle are permissible. Hence both desires play a necessary role in motivating action. It might be that the roles are identical, and that the role that the desire for *lokasaṃgraha* plays could be played by the desire to fight in the battle, and vice versa. It is more likely, however, that the roles that the desires play can only be played by desires of a certain type – the role that the desire for *lokasaṃgraha* plays can only be played by a desire for an end, and the role that the desire to fight in the battle plays can only be played by a desire for a means. If, instead of a desire for the means of fighting in the battle, Arjuna desires some other end – like heaven – the action of fighting does not arise.

One way to describe the different roles is to say that a desire for an end is the origin of motivation. A desire for a means, in contrast, connects the original motivation with action. So the roles that these desires play are specialized. No desire for an end can connect a desire for an end with action without becoming a desire for a means, and no desire for a means can be the origin of motivation without becoming a desire for an end.

What Condition Two says is that each type of desire is permissible only if it takes the most valuable state of affairs (available by means of some action of the agent) for a desire of its type. This means that in order for a desire for a means to be permissible, it need not necessarily take the most valuable state of affairs available by means of some action of the agent as its object; it need only take the most valuable means available by means of some action of the agent as its object. In order for a desire for an end to be permissible, in contrast, it must take the most valuable end available by means of some action of the agent as its object; it need not – and should not – take the most valuable means available by means of some action of the agent as its object.

Imagine, for example, that Arjuna desires the end of *lokasaṃgraha*, but is not yet motivated to act, because he lacks a desire for the means to *lokasaṃgraha*. In determining what to desire as a means, Arjuna must think about what the most valuable means to the end of *lokasaṃgraha* is. Whatever the most valuable means to the end of *lokasaṃgraha* is, that is what Arjuna should desire – so long as it is available by means of some action of his. If, instead, Arjuna thinks more generally about what the most valuable state of affairs is, he will come to a conclusion that is of no use to him in his circumstances – the conclusion that *lokasaṃgraha* is the most valuable state of affairs available by some action of his. Hence, in order to meet the second condition, a desire must take as its object the most valuable state of affairs available by means of some action of the agent appropriate to its desire type.

At this point conditions one and two can be combined. A desire is permissible only if it both (1) plays a necessary role in motivating the right action, and (2) takes as its object the most valuable state of affairs available by means of some action of the agent appropriate to the desire type.

An analysis of value

So far I have said relatively little about what I mean by the word 'valuable'. It might seem as if the notion of value is entirely unproblematic, and in no need of analysis. It is synonymous with words like 'good', 'important', 'desirable', and so on, and most people seem to have a firm intuitive grasp of what these words mean and how to use them.

Nonetheless, these words are notoriously difficult to define. G. E. Moore, for example, argues that 'good' is indefinable because it is a simple notion. For any definition of good – other than those that simply cite synonyms, like 'valuable' – "it may be always asked, with significance . . . whether it is itself good" (Moore 1903: 418). Moore offers the following example:

> It may easily be thought, at first sight, that to be good may mean to be that which we desire to desire . . . But if we carry the investigation further, and ask ourselves "Is it good to desire to desire A?" it is apparent, on a little reflection, that this question is itself as intelligible, as the original question "Is A good?"
>
> (Ibid.)

If it can be asked intelligibly whether it is good to desire to desire A, then 'I desire to desire A' cannot simply mean 'A is good'. If it did, then the question 'Is it good to desire to desire A?' would amount to the question 'Do I desire to desire to desire to desire A?', which it does not (ibid.).

Despite this difficulty, contemporary philosophers continue to develop accounts of value. One strategy for analyzing value is based on the intuition that in ordinary life, we often try to step out of our actual circumstances and assume the point of view of a more objective, balanced, and better informed person. Indeed, this intuition is what makes Arjuna's appeal to Kṛṣṇa – who is an incarnation of God, and therefore omniscient – for advice sensible. As Connie Rosati says, "[w]e wonder . . . whether there is some way to evaluate our options other than from within the standpoints of the lives with which they present us. For it seems that only such an evaluation could determine our real good" (Rosati 1995: 296).

Michael Smith develops an account of this sort. He claims that "it is a platitude to say that what it is desirable that we do is what we would desire to do if we were fully rational" (Smith 1994: 150). That is, it is an obvious truth that what it is valuable for an agent to do under certain circumstances is whatever the agent would desire to do if they were fully knowledgeable and fully rational.[12]

Rosati refers to these accounts as "Full Information Accounts of the Good." The basic claim is that something is valuable if and only if a fully knowledgeable person would desire it.[13] Peter Railton offers an account of this sort in his analysis of an agent's good. He draws a distinction between an agent's subjective and objective interests. An agent's subjective interests are simply the agent's desires. They "frequently reflect ignorance, confusion, or lack of consideration, as hindsight attests" (Railton 1986: 173). Often we think, after having done something imprudent, "If only I had known . . .". For this reason, subjective reasons do not capture the notion of an individual's good. As Railton says, "the fact that I am now so constituted that I desire something which, had I better knowledge of it, I would wish I had never sought, does not seem to recommend it to me as part of my good" (ibid.).

Objective interests, on the other hand, do capture the notion of an individual's good.

> Give to an actual individual A unqualified cognitive and imaginative powers, and full factual and nomological information about his physical and psychological constitution, capacities, circumstances, history, and so on. A will have become A+, who has complete and vivid knowledge of himself and his environment, and whose instrumental rationality is in no way defective. We now ask A+ to tell us not what he currently wants, but what he would want his non-idealized self A to want . . . were he to find himself in the actual condition and circumstances of A.
>
> (Ibid.)

Whatever A+ recommends that A desire is an objective interest of A, and whatever is an objective interest of A is part of A's good.

Neither Smith's nor Railton's account perfectly suits my purposes in the present context. Railton's analysis is limited to what is valuable for the agent. I am concerned, however, with value more generally – not just what is valuable to me, but what is valuable period. Smith's account, in contrast, is an analysis of what is valuable period. It leaves open the possibility that what is valuable for an agent to do is not relative to the agent's good (Smith 1994: 164–174). I want to do the same.

The problem with Smith's account is that it is only an analysis of what it is valuable for an agent to do. I am concerned more generally, however, with the question of which states of affairs are valuable. I do not mean to limit myself to the narrower question of which states of affairs among those that might be actions of the agent are valuable.

So rather than adopt either account, I want to offer an analysis that avoids both limitations. I propose the following analysis of value: Some state of affairs is valuable (under some set of circumstances) if and only if a fully knowledgeable agent would desire it (under those circumstances).[14]

Of course, in the present context, this analysis needs to be modified. Since we are under the assumption that the Some Desires Interpretation is correct, we must also assume that the fully knowledgeable agent knows that the Some Desires Interpretation is correct. Since the fully knowledgeable agent is rational, they draw the same inferences that I have above. In order for a desire to be permissible, it must (1) play a necessary role in motivating the right action, and (2) take as its object the most valuable state of affairs available by means of some action of the agent appropriate to the desire type. So every desire of a fully knowledgeable person will meet conditions (1) and (2).

This means that there might be a state of affairs that is valuable under the circumstances, but which the fully knowledgeable person would not desire. First, the valuable state of affairs might not be the most valuable state of affairs available to the agent appropriate to the desire type. If it is not, then the fully knowledgeable person would not desire it, even though it is valuable. Second, the desire for the valuable state of affairs might not play a necessary role in motivating the right action. If it does not, then the fully knowledgeable person would not desire it, even though it is valuable.

So, in the present context, it is false that some state of affairs is valuable if and only if a fully knowledgeable agent would desire it. Nonetheless, this kind of analysis can be put to good use in the present context. Rather than using the full information account as an analysis of the good, I want to use it as an analysis of permissible desires.

If a fully knowledgeable agent would desire some state of affairs, then the desire for that state of affairs both (1) plays a necessary role in motivating the right action, and (2) takes as its object the most valuable state of affairs available by means of some action of the agent appropriate to the desire type. Thus far I have said that conditions (1) and (2) are necessary conditions of a permissible desire. I have avoided the claim that conditions (1) and (2) are sufficient conditions of a permissible desire in order to leave open the possibility that permissible desires must meet some additional condition(s). If there is a third (fourth, and so on) condition, however, it will be met by any desire of a fully knowledgeable person for the same reasons that the first and second condition will be met. The fully knowledgeable person will know of the third (fourth, and so on) condition, and their desires will be in accord with it. Hence a desire is permissible if and only if a fully knowledgeable agent would have it.

There are, then, two ways of characterizing permissible desires. First, permissible desires can be characterized, at least in part, as desires that meet conditions (1) and (2). Second, permissible desires can be characterized as those desires that a fully knowledgeable agent would have. In what follows, it will be important to keep both of these characterizations in mind.

Permissible and impermissible desires in the *Yogasūtra*

In this section I argue that the *Yogasūtra* draws the distinction between permissible and impermissible desires in terms of desires that a fully knowledgeable agent would and would not have, respectively. I want to begin, however, with a disclaimer. In what follows, I continue to assume that the Some Desires Interpretation is correct. In the last chapter I argued that there are two justifications that might be offered for Premise Two of the argument for the Some Desires Interpretation. Premise Two reads: "Desire is a necessary condition of action." According to the first justification, Premise Two is analytically, or at least obviously true, hence the *Gītā* and other Indian texts must be consistent with it. I argued that this argument is unconvincing.

The second justification for Premise Two is that since desire is a necessary condition of action in the Indian philosophical traditions more generally, we should assume that the advice to act without desire in the *Gītā* amounts to the advice to act without a particular kind of desire. At this point I assume that the Some Desires Interpretation is correct because I assume that the claim that the Indian philosophical tradition in general accepts that desire is a necessary condition of action. Since I assume that the Indian philosophical tradition in general accepts the claim that desire is a necessary condition of action, I assume that desire is a necessary condition of action in the *Yogasūtra*.

The disclaimer is that there is no evidence in either the *Yogasūtra* or Vyāsa's *Yogasūtrabhāṣya* to support this claim. So while my analysis of the *Yogasūtra* assumes that the text takes desire to be a necessary condition of action, my analysis should not be taken as evidence for the second justification of the second premise of the argument for the Some Desires Interpretation.

If the argument for the Some Desires Interpretation is convincing, and the *Yogasūtra* draws a distinction between permissible and impermissible desires, then it defines permissible and impermissible desires in the way that I have outlined above, in terms of the desires that a fully knowledgeable agent would and would not have, respectively. Patañjali draws a distinction between two types of states, both of which might be translated as 'desire' in English. *Rāga* is a desire that something occur. *Dveṣa* is a desire that something not occur.[15] Patañjali defines the two terms concisely: "*rāga* is the consequence of pleasure" (*Yogasūtra* 2.7, Sārvabhauma and Nyāyaratna 1970: 154, line 4)[16] and "*dveṣa* is the consequence of pain" (*Yogasūtra* 2.8, Sārvabhauma and Nyāyaratna 1970: 155, line 2).[17] Vyāsa elaborates that

> one who has experienced pleasure, [and who has] a pre-existing memory of that pleasure, the desire (*gardha*), thirst (*tṛṣṇa*), or greed (*lobha*) toward that pleasure or the means to it, that is *rāga*.
>
> (*Yogasūtrabhāṣya* 2.7, Sārvabhauma and Nyāyaratna 1970: 154–155, lines 5 and 1)[18]

> One who has experienced pain, [and who has] a pre-existing memory of that pain, the aversion (*pratigho*), rage (*manyu*), wish to destroy (*jighāmsā*), or anger (*krodha*) which one has towards that pain or the means to it, that is *dveṣa*.
>
> (*Yogasūtrabhāṣya* 2.8, Sārvabhauma and Nyāyaratna 1970: 155, lines 3–4)[19]

Rāga and *dveṣa* are states that arise from past experiences of pleasure and pain, respectively, and which motivate an agent to pursue or avoid the source of that pleasure or pain, or that which they take to be the means to the source of pleasure or pain.[20] (As I mentioned earlier, these passages draw the distinction between a desire for a means and a desire for an end.)

Patañjali counts both *rāga* and *dveṣa* as *kleśas* (afflictions or hindrances), along with *avidyā* (ignorance), *asmitā* (a sense of self) and *abhiniveśa* (the will to live). "*Avidyā, asmitā, rāga, dveṣa,* [and] *abhiniveśa* [are] the five *kleśas*" (*Yogasūtra* 2.3, Sārvabhauma and Nyāyaratna 1970: 142, line 3).[21]

In his commentary to this verse, Vyāsa explains *kleśas* in terms of their causal role in both the manifestation of *prakṛti* (consisting of the *guṇas*) and the production of *karma*.

> The *kleśas* are the five errors (*viparyaya*). These [*kleśas*], [when] active, strengthen the dominance of the *guṇas*, cause the manifestation [of the *guṇas*], bring up a stream of cause and effect, and, having become mutually supporting, carry out the maturation of *karma*.
>
> (*Yogasū trabhāṣya* 2.3, Sārvabhauma and Nyāyaratna 1970: 142–143, lines 4 and 2–3)[22]

The state of *kaivalya* (liberation) is repeatedly described as a state in which the manifestation of the *prakṛti* associated with a particular person ceases, and in which *karma* no longer functions.[23] Hence the *kleśas* are fundamental to – and probably a necessary condition of – a person's persistence in *saṃsāra* (the cycle of rebirth). The elimination of the *kleśas* is crucial to the attainment of *kaivalya*. This implies that *rāga* and *dveṣa* – along with the other *kleśas* – are obstacles to *kaivalya*, and therefore ought to be eliminated. Hence any desire that can be classified as *rāga* or *dveṣa* is impermissible.

Among the five *kleśas, avidyā* is foundational. At *Yogasūtra* 2.4, Patañjali says, "*avidyā* is the field [*kṣetra*] of those that follow [it]" (Sārvabhauma and Nyāyaratna 1970: 143, line 3).[24] In his commentary to this verse, Vyāsa seems to go even further. "All these *kleśas* are divisions of *avidyā*. How so? With regard to all [of them], *avidyā* saturates them. That object that is affected by *avidyā*, the *kleśas* adhere closely to that very thing" (Sārvabhauma and Nyāyaratna 1970: 147, lines 4–6).[25] If desires that are based on *avidyā* are *rāga* and *dveṣa*, and *rāga* and *dveṣa* are impermissible, then any desire that is based on *avidyā* is impermissible. This, according to the *Yogasūtra*, is the essential criterion of an impermissible desire.[26]

This conclusion is further supported by the *Yogasūtra's* characterization of *vairāgya* (desirelessness). Just as *rāga* and *dveṣa* are not only explained by *avidyā*, but also identified as types of *avidyā*, likewise *vairāgya* is both explained by and identified with discrimination (*prasaṃkhyāna*) and knowledge (*jñāna*).

In verses 1.15 and 1.16, Patañjali distinguishes two types of *vairāgya*, a lower type and a higher type, respectively:

> The person who has an indifference to objects seen and described, that person is in the detached state that is *vairāgya*.
>
> (*Yogasūtra* 1.15, Sārvabhauma and Nyāyaratna 1970: 47, line 1)[27]

> The absence of the cravings for the *guṇas*, as a result of the discernment of *puruṣa*, that is the highest [*vairāgya*].
>
> (*Yogasūtra* 1.16, Sārvabhauma and Nyāyaratna 1970: 49, line 1)[28]

Vyāsa explains both types of *vairāgya* as a direct consequence of knowledge. His commentary on 1.15 reads,

> Of the mind [which is] impartial to objects seen, [such as] women, food, drink, [and] power, [and which is also] impartial to objects heard, [such as] the attainments of heaven, bodilessness, or dissolution into *prakṛti*, [which] even when there is a union [of the mind] with objects that are agreeable and not agreeable, is a seer of the faults of [these] objects, by means of the power of discrimination [*prasaṃkhyāna*], [whose] nature is non-enjoyment,[29] [for which there is] emptiness with regard to that which is to be abandoned and that which is to be gained, [whose] consciousness is subjugated, that [mind is said to be] *vairāgya*.
>
> (Sārvabhauma and Nyāyaratna 1970: 47–8, lines 2 and 1–3)[30]

A *vairāgin* (person who is desireless) is without desire for both things that might be experienced by means of the senses, and most things that cannot be. All of the normally alluring items of the world are categorized as objects seen (*dṛṣṭa*). The category of objects heard (*anuśravika*), in contrast, includes sublime, immaterial rewards for moral and spiritual progress, with the exception of *kaivalya*, none of which a human being can experience first-hand.[31]

This state of desirelessness is the direct consequence of the *vairāgin's* insight into the nature of reality. The most basic fault of each of the objects mentioned is that they are impermanent. Since they are impermanent, they are a source of pain, and a distraction from the attainment of more valuable ends.[32] Endowed with full knowledge of the nature of these objects, a fully knowledgeable person's desires for these things disappear, much as a typical person's desire for milk disappears when they realize the milk is sour. The ordinary person, ignorant of the nature of these things, continues to desire them.

Vyāsa makes the same basic point in his commentary to verse 1.16. Higher *vairāgya* is simply the consequence of a deeper knowledge of the nature of things.

> [One person] is impartial, seeing the fault in objects seen and heard about. [Another person] from the practice of seeing *puruṣa* (the true self), [whose] *buddhi* (discriminative faculty) is satisfied in detachment and truth, is impartial towards the manifest and unmanifest qualities of the *guṇas*.
>
> That *vairāgya* is two-fold. With regard to that [two-fold *vairāgya*], that which is higher, that is nothing but clarity of knowledge (*tajjñānaprasādamātram*). When that [clarity of knowledge] has arisen, the person [in] whom this knowledge has arisen thinks, "That which is to be attained is attained. Those *kleśas*, which are to be diminished, are diminished. Cut is the tight-fitting knot, the continuity of births, from the uninterruptedness of which [a person], having been born, dies, and having died,

is born." The highest *vairāgya* is the highest limit of knowledge (*jñānasyaiva parā kāṣṭā vairāgyam*). *Kaivalya* is not to be [understood as] distinct from this.

(Sārvabhauma and Nyāyaratna 1970: 49–51, lines 2–3 and 1–2)[33]

Vyāsa begins by restating the form of *vairāgya* described in the previous verse – *vairāgya* with regard to tangible objects or moral and spiritual accomplishments short of *kaivalya*. He then draws a distinction between this kind of *vairāgya* and higher *vairāgya*, in which the agent is indifferent to *prakṛti* altogether.

This higher *vairāgya* is a direct consequence of the knowledge of the distinction between *puruṣa* and *prakṛti*. Indeed, in this short passage Vyāsa twice says that higher *vairāgya* is nothing but perfect knowledge.

Since any desire based on *avidyā* is either *rāga* or *dveṣa*, and since any desire that is *rāga* or *dveṣa* is impermissible, any desire that is the result of *avidyā* is impermissible. If the words *rāga* and *dveṣa* are simply translated as 'desire' and 'aversion', and are taken to exhaust all of those states to which the English word 'desire' refers, then the *Yogasūtra* discourages all desire – contrary to the proponent of the Some Desires Interpretation's contention. If all desire is discouraged, and desire is a necessary condition of action, a fully knowledgeable person simply does not act.

This conclusion is contradicted, however, by Patañjali's description of Īśvara as both perfectly knowledgeable and motivated to help others. *Yogasūtra* 1.24 through 1.26 read,

> Īśvara is a distinct *puruṣa*, untouched by *kleśas*, *karmas*, *vipākas* (the *karmic* fruitions of actions), and their impressions (*āśaya*) (*Yogasūtra* 1.24, Sārvabhauma and Nyāyaratna 1970: 64, line 3).[34] In him, the seed of all knowledge is second to none (Yogasūtra 1.25, Sārvabhauma and Nyāyaratna 1970: 74, line 2).[35] Also, since [there is] no limitation by time, [he is] the *guru* of *puruṣas* (*Yogasūtra* 1.26, Sārvabhauma and Nyāyaratna 1970: 79, line 4).[36]

Īśvara is both perfectly knowledgeable, and entirely free from the *kleśas* and their *karmic* consequences in the form of impressions and their fruition. Hence Īśvara is entirely without both *rāga* and *dveṣa*. Nonetheless, Īśvara teaches teachers that have come before. He is the *guru* of *puruṣas*.

The action of teaching previous teachers, Vyāsa claims, is motivated by compassion for those living beings who might benefit from the teachings of the sages.

> [Īśvara has] the *prayojana* (motive) of the assistance of beings, even though there is no [possibility of the] promotion of his [own] self. At the dissolutions of the epochs and the great dissolutions, [he resolves,] "I will remove [those] *puruṣas* [who are] *saṃsārins* (those trapped in *saṃsāra*)

by teaching knowledge and *dharma*." And so it is said, "the first knower, from compassion, having inhabited a created mind, the venerable and great *ṛṣi* (seer) proclaimed [this] doctrine to Asuri, [who was] desirous to know [it]".

(*Yogasūtrabhāṣya* 1.25, Sārvabhauma and Nyāyaratna 1970: 77–79, lines 1, 1, and 1–2)[37]

Īśvara is motivated by compassion for those who persist in the cycle of *saṃsāra*. If desire is a necessary condition even of the actions of Īśvara, then presumably Īśvara has a desire to be compassionate, or a desire that *saṃsārins* no longer suffer, and this motivates the action of creating a mind, inhabiting the mind, teaching teachers, and so on.[38]

Since Īśvara is perfectly knowledgeable, however, he is without *kleśas*, because the *kleśas* are based on *avidyā*. If he is without *kleśas*, then he is without *rāga* and *dveṣa*, since *rāga* and *dveṣa* are *kleśas*. If he is without *rāga* and *dveṣa*, but nonetheless acts, then the category of desire is not exhausted by *rāga* and *dveṣa*.

This is not to say that only Īśvara acts on permissible desires. If the *Yogasūtra* admits the possibility of *jīvanmukti* (the state of living liberation) – as Ian Whicher (1998) and others claim – presumably the *jīvanmukta's* actions will be motivated by desires that are in accord with knowledge as well. Indeed, if *rāga* and *dveṣa* have the consequences of strengthening the dominance of the *guṇas* and carrying out the maturation of *karma*, as Vyāsa claims in his commentary to 2.3 (see above), then even the ordinary person must be capable of acting without *rāga* and *dveṣa* in order to make progress towards *kaivalya*. This is the conclusion that the Some Desires Interpretation demands.

If this is right, then in the context of the *Yogasūtra*, the words *rāga* and *dveṣa* should be translated as something like 'impermissible desire' and 'impermissible aversion', respectively, rather than simply as 'desire' and 'aversion' – at least if the Some Desires Interpretation is correct. This leaves room for desires that are neither *rāga* nor *dveṣa* – permissible desires and aversions.

Hence the *Yogasūtra* accepts the analysis of permissible and impermissible desires that I developed in the first three sections of this chapter. A desire is either based on *avidyā* or it is based on *jñāna*. If it is based on *avidyā*, then it is impermissible. If it is based on *jñāna*, then it is permissible. Hence a desire is permissible if and only if it is a desire that a fully knowledgeable agent would have.

As I point out in subsequent chapters, most proponents of the Some Desires Interpretation argue for a more specific criterion that all permissible desires share. Nonetheless, any Some Desires Interpretation must be consistent with the conclusion that all permissible desires are desires that a fully knowledgeable agent would have under the circumstances. If all permissible desires share some additional criterion as well, then some additional argument is needed.

The problem of desirelessness, then, at least as it is found in the *Yogasūtra*, has a straightforward – albeit perhaps only partial – solution. An agent ought to eliminate all desires that a fully knowledgeable agent would not have, and act motivated by desires that a fully knowledgeable agent would have. In order to become desireless, then, an agent must come to have true beliefs about the relative value of things, and desire accordingly.

In Chapter 1 I considered Teschner's and Brodbeck's No Action interpretations. One of the objections that I offered to these views was that they take the advice to act without desire as advice about what to believe, rather than what to desire. Now it is clearer why this interpretation might seem plausible. In order to become desireless, an agent must come to have true beliefs, not only about the faulty nature of material objects and heavenly rewards, but also about the distinction between *puruṣa* and *prakṛti*. It is this last belief in particular that Teschner and Brodbeck identify with desirelessness in the context of the *Bhagavadgītā*. The word 'desireless' does not simply mean fully knowledgeable, but the two are so closely related that it is impossible to achieve one without achieving the other. A person is desireless just in case they both have no desires that a fully knowledgeable person would not have, and act on only those desires that a fully knowledgeable person would have.

3 The desire for *Mokṣa*

In the last chapter I argued that a permissible desire must meet two conditions. First, the desire must play a necessary role in motivating the right action. Second, the desire must take as its object the most valuable state of affairs available to the agent appropriate to the desire type. I also argued that a desire is permissible if and only if it is a desire that a fully knowledgeable agent would have.

I also argued that according to the *Yogasūtra*, the distinction between permissible and impermissible desires amounts to the distinction between desires that a fully knowledgeable agent would have and desires that a fully knowledgeable agent would not have. Hence the problem of desirelessness – at least in the *Yogasūtra* – seems to have a straightforward solution. An agent ought to eliminate all desires that a fully knowledgeable agent would not have, and act on those that a fully knowledgeable agent would have.

Of course, most proponents of the Some Desires Interpretation insist that permissible desires share some additional, more specific criterion. Just those passages from the *Yogasūtra* that I considered in the last chapter seem to support at least three more specific versions of the Some Desires Interpretation. First, all permissible desires lack phenomenological saliency. Second, all permissible desires are unselfish. Third, the only permissible desire is the desire for *mokṣa*.

In this chapter, I consider the view that the only permissible desire is the desire for *mokṣa*. I consider five arguments for this position. According to the first argument, the *Gītā* denies that anything other than *mokṣa* has value of any sort. If *mokṣa* is the only state of affairs that is valuable, then it is always the most valuable state of affairs available by means of some action of the agent appropriate to any desire type. Hence only the desire for *mokṣa* is permissible. I object that according to the *Gītā*, states of affairs other than *mokṣa* are valuable. Minimally, other states of affairs are instrumentally valuable, as a means to *mokṣa*.

According to the second argument, only a desire for intrinsically valuable states of affairs is permissible. Since *mokṣa* is the only intrinsically valuable state of affairs, the desire for *mokṣa* is the only permissible desire. I object that at least some of those states of affairs that are a means to *mokṣa* are intrinsically valuable as well. Otherwise there is no sensible explanation for why certain actions, rather than their opposites, lead to *mokṣa*.

The third argument states that only desires for the most valuable states of affairs available to the agent – regardless of the desire type – are permissible. Since *mokṣa* is always the most valuable state of affairs available to the agent, only a desire for *mokṣa* is permissible. I object that the means to an end can be as valuable as the end itself. In some cases, a means to a valuable end is even more valuable than the end itself.

The fourth argument states that only desires for the most intrinsically valuable states of affairs available to the agent – regardless of the desire type – are permissible. Since *mokṣa* is always the most intrinsically valuable state of affairs available to the agent, only a desire for *mokṣa* is permissible. I object that if this stipulation is accepted, neither the *jīvanmukta* nor God has desires. Hence neither the *jīvanmukta* nor God acts.

Finally, the proponent of the *Mokṣa*-only Interpretation might say that the desire for *mokṣa* should be understood broadly, to refer not only to the desire for *mokṣa* itself, but also to the desire for anything that is a means to *mokṣa*. I argue that this version of the *Mokṣa*-only Interpretation is importantly misleading. Since none of these arguments are convincing, the *Mokṣa*-only Interpretation is implausible.

Three versions of the Some Desires Interpretation

Most proponents of the Some Desires Interpretation insist that all permissible desires share some additional, more specific criterion. They tend to disagree, however, about what the additional criterion is. It is easy to see why. In just those passages from the *Yogasūtra* that I considered in the last chapter, there seems to be evidence for at least three more specific versions of the Some Desires Interpretation.

First, in his commentary to *Yogasūtra* 2.7, Vyāsa seems to say that *rāga* is synonymous with thirst (*tṛṣṇa*) and greed (*lobha*). In his commentary to *Yogasūtra* 2.8, he seems to say that *dveṣa* is synonymous with rage (*manyu*), the wish to destroy (*jighāmsā*), and anger (*krodha*). If *rāga* and *dveṣa* constitute the impermissible class of desires, then perhaps impermissible desires are simply those that are phenomenologically salient, and permissible desires are those that are not phenomenologically salient.

In the *Gītā*, Kṛṣṇa seems to equate *kāma* and *krodha* (anger). Arjuna asks, "moved by what, then, does a person act [in a way that is] blameworthy?" (3.36, Sadhale 1985a: 337, lines 17–18).[1] Kṛṣṇa responds,

> this is *kāma* (desire). This is *krodha* (anger). Its cause is the *guṇa rajas*. Know this [which is] all consuming, and greatly destructive to be the enemy. As fire is covered by smoke, and a mirror by dust, as an embryo is covered by the membrane, in the same way, that [knowledge] is covered by this [*kāma*]. The knowledge of the wise ones is [even] covered

> by this eternal nemesis with the form of *kāma*, O Arjuna, [which is] an insatiable fire.
>
> (3.37–3.39, Sadhale 1985a: 338, 342, lines 36–37 and 12–15)[2]

If impermissible desires are like an "all consuming," "insatiable fire" and obstruct knowledge, then perhaps impermissible desires are those that the agent can feel. Perhaps they are something like a craving, or intense urge. It is well known that desires of this sort tend to obstruct deliberation and knowledge. So the rationale for eliminating desires of this type is straightforward.

A second view that seems supported by the *Yogasūtra* passages in the last chapter is the view that only unselfish desires are permissible. Patañjali says that Īśvara is omniscient. "In him, the seed of the knowledge of everything is second to none" (*Yogasūtra* 1.25, Sārvabhauma and Nyāyaratna 1970: 74, line 2).[3] Īśvara is motivated exclusively by the desire to help others. He has no desire whatever for his own benefit. If the desires of an omniscient being are perfectly unselfish, then presumably unselfish desires are permissible. Since Īśvara has no desires for his own benefit, presumably selfish desires are impermissible.

In the *Gītā*, Kṛṣṇa describes his own motivation in a way that parallels Vyāsa's description of Īśvara's motivation.

> For me, O Arjuna, there is nothing to be done in the three worlds. Nor [is there something] to be attained that is not attained. Nonetheless, I perform actions. For if I, [who am] untiring, would never perform actions, O Arjuna, humankind everywhere follows my path.
>
> (3.22–3.23, Sadhale 1985a: 315, lines 11–12 and 316, lines 13–14)[4]

Like Īśvara, Kṛṣṇa does not act for his own benefit. He acts only for the sake of others. He explains that "If I did not act, these worlds would fall into ruin, and I would be an agent of confusion. I would destroy these creatures [by not acting]" (3.24, Sadhale 1985a: 316, lines 15–16).[5]

Kṛṣṇa instructs Arjuna to be motivated in the same way: "As the unwise perform actions with attachment, O Arjuna, so the wise should act without attachment, desiring *lokasaṃgraha* . . . You must act [with] *lokasaṃgraha* alone in mind" (3.25 and 3.20, Sadhale 1985a: 318, lines 25–26 and 310, line 29).[6] These passages suggest that to act without attachment is to act motivated by the well-being of others. Hence only unselfish desires are permissible.

Other passages suggest a third view – that only a desire for liberation is permissible. In defining *vairāgya*, Vyāsa says that a desireless person is without desires for impermanent things. Since everything that is constituted by *prakṛti* is impermanent, a desireless person is without desires for anything constituted by *prakṛti*.

Likewise, Vyāsa describes the person who has attained the higher state of *vairāgya* as indifferent to anything that is constituted by the *guṇas*. Again, since all *prakṛti* is constituted by the *guṇas*, the desireless person is without desires for anything constituted by *prakṛti*. According to Yoga, the only thing that is not constituted by *prakṛti* is *puruṣa*. Hence if the desireless person desires anything, they desire to realize their true self and attain *kaivalya*. Hence only the desire for *kaivalya* is permissible.

In a verse that parallels Vyāsa's description of the *vairāgin* as indifferent to the *guṇas*, Kṛṣṇa enjoins Arjuna to be indifferent to the *guṇas*: "The Vedas are the domains of the three *guṇas*. O Arjuna, be without the three *guṇas*!" (2.45, Sadhale 1985a: 183, line 36).[7] He advises Arjuna to be indifferent to the *prakṛtic* world of opposites, and possessed of the true self. "Unconcerned with the opposites, standing forever in truth, free from acquiring and keeping, [be] possessed of the true self (*ātmavān*)" (2.45, Sadhale 1985a: 183, line 37).[8] Again, since all *prakṛti* is constituted by the *guṇas*, the desireless person is without desires for anything constituted by *prakṛti*. Since, according to the *Gītā*, the only things that are not constituted by *prakṛti* are *ātman* and *Īśvara*, if the desireless person desires anything, they desire to realize the true self and/or God, and attain *mokṣa*.

Hence there are at least three seemingly plausible versions of the Some Desires Interpretation. According to the first, all permissible desires lack phenomenological saliency. According to the second, all permissible desires are unselfish. According to the third, the only permissible desire is a desire for *kaivalya* or *mokṣa*.

The *Mokṣa*-only Interpretation

Throughout this book, I consider each of these three versions of the Some Desires Interpretation. I want to begin, however, with the interpretation according to which the only permissible desire is the desire for *kaivalya* or *mokṣa*. I will call this the '*Mokṣa*-only Interpretation'.

The argument for the *Mokṣa*-only Interpretation – at least in the context of the *Gītā* – can be schematized in the following way:

> Premise One: Kṛṣṇa advises Arjuna to act without desire.
> Premise Two: Desire is a necessary condition of action.
> Conclusion One: Hence Kṛṣṇa's advice is a contradiction.
> Conclusion Two: So this cannot be Kṛṣṇa's advice.
> Conclusion Three: Kṛṣṇa advises Arjuna to act without some desires. He permits others.
> Conclusion Four: Kṛṣṇa advises Arjuna to act motivated by the desire for *mokṣa*.

The argument through Conclusion Three is the same for any Some Desires Interpretation. Only Conclusion Four is unique to the *Mokṣa*-only Interpretation.

In order for this interpretation to be at all plausible in the case of the *Gītā*, the desire for *mokṣa* must be equivalent in some way with both the desire for the true self and the desire for God. The latter goals are both mentioned and enjoined much more often than the goal of *mokṣa*, so if they are importantly distinct, the *Mokṣa*-only Interpretation must be dismissed outright. I will assume in what follows that the *Gītā's* injunctions to pursue God and the true self either entail, or are practically equivalent to, injunctions to pursue *mokṣa*.[9]

In some of the earliest philosophical texts of the tradition, desirelessness is mentioned as a characteristic of the successful *mumukṣu* (liberation seeker). In many cases, desirelessness is defined as the absence of certain paradigmatic desires. *Bṛhadāraṇyaka Upaniṣad* 3.5.1, for example, states:

> [i]t is when they come to know this [true] self that Brahmins give up the desire for sons, the desire for wealth, and the desire for worlds, and undertake the mendicant life. The desire for sons, after all, is the same as the desire for wealth, and the desire for wealth is the same as the desire for worlds – both are simply desires.
>
> (Olivelle 1998: 39)

Here the desires for sons and wealth stand for earthly desires more generally. The phrase 'desire for worlds' refers to desires for heaven, and so on. The division corresponds with Vyāsa's distinction between objects seen and objects heard (see Chapter 2). As I said in the last chapter, the characteristic that all of these objects share is impermanence. Since they are impermanent, the desires for them are impermissible.

Bṛhadāraṇyaka Upaniṣad 4.4.6 reads:

> Now, a man who does not desire – who is without desires, who is freed from desires, whose desires are fulfilled, whose only desire is his self – his vital functions (*prāṇa*) do not depart. *Brahman* he is, and to *brahman* he goes.
>
> (Olivelle 1998: 65)

Hence to be desireless is to desire only the true self. Any desire other than the desire for the true self is impermissible.

This also seems to be the sense of the following passage from the *Gītā*:

> [The person whose] self is unattached to contacts with [that which is] external (*bāhya*) [to the self], who finds happiness in the self, whose self is joind by means of yoga to Brahman, that person attains eternal happiness . . . The person who, [having] happiness from within, contentment from within, [and] radiance from within, that person is a yogin, who attains *Brahmanirvāṇa* (extinction in Brahman), [and] becomes Brahman.
>
> (5.21 and 5.24, Sadhale 1985a: 499, lines 23–24, and 506, lines 19–20)[10]

Any desire for that which is external to the true self is impermissible. A person attains *mokṣa* motivated by a desire for union with the true self and God alone.

Some of the most important classical commentators on the *Gītā* also seem to endorse this interpretation. In their commentaries to *Gītā* 2.55, for example, both Śaṅkara and Rāmānuja seem to say that only a desire for the true self is permissible. The *Gītā* verse reads: "When one fully abandons all desires existing in the mind, O Pārtha, satisfied only in the self, by the self, [then] one is called 'established in wisdom' (*stithaprajña*)" (Sadhale 1985a: 214, lines 2–3).[11]

Śaṅkara explains that the phrase *kāmān sarvān* (all desires) means the "complete abandonment" (*prakarṣeṇa jahāti*) of "all various desires" (*samastān kāmān icchābhedān*). An opponent objects that without desire, one would act like an insane person (*unmatta*). If one wants nothing, what directs one's actions?[12] Śaṅkara clarifies that the verse endorses the elimination of the desire for external objects (*bāhyalābhanirapekṣaḥ*) – that is, objects other than the self (Sadhale 1985a: 214, lines 8–11).

In his commentary to *Gītā* 2.48, Śaṅkara considers a similar objection: "If action is not to be done by one driven by the *phala* (consequence) of action, then how is it to be done?" (Sadhale 1985a: 191, line 10).[13] He explains that this is why Kṛṣṇa advises, "perform actions for the sake of Īśvara alone, even having abandoned the desire that Īśvara be pleased by me" (Sadhale 1985a: 195, lines 11–12).[14] This suggests that the only legitimate goal is *mokṣa*, and hence that the only permissible desire is a desire for *mokṣa*. A desire for anything other than *mokṣa* is impermissible.

In his commentary to *Gītā* 2.55, Rāmānuja explains,

> satisfied only in the self, by the self, with mind fixed on the self alone, on account of this satisfaction, all desires other than that [that is, other than the desire for self] which rest in the mind [are abandoned]. As one abandons [those other desires] to the highest degree, thus one is called *stithaprajña*.
>
> (Sadhale 1985a: 214, lines 30–32)[15]

Again, the desire for the self is the only permissible desire, and any desire other than the desire for the self is to be eliminated.

There is also a well-known passage from Śaṅkara's *Brahmasūtrabhāṣya* 1.1.1, in which he lists the qualities of a promising *mumukṣu*. The final criterion is the desire for *mokṣa* (*mumukṣutva*). Rāmānuja's list of qualities is slightly different, but it also concludes with the desire for *mokṣa*. If the desire for *mokṣa* is a prerequisite for its attainment, then surely the desire is not to be eliminated along with all of the others.

Four arguments for the *Mokṣa*-only Interpretation

If the *Mokṣa*-only Interpretation is correct, then only a desire for *mokṣa* is permissible. If only a desire for *mokṣa* is permissible, then the only desire that a fully knowledgeable agent has under any circumstances is the desire for *mokṣa*. If the only desire that a fully knowledgeable agent has under any circumstances is the desire for *mokṣa*, then under all circumstances the only desire that both (1) plays a necessary role in motivating the right action, and (2) takes as its object the most valuable state of affairs available by means of some action of the agent appropriate to the desire type, is the desire for *mokṣa*.

Argument One: Only Mokṣa *is valuable*

There are at least four arguments that might be offered in support of this conclusion. First, one might argue that no state of affairs other than *mokṣa* is valuable under any circumstances. If no state of affairs other than *mokṣa* is valuable under any circumstances, then a desire for any state of affairs other than *mokṣa* can never meet condition (2). If a desire for any state of affairs other than *mokṣa* can never meet condition (2), then no desire for a state of affairs other than *mokṣa* is permissible. The only permissible desire, then, is the desire for *mokṣa*. The argument can be schematized as follows:

(MO1)

Premise One: A desire is permissible only if it takes as its object the most valuable state of affairs available by means of some action of the agent appropriate to the desire type.
Premise Two: *Mokṣa* is valuable.
Premise Three: Nothing other than *mokṣa* has any value.
Conclusion One: Hence nothing other than *mokṣa* can be the object of a permissible desire.
Conclusion Two: Hence *mokṣa* is the only permissible desire.

In this argument, Premise Three is crucial. If states of affairs other than *mokṣa* have value, the conclusion that *mokṣa* is the only permissible desire does not follow.

There are two distinct arguments that might be offered for Premise Three. The first is an argument from illusion. Everything other than *mokṣa* – all earthly and heavenly matters – is a product of *māyā* (illusion). Anything that is a product of *māyā* is without value. Just as the apparent water in a distant mirage is without value because it does not really exist (and therefore cannot quench thirst, cleanse, and so on), likewise all of the apparent entities and events of the world are without value, because they do not really exist. Hence nothing other than *mokṣa* has any value. If nothing other than *mokṣa* has any value, then a desire for anything other than *mokṣa* does not meet condition (2) of a permissible desire. Hence only a desire for *mokṣa* is permissible.

The second argument is an argument from pain. Since the world of *saṃsāra* and everything in it is inherently painful and unsatisfactory, the world of *saṃsāra* and everything in it – including heaven, and so on – is of only negative value. Hence nothing other than *mokṣa* has any value. If nothing other than *mokṣa* has any value, then a desire for anything other than *mokṣa* does not meet condition (2) of a permissible desire. Hence only a desire for *mokṣa* is permissible.

Lance Nelson seems to attribute each of these arguments to both the *Gītā* and Advaita Vedānta. In a paper on the ecological implications of Advaita, Nelson says,

> Śaṅkara and his disciples see the universe of birth and rebirth (*saṃsāra*) as a "terrible ocean" infested with sea-monsters. In it we are drowning, and from it we need rescue . . . Individual selves trapped in *saṃsāra* go from birth to birth without attaining peace. They are like worms, caught in a river, being swept along from one whirlpool to another . . . The sole purpose of the Advaitic guru is to overcome the monster of ignorance, together with its manifestation, the world . . . What should our attitude to participation in life be? Śaṅkara answers that we should regard *saṃsāra* as a terrible (*ghora*) and vast ocean, existence in which should be feared, even despised.
>
> (Nelson 1998: 67)

Since the world of *saṃsāra* is based on ignorance (the argument from illusion), and since *saṃsāra* is horrific (the argument from pain), the proper attitudes toward it are fear and hatred. Nelson concludes that "[f]ar from being worthy of reverence, all that is other than the *ātman*, including nature, is without value" (Nelson 1998: 66). If this is right, then *mokṣa* – the state in which *ātman* is attained – is the only valuable state of affairs. If *mokṣa* is the only valuable state of affairs, then only a desire for *mokṣa* can meet condition (2) of a permissible desire. Hence the only permissible desire is a desire for *mokṣa*.

Nelson's interpretation of the *Gītā* roughly parallels his analysis of Advaita. He points out that certain *Gītā* verses imply that the author takes the natural world to be an illusion. He claims that at *Gītā* 2.16, Kṛṣṇa identifies the three *guṇas* of *prakṛti* with *māyā* (Nelson 2000: 137) (the argument from illusion).[16] Additionally, the world of *prakṛti* is an "abode of pain" according to *Gītā* 8.15, and "escape is an urgent desideratum" according to *Gītā* 14.5 and 14.20 (ibid.) (the argument from pain). Nelson points out that neither Śaṅkara nor Rāmānuja, commenting on some of the supposedly eco-friendly verses of the *Gītā*, suggest that the natural world has any value. "Śaṅkara's reading . . . gives no suggestion whatsoever that the particulars of the natural world are to be valued" (Nelson 2000: 138). If the particulars of the natural world are not to be valued, presumably they are never at all valuable.

If Nelson is correct, and the *Gītā* takes the material world to be perfectly devoid of positive value, it seems natural to conclude in this case as well that any desire for earthly things is impermissible. As Nelson says,

> the ascetic must practice "seeing the defects" in [his false phenomenal

> supports] (*doṣa-darśana*). The body, he must convince himself, is inert (*jaḍa*) and "besmeared with endless impurities" . . . Indeed, he must cultivate positive disgust for it and all other phenomena.
>
> (Nelson 1998: 70)

If a person must desire something in order to act, then presumably the desire that is permissible is a desire for that which is neither deficient nor impure. Since everything other than *mokṣa* is deficient, only a desire for *mokṣa* is permissible. Nelson draws the conclusion that "in this way of thinking, value is located in the Self alone" (Nelson 1998: 67).[17] Presumably a desire for *mokṣa*, then, is the only desire that is permissible. Any desire other than the desire for *mokṣa* is impermissible.

There are at least two problems with these arguments. First, if the world is an illusion, then it is not obvious how it can have negative value. If it can have negative value despite being an illusion, then it is not obvious that its illusoriness entails that it is without positive value. Hence the two arguments for Premise Two are not obviously consistent.

Second, Kṛṣṇa endorses a wide range of states of affairs other than *mokṣa*. This implies that these states of affairs are valuable. Minimally, they are instrumentally valuable, as a means to *mokṣa*. Kṛṣṇa emphasizes the value of knowledge in attaining *mokṣa*. He says, in a seemingly controversial verse, that "even if you are the evil doer of all evil doers, you pass over all wrong-doing by the boat of knowledge" (4.36, Sadhale 1985a: 444, lines 10–11).[18] Faith (*śraddha*), in turn, is a means to knowledge: "The person possessed of faith attains knowledge. Devoted to that [knowledge], senses controlled, having attained knowledge, one goes to the highest peace without delay" (4.39, Sadhale 1985a: 447, lines 3–4).[19] This suggests that knowledge, faith and restraint of the senses are all valuable, at least as a means to the valuable end of *mokṣa*.

Indeed, each characteristic that Kṛṣṇa ascribes to the successful *mumukṣu* might be taken as a means to *mokṣa*. The successful *mumukṣu* is described as impartial (2.15, 5.19, 12.17–18), disciplined (2.39, 5.12), equanimous (2.65, 2.70), concentrated (2.41, 6.10, 8.12), purified (6.12, 13.7), chaste (6.14, 8.11), moderate towards food, sleep, and play (6.17), devoted (8.10, 8.22, 12.2, 13.10), meditating (2.53, 12.6, 12.12), non-harming (13.7), patient (13.7), and so on. Each of these qualities is valuable, then, at least as a means to *mokṣa*.

Additionally, Kṛṣṇa endorses the performance of *svadharma* (one's own *dharma*) (3.35). For Arjuna, this means fighting in the battle. For the farmer, it means plowing, seeding, milking, and so on. For the entrepreneur, it means buying, selling, investing, researching, and so on. For all three, *svadharma* includes providing for family, respecting elders, performing certain ritual actions, and so on. Presumably each of these actions and all of the others that might be inferred from this advice – a perhaps infinite range of events – have some value. If they were without any value at all, presumably Kṛṣṇa would not advise them.

Indeed, in a number of verses Kṛṣṇa ranks various paths to *mokṣa* in terms of their value: "Renunciation [of action] and the Yoga of action both bring about the highest bliss, but of the two, the Yoga of action is more valuable (*niḥśreyasa*) than the renunciation of action" (5.2, Sadhale 1985a: 464, lines 14–15).[20] This implies that both paths have some value, and that the value of the Yoga of action is significant enough that it outweighs that of renunciation. Kṛṣṇa also claims that "for the *kṣatriya*, [some] other [action] more valuable than battle in accord with *dharma* is not found" (2.31, Sadhale 1985a: 156, lines 28–29).[21] This implies that battle in accord with *dharma* is indeed valuable. These claims are not consistent with the claim that nothing other than *mokṣa* has any value.[22]

Basant K. Lal agrees with Nelson's claim that Hinduism denies the value of the material world. Many of his comments imply that he is a proponent of the *Mokṣa*-only Interpretation: "Doctrinal Hinduism, strictly interpreted, teaches that the attainment of final bliss and peace [that is, *mokṣa*] is possible if and only if one transcends all worldly considerations" (Lal 1986: 208).

He is careful to point out, however, that worldly states of affairs may have instrumental value. "They are like rungs on a ladder: each has value only in the sense that, by mounting them, the climber goes higher [towards *mokṣa*]" (Lal 1986: 200). This means that states of affairs other than *mokṣa* have value, and therefore should be pursued, even if their value is derived exclusively from the value of *mokṣa*. "From the ultimate or transcendental point of view . . . neither the sacrifice nor the attitude [of *ahiṃsā*] has any value or dis-value in itself: From that point of view, like the rungs of a ladder, neither has any intrinsic significance" (Lal 1986: 200–201).[23] Yet these things are better than their alternatives, at least in part because they are a means to *mokṣa*.[24]

Tara Chatterjea makes a similar point.

> Perfection of the individual person is considered to be the highest value. Such perfection is achieved through cultivation of moral and religious goodness. "Doing good to others" has been accorded a very high instrumental value, for that is one of the basic ways which leads to moral uplift.
> (Chatterjea 2002: 146)

Even if morality and the performance of ritual are valuable only as a means to the end of *mokṣa*, they are nonetheless instrumentally valuable.[25]

If states of affairs other than *mokṣa* are valuable, then under the right circumstances a state of affairs other than *mokṣa* might be the most valuable state of affairs available by means of some action of the agent appropriate to the desire type. If a state of affairs other than *mokṣa* might be the most valuable state of affairs available by means of some action of the agent appropriate to the desire type, then a desire for a state of affairs other than *mokṣa* might be permissible. It may be, for example, that under some set of circumstances *mokṣa* is the most valuable end available by means of some action of mine, and that my action of performing some ritual action is the best means to *mokṣa*. Hence it may be that my desire to perform the ritual is permissible.

Indeed, if a desire for a means ever plays a necessary role in motivating action, the state of affairs that the desire for a means takes as its object is a state of affairs other than *mokṣa*. Hence (MO1) is not convincing, absent any additional argument.

Argument Two: Only **mokṣa** *is intrinsically valuable*

At this point a proponent of the *Mokṣa*-only Interpretation might admit that all of the states of affairs that are a means to *mokṣa* are instrumentally valuable, but then claim that only desires for intrinsically valuable states of affairs are permissible, and that desires for instrumentally valuable states of affairs are impermissible.

In other words, the proponent of the *Mokṣa*-only Interpretation might insist that the conditions of a permissible desire must be revised to read: A desire is permissible only if it both (1) plays a necessary role in motivating the right action, and (2) takes as its object the most intrinsically valuable state of affairs available by means of some action of the agent appropriate to the desire type. Since the only intrinsically valuable state of affairs is *mokṣa*, the desire for *mokṣa* is the only permissible desire. The argument can be schematized as follows:

(MO2)

Premise One: A desire is permissible only if it takes as its object the most intrinsically valuable state of affairs available by means of some action of the agent appropriate to its desire type.
Premise Two: *Mokṣa* is intrinsically valuable.
Premise Three: Nothing other than *mokṣa* has intrinsic value.
Conclusion One: Hence *mokṣa* is always the most intrinsically valuable state of affairs available by means of some action of the agent appropriate to the desire type.
Conclusion Two: Hence only a desire for *mokṣa* is permissible.

There are at least three problems with this argument. First, the solution seems ad hoc. The proponent of the *Mokṣa*-only Interpretation simply stipulates that only a desire for an intrinsically valuable state of affairs is ever permissible. While this serves the purpose of preserving the *Mokṣa*-only Interpretation, there are no obvious independent reasons for accepting this stipulation.

Second, the argument entails that no desires for means are permissible. Since, according to the proponent of this version of the argument for the *Mokṣa*-only Interpretation, *mokṣa* is the only intrinsically valuable state of affairs, the only states of affairs that a permissible desire for a means might take are states of affairs that are a means to *mokṣa*. If, in order to be permissible, a desire must take an intrinsically valuable state of affairs as its object, however – as the argument stipulates – then the only state of affairs that a permissible desire for a means might take is *mokṣa*. Since *mokṣa* is never a means to itself, however, no desire for a means is ever permissible. This seems counter-intuitive.

Additionally, there is little evidence for this view in the *Gītā* or elsewhere. Rāmānuja explains Kṛṣṇa's injunction to be *niryogakṣema* (free from acquiring and keeping) at *Gītā* 2.45 (cited above) in the following way:

> Having abandoned [both] the acquiring of objects [which are not yet attained] and the keeping of objects [already] attained [which are] neither the true self nor the means (*upāya*) to the attainment of [the true self], be possessed of the true self!
>
> (Sadhale 1985a: 185–186, lines 42 and 1–2)[26]

This suggests that not only a desire for the true self, but also a desire for that which is a means to the true self – that is, knowledge, faith, and so on – are permissible. The desires that are impermissible are desires outside of (*bahiḥ*) this class.

If this is right, then at least one of the premises in (MO2) is false. It cannot be that *mokṣa* is the only intrinsically valuable state of affairs (Premise Three) and that a desire is permissible only if it takes an intrinsically valuable state of affairs as its object (Premise One). Hence (MO2) is not convincing.

The third problem with this argument is that the distinction between states of affairs that are instrumentally and intrinsically valuable is dubious in this context. Even if *mokṣa* is the highest human goal and the most valuable state of affairs available by means of some action of the agent, the value of the states of affairs that are a means to *mokṣa* cannot derive entirely from the value of *mokṣa*. It must be either that these states of affairs are themselves intrinsically valuable, or their instrumental value is derived from some intrinsically valuable state of affairs other than *mokṣa*.[27] I make this point elsewhere, in the context of animal ethics in the Hindu tradition, so I will review that basic argument here.[28]

One prominent theory of the value of animals in Hinduism is that animals have only instrumental value. Animals are only valuable as a means to the attainment of *mokṣa*. If an agent harms an animal, the agent accumulates demerit, and this demerit is an obstacle to liberation. A person ought not to harm animals, then, for this reason alone.[29] The same will be true of harming humans, and any other type of wrongdoing, so the argument is easily generalizable.[30]

This account entails unacceptable consequences, however. If animals are valuable only as a means to *mokṣa*, then there is no explanation for why demerit – that is, bad *karma* – arises from harming animals in the first place. It cannot be that harm to animals produces bad *karma* because it postpones *mokṣa*, because harming animals postpones *mokṣa* only because it produces bad *karma*. If anything that produces bad *karma* postpones *mokṣa*, and nothing besides postponing *mokṣa* makes it the case that an action produces bad *karma*, then bad *karma* arises willy-nilly from some actions but not from others – from crushing an animal but not from crushing a can.

Consider an analogy. A young child asks his older sister why she shoves him when he enters her bedroom without asking permission, and when he crosses the imaginary line that divides the back seat of the car in two, but in no other circumstances. His sister explains that she shoves him when he does these things because when she shoves him she is punished by their parents. Assume also that his sister would be punished by their parents for shoving her brother regardless of her reason for shoving him.

It should be obvious that this is no justification at all, because the punishment that follows from the sister's act of shoving results regardless of what the brother has done. Likewise, however, the postponement of *mokṣa* that follows from the production of bad *karma* results from the bad *karma* regardless of what, in turn, produces the bad *karma*. So, just as the punishment from her parents cannot justify the sister's choice of when to shove her brother, the postponement of *mokṣa* (the analogue of the parents' punishment) cannot justify the connection between bad *karma* (the boy being struck by his sister) and harm to animals (the analogue of the brother entering the room or crossing the imaginary line) – or anything else.

As long as there is no additional element in the explanation, the distinction between right and wrong is arbitrary. It might just as well be that murder and lying lead to *mokṣa*, rather than their opposites, if there is nothing really wrong with the actions of murder and lying in themselves.[31] It cannot be that truth telling is valuable because it leads to *mokṣa*, because the explanation of why truth telling leads to *mokṣa* in the first place is that truth telling is valuable. This kind of claim should seem absurd to us, and it is. It is not absurd at all, however, if one takes seriously the claim that the value of any state of affairs derives exclusively from its contribution to the attainment of *mokṣa*.

In order to avoid this problem, all that is required is to concede that something other than *mokṣa* is intrinsically valuable. If, for example, the avoidance of the animal's experience of pain is intrinsically valuable, as Roy W. Perrett argues quite convincingly (Perrett 1993: 88),[32] then it is easily explained why harming the animal unnecessarily is wrong, why bad *karma* arises from the harming of animals, and why the action postpones *mokṣa*.[33]

More generally, if those states of affairs that are a means to *mokṣa* are intrinsically valuable, then it is easily explained why performing the actions that are a means to these ends is right, why good *karma* – or no *karma* – arises from them, and why *mokṣa* is incrementally attained by means of them. Otherwise the doctrine of *karma*, and the distinction between right and wrong, are indefensible.[34] Additionally, this kind of account allows that the sage helps an animal in order to help an animal, rather than exclusively as a means to attaining their own *mokṣa*. This is in accord with our intuitions about a sage's motivation.

If states of affairs other than *mokṣa* are intrinsically valuable, however, then the claim that nothing other than *mokṣa* has intrinsic value – Premise Three of (MO2) – is false. If states of affairs other than *mokṣa* are intrinsically valuable, then the state of affairs might be the most intrinsically valuable state of affairs available by means of some action of the agent appropriate to the desire type. If a state of affairs is the most intrinsically valuable state of affairs available by means of some action of the agent appropriate to the desire type, then it might be the object of a permissible desire – even if we grant the dubious claim that a state of affairs must be intrinsically valuable in order for a desire that takes it as its object to be permissible. Hence (MO2) is not convincing.

Argument Three: **Mokṣa** *is most valuable*

The proponents of the *Mokṣa*-only Interpretation might adopt a third strategy. They might admit that states of affairs other than *mokṣa* are intrinsically valuable, but then claim that only a desire for the most valuable state of affairs available by means of some action of the agent is permissible – regardless of the role that the desire plays in motivating action. That is, the proponent of the *Mokṣa*-only Interpretation might insist that the conditions of a permissible desire must be revised to read: A desire is permissible only if it both (1) plays a necessary role in motivating the right action, and (2) takes as its object the most valuable state of affairs available by means of some action of the agent. The proponent might then argue that since, in all circumstances, *mokṣa* is the most valuable state of affairs available by means of some action of the agent, only a desire for *mokṣa* is permissible. The argument may be schematized as follows:

(MO3)

Premise One: A desire is permissible only if it takes as its object the most valuable state of affairs available by means of some action of the agent.
Premise Two: *Mokṣa* is valuable.
Premise Three: While states of affairs other than *mokṣa* have value, *mokṣa* is always the most valuable state of affairs available by means of some action of the agent.
Conclusion One: Hence *mokṣa* is always the most valuable state of affairs available by means of some action of the agent.
Conclusion Two: Hence only a desire for *mokṣa* is permissible.

This argument faces a number of objections as well. First, *mokṣa* typically cannot be attained by a single action. In those cases in which a single action will have this consequence, *mokṣa* is not really the consequence of this action by itself, but the consequence of a long series of actions. So typically what is really at stake is some bit of progress towards *mokṣa*, not the attainment of *mokṣa*. So Premise Three is false. Since, in most circumstances, *mokṣa* is not available by means of some action of the agent, *mokṣa* is not always the most valuable state of affairs available by means of some action of the agent.

This objection can be avoided by revising Premise Three to read: While states of affairs other than *mokṣa* have value, some incremental progress towards *mokṣa* is always the most valuable state of affairs available by means of some action of the agent. Read this way, however, the premise is at least less obviously true, just because the value of some incremental – and often infinitesimal – progress towards *mokṣa* is not obviously valuable enough to outweigh the value of any other state of affairs available to the agent. Imagine, for example, that an agent might make some incremental progress towards *mokṣa* by raising their children in a responsible and unselfish way. Is it obvious that the agent's progress towards *mokṣa* at the end of that life is more valuable than the improved well-being of their children, which resulted from the same acts that produce the incremental progress towards *mokṣa*? Is it possible that whatever progress towards *mokṣa* Gandhi might have made in his lifetime – perhaps he actually even attained *mokṣa* – clearly outweighs the value of the benefit that his actions had – and continue to have – on others?

Second, the argument remains vulnerable to the ad hoc objection I raised against (MO2). The proponent of the *Mokṣa*-only Interpretation simply stipulates that only a desire for the most valuable state of affairs available by means of some action of the agent is ever permissible. While this serves the purpose of preserving the *Mokṣa*-only Interpretation, there are no obvious independent reasons for accepting this stipulation.

Third, again like (MO2), the argument entails that no desires for means are permissible. Since *mokṣa* is always the most valuable state of affairs available to the agent, the only states of affairs that a permissible desire for a means might take are states of affairs that are a means to *mokṣa*. If, in order to be permissible, a desire must take the most valuable state of affairs available by means of an action of the agent as its object, however – as the argument stipulates – then the only state of affairs that a permissible desire for a means might take is *mokṣa*. Since *mokṣa* is never a means to itself, no desire for a means is ever permissible. Besides being counter-intuitive, the account lacks textual support. As I said, Rāmānuja, for example, seems to say that some desires for means are permissible.

Fourth, if some state of affairs is the most valuable available by means of some action of the agent, then that which is a means to that state of affairs is equally valuable, all other things being equal. Suppose, for example, that I can file an amendment to a previous year's tax return, and receive an extra $100. I fill out the form, put it in a stamped addressed envelope, and then lose it, just ten minutes before the post office closes on the day of the deadline for an amended form. (I have gotten every extension available.)

In these circumstances, the value (at least to me) of the state of affairs in which I hand the clerk the letter before the post office closes is easy to calculate in dollars – its value is $100. Since the only way that the valuable state of affairs will occur is if I find the letter right away, it seems that the value of the state of affairs in which I find the letter is also $100. (We might assume that if I find it right away, I will certainly hand it to the clerk in time.) Surely my desire that I find the letter is as permissible as my desire to hand the letter to the clerk, since the same basic reasons for handing the letter to the clerk are also reasons for finding the letter.

Likewise, if, under some particular circumstances the most valuable state of affairs that I can bring about is the one in which I make some incremental progress towards *mokṣa*, and avoiding harm to an animal is the means to this progress, then the avoidance of harm to the animal is as valuable as my incremental progress towards *mokṣa*, even if the first state of affairs is only instrumentally valuable as a means to the latter (which, as I argued above, is dubious).

If this is right, then desires for states of affairs other than *mokṣa* might be permissible, even if only a desire for the most valuable state of affairs available is permissible, since, all other things being equal, the means is as valuable as the end to which it is a means. Indeed, this is true even if *mokṣa* is the only intrinsically valuable state of affairs. Hence premise three of (MO3) is false, and (MO3) is not convincing.

The fifth problem with (MO3) is that if the action of an agent is both a means to *mokṣa* and a means to some state of affairs that is valuable for other reasons – as would typically, and perhaps always, be the case – then the performance of the action is more valuable than the progress towards *mokṣa* that the agent makes by means of the action. The action's value derives from the value of the agent's progress towards *mokṣa* itself, and is therefore equivalent to the value of this progress. But it also derives value from the value of the state of affairs that it causes – say, the non-harm of an animal. Its total value, then, is greater than the value of the progress towards *mokṣa* alone. Hence under the circumstances, the state of affairs in which I avoid harming the animal is more valuable than my incremental progress towards *mokṣa*, because the state of affairs in which I avoid harming the animal is the most valuable – the pain of the animal is avoided, and I make incremental progress towards *mokṣa*. In this case, if the stipulation on which (MO3) is based is correct, the desire for *mokṣa* is sometimes impermissible!

Argument Four: **Mokṣa** *is most intrinsically valuable*

The proponent of the *Mokṣa*-only Interpretation might combine the requirements of (MO2) and (MO3), and offer the following argument:

(MO4)

Premise One: A desire is permissible only if it takes as its object the most intrinsically valuable state of affairs available by means of some action of the agent.

Premise Two: *Mokṣa* is intrinsically valuable.
Premise Three: While states of affairs other than *mokṣa* have intrinsic value, *mokṣa* is always the most intrinsically valuable state of affairs available by means of some action of the agent.
Conclusion One: Hence *mokṣa* is always the most intrinsically valuable state of affairs available by means of some action of the agent.
Conclusion Two: Hence only a desire for *mokṣa* is permissible.

In other words, the proponent of the *Mokṣa*-only Interpretation might revise the conditions of a permissible desire to read: A desire is permissible only if it both (1) plays a necessary role in motivating the right action, and (2) takes as its object the most intrinsically valuable state of affairs available by means of some action of the agent. Since *mokṣa* is always the most intrinsically valuable state of affairs available to the agent, the desire for *mokṣa* is the only permissible desire.

This version of the argument is undoubtedly the strongest of the four. Nonetheless, it faces at least three objections. The first two are familiar enough. First, the stipulation in Premise One seems ad hoc. The proponent of the *Mokṣa*-only Interpretation simply stipulates that only a desire for the most intrinsically valuable state of affairs available by means of some action of the agent is ever permissible, without offering independent reasons for accepting the stipulation.

Second, the argument entails that no desires for means are permissible. Since *mokṣa* is always the most intrinsically valuable state of affairs available to the agent, the only states of affairs that a permissible desire for a means might take as its object are states of affairs that are a means to *mokṣa*. If, in order to be permissible, a desire must take the most intrinsically valuable state of affairs available by means of an action of the agent as its object, however – as the argument stipulates – then the only state of affairs that a permissible desire for a means might take is *mokṣa*. Since *mokṣa* is never a means to itself, no desire for a means is ever permissible.

The third problem with this account is that it entails that neither God nor the *jīvanmukta* ever acts. Both God and the *jīvanmukta* have already attained *mokṣa*. If the attainment of *mokṣa* is the only possible object of a permissible desire, presumably neither God nor the *jīvanmukta* has any desires. Without desires, neither God nor the *jīvanmukta* acts. While there is some debate over whether the state of *jīvanmukti* can actually be attained,[35] it is explicit in both the *Gītā* and the *Yogasūtra* (see above), among many others, that God acts. Hence (MO4) is unconvincing.

A fifth argument for the *Mokṣa*-only Interpretation

The proponent of the *Mokṣa*-only Interpretation might adopt a fifth strategy. They might say that the desire for *mokṣa* should be understood broadly, to refer not only to the desire for *mokṣa* itself, but also the desire for anything that is a means to *mokṣa*. Since any permissible desire is a desire for the most valuable state of affairs appropriate to its desire type (available by means of some action of the agent), and since any state of affairs that is the most valuable state of affairs appropriate to its desire type (available by means of some action of the agent) is either *mokṣa*, or a means to *mokṣa*, all permissible desires are desires for either *mokṣa* or a means to *mokṣa*. The argument can be schematized as follows:

(MO5)

Premise One: A desire is permissible only if it takes as its object the most valuable state of affairs appropriate to the desire type available by means of some action of the agent.
Premise Two: Any state of affairs that is the most valuable available by means of some action of the agent appropriate to its desire type is either *mokṣa* or a means to *mokṣa*.
Conclusion One: Hence only the desire for *mokṣa* and desires for states of affairs that are a means to *mokṣa* are permissible.
Conclusion Two: Hence only a desire for *mokṣa* is permissible.

In the example of avoiding harm to animals, for example, the agent's desire to avoid harming the animal can be classified as a desire for *mokṣa*, since avoiding harm to animals is a means to *mokṣa*. Likewise, any state of affairs other than *mokṣa* that is the most valuable available to the agent is a means to *mokṣa*. Hence all permissible desires are either a desire for *mokṣa* or a desire for the means to *mokṣa*.

Even if this formulation of the *Mokṣa*-only Interpretation is technically correct, it is importantly misleading. Just because the state of affairs that I desire to bring about is a means to *mokṣa*, it does not follow that I bring about that state of affairs in order to bring about *mokṣa*.

Joel Feinberg makes a similar point in his paper "Psychological Egoism". A proponent of egoism might argue as follows:

> It is a truism that when a person gets what he wants he characteristically feels pleasure. This has suggested to many people that what we really want in every case is our own pleasure, and that we pursue other things only as a means.
>
> (Feinberg 2005: 477)

Even when a person does something extremely unpleasant, they experience some pleasure, simply as a result of fulfilling their desire. I may hate cutting the lawn, but I feel some satisfaction as I finish the chore. If pleasure is an inevitable consequence of any successful action, then it follows that the only reason that any agent ever acts is to feel this inevitable pleasure.[36]

Likewise, every action motivated by a desire for the most valuable state of affairs available to the agent – either as an end or a means – has the consequence of *mokṣa*. If progress towards *mokṣa* is an inevitable consequence of bringing about the most valuable state of affairs available to the agent, then this incremental progress towards *mokṣa* is what the agent always wants in bringing about the most valuable states of affairs.

Feinberg offers the following objection to the argument for egoism:

> Pleasure may well be the usual accompaniment of all actions in which the agent gets what he wants; but to infer from this that what the agent always wants is his own pleausre is like arguing, in William James's example, that because an oceanliner constantly consumes coal on its trans-Atlantic passage that therefore the *purpose* of its voyage is to consume coal. The immediate inference from constant accompaniment to purpose (or motive) is always a *nonsequitur*.
>
> (Feinberg 2005: 479)

If the inference from constant accompaniment to purpose is unjustified in the oceanliner case, then it is unjustified in the egoism case. Just because pleasure inevitably follows successful action, it does not follow that all actions are motivated by a desire for this pleasure.

The same analogy demonstrates that the inference that the proponent of the *Mokṣa*-only Interpretation draws is unjustified. Just because incremental progress towards *mokṣa* inevitably follows actions that bring about the most valuable state of affairs available to the agent, it does not follow that all actions that bring about the most valuable states of affairs are motivated by a desire for this incremental progress towards *mokṣa*. Hence this fifth argument is unconvincing as well.

Since none of the five arguments for the *Mokṣa*-only Interpretation succeeds, the *Mokṣa*-only Interpretation is implausible. It is almost certainly true that the desire for *mokṣa* is often permissible. It may even be true that a desire for *mokṣa* ought to guide many, and perhaps most, of an agent's actions. To say, however, that any desire other than the desire for *mokṣa* is impermissible is to ignore the wide range of valuable states of affairs that an agent might play some role in bringing about. A fully knowledgeable agent will desire states of affairs other than *mokṣa*.

4 Unselfish desires

In the last chapter I argued that there is textual evidence for at least three versions of the Some Desires Interpretation. First, it might be that all permissible desires lack phenomenological saliency. Second, it might be that all permissible desires are unselfish. Third, it might be that only a desire for *mokṣa* is permissible. I argued that the third view, the *Mokṣa*-only Interpretation, is implausible. Since states of affairs other than *mokṣa* are valuable, desires for states of affairs other than *mokṣa* are permissible.

In this chapter I consider the view that all permissible desires are unselfish. The basic argument for this version of the Some Desires Interpretation is that since the *Gītā* and other Indian texts advise the elimination of selfishness, the advice to eliminate desire amounts to the advice to eliminate selfish desires.

I point out that the word 'selfish' is ambiguous. In one sense it means self-interested. In another sense it means excessively self-interested. So there is some question as to what the proponents of this view mean when they say that all selfish desires are to be eliminated.

If by 'selfish' proponents of this view mean self-interested, then the basic argument is that since the *Gītā* and other Indian texts advise the elimination of self-interest, the advice to eliminate desire amounts to the advice to eliminate self-interested desires. The problem with this version of the argument is that the *Gītā* advises the elimination of excessive self-interest, not self-interest more generally. While the empirical self is certainly less valuable than the typical person believes, it is not entirely without value. Hence some self-interested desires might be permissible.

If by 'selfish' proponents of this view mean excessively self-interested, then the basic argument is that since the *Gītā* and other Indian texts advise the elimination of excessive self-interest, the advice to eliminate desire amounts to the advice to eliminate excessively self-interested desires. The problem with this version of the argument is that it reduces the advice to eliminate desire to insignificance. Very few selfish actions are motivated by excessively selfish desires.

One alternative is to claim that since the *Gītā* and other Indian texts advise the elimination of excessive self-interest, the advice to eliminate desire amounts to the advice to eliminate all self-interested desires. This avoids the problem of reducing the advice to eliminate desire to insignificance, but the inference is unjustified. Similar reasoning supports the elimination of altruistic desires.

Finally, the proponents of this view might claim that 'selfish' means something like based on false beliefs about the self. Hence the advice to eliminate desire amounts to the advice to eliminate desires based on false beliefs about the self. I argue that the advice to eliminate desire does entail the elimination of desires based on false beliefs about the self. It is misleading, however, to call these desires 'selfish', because there are excessively altruistic desires that are impermissible for the same reason. Additionally, desires based on false beliefs about things other than the self are impermissible. The advice to eliminate desire amounts to the advice to eliminate impermissible desires, only some of which are selfish in any normal sense of the word. Hence the view that only unselfish desires are permissible is implausible.

Unselfishness

There are a number of important contemporary authors who claim that the *Gītā's* advice to act without desire amounts to the advice to eliminate selfish desires, and act on unselfish desires. Indeed, this is probably the most common contemporary interpretation of the doctrine.

K.N. Upadhyaya, for example, says, "[d]evotion . . . does not require abandonment of work but only the abandonment of selfish desires" (Upadhyaya 1969: 162). Chatterjea claims "that according to the *Gītā* a desire is a desire when it aims only at self-centered gains" (Chatterjea 2002: 134). B. K. Matilal, among others,[1] also seems to endorse this position (Matilal 2002: 130).

The argument for the No Selfish Desires Interpretation – at least in the context of the *Gītā* – can be schematized in the following way.

(NSDI)

Premise One: Kṛṣṇa advises Arjuna to act without desire.
Premise Two: Desire is a necessary condition of action.
Conclusion One: Hence Kṛṣṇa's advice is a contradiction – at least prima facie.
Conclusion Two: So this cannot be Kṛṣṇa's advice.
Conclusion Three: Kṛṣṇa advises Arjuna to act without some desires. He permits others.
Conclusion Four: Kṛṣṇa advises Arjuna to act without selfish desires. He permits unselfish desires.

Again, the argument through Conclusion Three is common to any version of the Some Desires Interpretation. Only Conclusion Four is unique to the No Selfish Desires Interpretation.

As I mentioned in Chapter 2, the first piece of evidence for this interpretation is that Kṛṣṇa's own motives are perfectly unselfish. He has nothing to attain by acting, but acts nonetheless, to prevent the ruin of the world. Kṛṣṇa also advises Arjuna to act for the same reason. "You must act [with] *lokasaṃgraha* alone in mind." This suggests that only unselfish desires are permissible. Selfish desires are not.

Another reason to believe that the distinction between permissible and impermissible desires amounts to the distinction between unselfish and selfish desires is that selfishness (*nirahaṅkāra, nirmama*) is generally discouraged in the *Gītā* and elsewhere. If selfishness is to be eliminated, surely selfish desires are to be eliminated as well.

In order to see whether this is the right interpretation of the advice, it is important to be as clear as possible about what selfishness is, what selfish desires are, and what the relationship is between the two. The word 'selfish' is ambiguous. In ordinary language 'selfish' usually means something like more self-interested than one should be, but sometimes it just means self-interested.

A business partner is referred to as selfish when they seek more than their share of the profits, but not because they seek some benefit. A person who chooses to watch a certain movie because they expect to enjoy it is not normally regarded as selfish, but if they overrule the preferences of others without justification, they are. In these cases 'selfish' means excessively self-interested – more self-interested than one should be.

On the other hand, an agent who donates to charity might be called selfish if it is discovered that their purpose in doing so is lowering their tax bracket. "They had selfish reasons for doing so," one might say. In this sense 'selfish' just means self-interested; their self-interest is not necessarily inappropriate, even if it is better to donate to charity motivated by a desire for the well-being of others.

There is some question, then, about what the proponent of the No Selfish Desires Interpretation means when they claim that selfish desires are impermissible. They could mean that self-interested desires are impermissible, or they could mean that excessively self-interested desires are impermissible.

Three versions of the No Selfish Desires Interpretation

The first version of the No Selfish Desires Interpretation

The crucial inference in (NSDI) is the inference from Conclusion Two – Kṛṣṇa advises Arjuna to act without some desires, and permits others – to Conclusion Three – hence Kṛṣṇa advises Arjuna to act without selfish desires, and permits unselfish desires. As I mentioned, the supplemental argument for this inference is:

(SA)

Premise One (Conclusion Three from NSDI): Kṛṣṇa advises Arjuna to act without some desires. He permits others.
Premise Two: The *Gītā* advises the elimination of selfishness (*nirmama* and *nirahaṅkāra*).
Conclusion (Conclusion Four from NSDI): Hence Kṛṣṇa advises Arjuna to act without selfish desires. He permits unselfish desires.

Since the word 'selfish' is ambiguous, this argument can be taken in at least three ways. First, the word 'selfish' might mean self-interested. In this case the basic inference is: since self-interest is impermissible, self-interested desires are impermissible as well. This interpretation of the argument reads:

(SA1)

Premise One: Kṛṣṇa advises Arjuna to act without some desires. He permits others.
Premise Two: The *Gītā* advises the elimination of self-interest (*nirmama* and *nirahaṅkara*).
Conclusion: Hence Kṛṣṇa advises Arjuna to act without self-interested desires. He permits desires that are not self-interested.

By 'self-interested desire' I mean a desire that meets one of the two following criteria (which I adopt from Bernard Williams). The desire is either

(1) "of the form 'I want that I . . .', where this is followed by something which specifies [the agent's] getting something, entering into a desirable state, or whatever" or

(2) "depend[s] on a desire which is of that form, in the sense that it is only because he has the latter desire that he has the former".

(Williams 1973: 260)

The only qualification worth adding is that if the desire is selfish because it meets criterion (1), it does not "depend on" – that is, it is not derived from – a desire which is not of that form. If an agent desires to eat chocolate cake and they have no further reason for desiring to eat it, then the desire is selfish in this sense. If, however, they want it only to give to a sibling, the desire is not selfish. If the person desires that their colleague succeed, but this desire is derived from the desire that they replace their colleague at their present position, the desire is selfish, even though its propositional content does not refer to the agent. In this sense, 'selfish' is synonymous with the word 'egoistic' as it is used in discussions of psychological and ethical egoism.[2]

These criteria make it clear that both a desire for an end and a desire for a means may be either unselfish or selfish in this sense, and therefore permissible or impermissible. If I desire the end of chocolate cake, the desire is selfish. If I desire the end that my sister have chocolate cake, the desire is unselfish. If I desire chocolate cake as a means to the end of my sister having chocolate cake, then it is unselfish. If I desire that my sister have chocolate cake as a means to the end of my having chocolate cake, then it is selfish. If the desire for an end that motivates the action is selfish, the desire is selfish. If it is not, the desire is unselfish.

If this is the sense in which the proponent of the No Selfish Desires Interpretation uses the word 'selfish', then the account is appealing for a number of reasons. First, the concept of a selfish desire is straightforward – it is just a desire that meets one of the criteria above. Second, the concept of a selfish action is straightforward – it is just an action motivated by a selfish desire. Third, there is a very tight connection between the advice to eliminate selfishness and the advice to eliminate selfish desires. A selfish action is just an action motivated by a selfish desire, and the elimination of selfish desires precludes all selfish actions. On this reading, the inference from no selfishness to no selfish desires is justified.

One problem with this version of the argument for the No Selfish Desires Interpretation is that the *Gītā* does not advise the elimination of self-interest, as Premise Two claims. The *Gītā* characterizes the liberated person as unselfish in a number of places, and an analysis of these verses and their commentaries suggests that the advice to eliminate unselfishness does not amount to the advice to eliminate self-interest in general.

There are a number of verses in which the *Gītā* either characterizes the liberated person[3] as unselfish or enjoins those who are not unselfish to become so. Verse 2.71 reads:

> The person who has eliminated all desires and acts desirelessly, free from [the conception of] mine-ness (*nirmamaḥ*), and without a sense of self (*nirahaṅkāraḥ*), they achieve peace.
>
> (Sadhale 1985a: 242, lines 8–9)[4]

At 3.30, Kṛṣṇa enjoins Arjuna:

> Having given up all actions to me, with the highest self in mind, having become desireless and free from [the conception of] mine-ness (*nirmamaḥ*), fight unimpassioned!
>
> (Sadhale 1985a: 325, lines 34–35)[5]

I translate the Sanskrit words *nirmama* and *nirahaṅkāra*[6] – literally, no mine and no I constructing – as "free of a sense of mine-ness" and "without a sense of self," respectively. In each verse selfishness in action is emphasized.

Nonetheless, both *nirahaṅkāra* and *nirmama* are first and foremost epistemic achievements. An agent who is *nirahaṅkāra* or *nirmama*[7] does not confuse their empirical self with their real self – the *ātman* or *puruṣa*.

Rāmānuja explains that to be *nirahaṅkāra* is to be "without the thought that the body, [which is] not the self, is the self" (2.71, Sadhale 1985a: 242, line 25).[8] Likewise, to be *nirmama* is to be "without the thought that whatever is not the self is the self" (18.53, Sadhale 1985c: 376, line 24).[9] In his commentary to *Gītā* 3.27, Rāmānuja says that the agent who is *ahaṅkāra* (which is the opposite of *nirahaṅkāra*) "thinks 'I' with regard to *prakṛti* (physical matter) and objects that are not I" (Sadhale 1985a: 320, line 29).[10] The knowledgeable person does not misidentify with their body, feelings, dispositions, or anything else that can be the object of consciousness. They know that their true self is distinct from all that is fleeting. Rāmānuja explains that each of the two characteristics (*nirmama* and *nirahaṅkāra*) has to do in part with the agent qua knower. To be unselfish is to be without false beliefs about the nature of the self.

Śaṅkara makes the same point in his commentary to the *Gītā*. He explains that the *nirahaṅkāra* agent is "without the thought 'I' " (12.13, Sadhale 1985b: 375, line 5),[11] and without esteem for the self that arises from learning and other accomplishments (2.71, Sadhale 1985a: 242, line 13).[12] This too means that the agent does not misidentify with their body, feelings, dispositions, and so on. To be *nirmama*, according to Śaṅkara, is to be "without mineness even with regard to one's body and life" (18.53, Sadhale 1985c: 376, lines 8–9).[13,14]

This conception of selfishness is similar to that found in the *Yogasūtra*. As I mentioned in Chapter 2, the *Yogasūtra* lists *asmitā* – literally I am-ness – among the five *kleśas* (defilements), and states that the first *kleśa* – ignorance (*avidyā*) – is the ground from which the others are generated. Hence I am-ness is the result of false beliefs. In his commentary to *Yogasūtra* 2.6, Vyāsa characterizes *asmitā* as the mistaken identification of *puruśa* (the real self) and *buddhi* (intellect), which is a particular evolute of *prakṛti* (matter) typically taken to stand for the *prakṛtic* self more generally. Hence I am-ness is the result of false beliefs about the distinction between *puruṣa* and the *prakṛtic* self.

I also pointed out in Chapter 2 that Vyāsa defines higher *vairāgya* primarily in terms of the realization of the distinction between *puruṣa* and the *prakṛti*. Hence in both texts, this kind of epistemological selfishness is the foundation of desire, and the elimination of this epistemological selfishness is essential to the attainment of complete desirelessness.

Rāmānuja concludes his commentary to 2.71 by saying, "the person who acts having seen the self achieves peace" (Sadhale 1985a: 242, lines 25–26).[15] The thought here and elsewhere is that knowledge about the true nature of the self is the foundation of living rightly and achieving the highest goal of *mokṣa*. To be unselfish is to be without false beliefs about the nature of the self – to identify with the true self rather than the empirical self – but it is also to act; an agent who knows the self acts accordingly.

While the epistemic aspect of *nirahaṅkāra* and *nirmama* are relatively straightforward, there are a number of possible interpretations of their implications for action. As I mentioned above, Śaṅkara claims that the *nirahaṅkāra* agent is without the thought 'I', and elsewhere says that to be *nirmama* is to be "without mineness." Rāmānuja says the same thing in his commentary to these two verses: the *nirmama* agent is "without mineness". Śaṅkara is somewhat clearer when he explains *nirmama* as being "without the thought 'this is mine' " (2.71, Sadhale 1985a: 242, lines 25–26).[16]

There are a number of ways to interpret the claim that the unselfish agent is without the thought "this is mine". It might mean that the liberated person is, and the rest of us should be, perfectly incapable of the thought 'this is mine'. If this were the meaning of the claim, however, the liberated person would be incapable of identifying things that are certainly theirs. Neither Śaṅkara nor Rāmānuja wants to say that the liberated person cannot identify the woman who birthed and raised them as their mother. They do not respond to the question "Is this your robe?" with utter incomprehension. So "without the thought 'this is mine' " should not be taken too literally.

A slightly less literal interpretation is that the liberated person thinks 'this is mine' but never allows it to enter into their practical deliberations. They are capable of the thought, but their actions never reflect this. If this is the meaning of the claim, the agent still cannot respond sensibly to the question "Is this your robe?" If they end up dressing in their own clothes rather than someone else's, it is random chance. So this interpretation of the claim is also too extreme.

There are at least two more interpretations of the claim that the liberated agent does not have the thought 'this is mine'. It makes sense to consider them simultaneously because they both seem initially plausible, and I suspect that any doubt about the position that I favor will be due in part to a suspicion that the other is more accurate. The first position is that the liberated agent has the thought 'this is mine' and therefore disregards whatever it is that 'this' refers to. This is the interpretation that the proponent of this first version of the No Selfish Desires Interpretation must defend. The second position is that the liberated agent has the thought 'this is mine' but does not privilege that which is theirs without justification. In order to clarify and assess the plausibility of the two positions, consider an example.

Suppose that a sage is traveling in a group. When the group stops to rest, the sage notices a spot of blood on the ground and believes that some member of the party is injured and in need of treatment. As a consequence, the sage is motivated to do whatever needs to be done to get the injured person the needed treatment. If that means bandaging the person, the sage will do it. If it means retrieving the first aid kit, the sage will do that. In short, the sage is disposed towards doing what they can to help the injured person. They count the injury as a reason to help, and they are motivated by that fact. We might say the sage desires to help the injured person. So the sage sets out to determine who is injured.

The sage looks at each of the people standing nearby and sees that none are injured. The sage then looks down and sees that they have a large cut on their own heel that they had not noticed, and that they are the one in need of treatment. What does the sage do now, given that they are "without the thought 'this is mine' "?

On the first of the two interpretations, the agent loses the desire to help the injured person, since the desire is self-interested. They think, "this wound is mine" and therefore disregard the wound. They are not motivated to bandage the wounded person or retrieve the first aid kit, or even tell anyone about the wound, because they do not take the fact that the wound is theirs as a reason to do anything. In short, they allow the wound to continue bleeding, no matter how serious it is, at least in the absence of other reasons for treating it that are not related to them.

On the second interpretation, the sage will, under most circumstances, remain motivated to help the injured person, even in light of the fact that they are the one who is injured. That is, they will continue to desire to help the injured person, find the first aid kit, and so on. In short, under the circumstances, the sage will have self-interested desires.

On this second interpretation, the sage might neglect their own well-being if there are other considerations that should override their injury. If, for example, there is another person in the group who is more seriously injured, they will not count the fact that the first injury is theirs as an overriding reason to treat their wound first. In the absence of countervailing reasons, however, they will count their own injury as a reason for treating the injury.

Even if there are no countervailing reasons, and the sage is motivated to treat the wound, they will not be more motivated to treat their own wound than they would have been motivated to help someone else if it had turned out that not they but someone else had been injured. Nor is the sage more motivated now, knowing that they are injured, than they had been before they knew the identity of the injured person.[17] They do not count the fact that they are the injured person as an additional reason or a stronger reason for helping – at least not without justification.

This is not to say that there cannot be cases in which privileging that which is one's own is justified. If, for example, the sage has the coagulation disorder von Willebrand Disease, and is at greater risk of bleeding to death than the average person in the group, the fact that they are the one who is injured will strengthen their disposition to contribute to the treatment of the wound. They will consider it more urgent than they may otherwise have done – but rightly so.

Often the sage might be in a privileged position to help their own self, and in cases like this they might be justified in privileging that which is theirs. The sage is one of two people who are thirsty, but because they do not know where the other person has gone, they are only motivated to alleviate their own thirst. Thomas Nagel makes this point (Nagel 1970: 129). One should not prefer one's own well-being to another's simply because it is one's own – this would amount to some version of solipsism, according to Nagel – but this does not preclude a person from privileging their own well-being for other reasons.

A comparison of the implications of the two interpretations suggests that the second account is much more plausible, just because the first account must defend the implausible claim that the injury to the sage is not in itself a reason for the sage to treat the wound. Even if the body is much less valuable than is ordinarily thought – and the Indian traditions certainly say this much – perfect indifference to it is excessive. It turns a reasonable and conceivable – albeit supererogatory – form of unselfishness into something quite bizarre.[18] As M. M. Agrawal says, "[i]t would be the limit of senselessness to suggest that, e.g., a true saint should not be concerned with avoiding injury to himself, when he easily can by making an appropriate move" (Agrawal 1982: 41).

The so-called orthodox Indian traditions, and the *Gītā* in particular, seem to conceive of virtue as a means between extremes. Kṛṣṇa explains, for example, that

> Yoga is not to eat too much. Nor, however, is it to not eat altogether. And [yoga is not] the habit of sleeping too much. Nor, however, [the habit] of staying awake, O Arjuna. [Of the person whom is] disciplined (*yukta*) with regard to food and play, [whom] with regard to actions, has disciplined effort, [and whom] is disciplined with regard to sleeping and waking, [of that person] yoga is destructive of *duḥkha*.
>
> (6.16–6.17, Sadhale 1985a: 543, lines 1–4)[19]

If unselfishness is a virtue, it is the means between egomania and complete self-abnegation, not one of these extremes. Yet the proponent of the first version of the argument for the No Selfish Desires Interpretation must say just this – unselfishness is a complete disregard for one's own person; the sage might simply bleed to death.

One might reply that the sage still drinks, eats, and cares for their body, but only as a means to helping others. Even this view, however, entails that the sage does not count the fact that they are in a burning building as a reason in itself to flee; it is only a reason to flee if it will somehow help others. If this is their judgment of the value of their own well-being, it is difficult to see why they judge the well-being of others so highly.

One might insist that there is something about the distinction between liberated and non-liberated people that allows this, but even if this is granted, there is the unacceptable consequence that a liberated person will not count the fact that another liberated person is trapped in a burning building as a reason in itself to save that person. Nor will they count the fact that they are trapped as a reason for someone else to save them. If the well-being of their empirical self is irrelevant on account of their being liberated, then securing it should not count as a reason for others, and the well-being of other liberated people should not count as a reason to secure it or for others to secure it.[20]

In Chapter 3 I argued that unless some state of affairs other than *mokṣa* is valuable, bad *karma* might just as well arise from helping others, rather than hurting them. I argued that the most plausible explanation for the correlation between demerit and harm is that the well-being of sentient beings is intrinsically valuable. The reason that bad *karma* accrues as a result of harming others, rather than helping others, is that helping others is meritorious, and harming others is demeritorious. This only makes sense, however, if the well-being of others is valuable. If others are valuable, however, then the agent is also valuable, and should not entirely disregard their own well-being.

The proponent of this view might be tempted to persist in its defense, but there is no need to do so. All of the unselfish actions that are expected of the liberated person can be accounted for under the second interpretation without the odd consequences of the first view. This means that the second interpretation is the more plausible. The advice to eliminate selfishness amounts to the advice to avoid privileging that which is one's own without justification.

Śaṅkara's gloss of *nirmama* at 2.71 supports this interpretation. It reads: "*nirmama* means without clinging (*abhiniveśa*) to the thought 'this is mine' " (Sadhale 1985a: 242, lines 12–13).[21] The word 'clinging' here suggests that it is not concern for oneself, but excessive concern for oneself that is problematic.

This suggests that the liberated person counts the fact that something is theirs as a reason for acting, but only under the right circumstances and in the right way. That the thirst is theirs justifies drinking water under most circumstances, but not if they are stranded in the desert with someone else, and the two have just enough water for both to survive, and the sage has already had their share. To say that they do not cling to the thought 'this is mine' is to say that they do not make more of the fact that something is theirs than they should.

In verse 7.4 of the *Gītā* Kṛṣṇa lists eight evolutes of *prakṛti* (matter) – earth, water, fire, air, ether, mind, intellect, and selfhood (*ahaṅkāra*) (Sadhale 1985b: 11, lines 32–33).[22] These correspond to the first eight evolutes of the Sāṃkhya system. In the earliest (existent) Sāṃkhya text, the *Sāṃkhyakārikā*, ĪśvaraKṛṣṇa explains *ahaṅkāra* as *abhimāna* (Larson 1969: 263),[23] which is best translated as "self-conceit". It is *ahaṅkāra* in this sense – the sense of an exaggerated (that is, unjustified) sense of one's own importance – that is discouraged in the *Gītā*.

Verses 16.12–16.18 of the *Gītā* describe the person who is destined for the worst rebirth. They believe that they are superior to everyone else, and they gloat about their accomplishments. Kṛṣṇa describes this kind of person as "self-conceited, arrogant, and proud" (16.10, Sadhale 1985c: 217, line 10).[24] They are willing to achieve their ends by unjust means. These verses suggest that unjustified self-interest, not self-interest more generally, is the problem. Cheating others incurs demerit. Eating in order to sustain one's body does not (4.21). At one point, Kṛṣṇa says that those who harm the body lack discrimination: "Those [who are] unthinking, harming the group of elements in the body, and therefore me within the body as well, know them to be of demonic intention" (17.6, Sadhale 1985c: 248, lines 3–4).[25] Hence excessive self-interest, not self-interest more generally, is impermissible.

The version of the No Selfish Desires Interpretation that is under consideration in this section is the view that self-interested desires are impermissible because self-interest in general is impermissible. The plausibility of this view depends on the truth of the claim that the advice to eliminate selfishness amounts to the advice to eliminate self-interest. Since the advice to eliminate selfishness is advice to eliminate excessive self-interest, and not self-interest more generally, this version of the argument for the No Selfish Desires Interpretation is not convincing. Some self-interest is justified, hence some self-interested desires are permissible.

The second version of the No Selfish Desires Interpretation

Since the advice to eliminate selfishness amounts to the advice to eliminate excessive self-interest, it does not support the conclusion that all self-interested desires are impermissible – at least not in the straightforward way that it would if it were a prohibition on self-interest period.[26] Instead, the proponent of the No Selfish Desires Interpretation might accept this analysis of the advice to eliminate selfishness and argue that it supports the conclusion that excessively self-interested desires are impermissible. The impermissible selfish desires, then, are just these excessively self-interested ones. This version of the argument may be schematized as follows:

(SA2)

Premise One: Kṛṣṇa advises Arjuna to act without some desires. He permits others.
Premise Two: The *Gītā* advises the elimination of excessive self-interest (*nirmama* and *nirahaṅkara*).
Conclusion: Hence Kṛṣṇa advises Arjuna to act without excessively self-interested desires. He permits desires that are not excessively self-interested.

The authors cited above seem, at times, to advance this kind of view. Matilal, for example, uses the word ‘selfish’ to describe the discouraged class of desires and elaborates its meaning in terms of justification.

> The real *karmayogin* [the individual who acts without desire] . . . would do whatever is expected of him by society and he would exercise unbiased reason to decide conflicting alternatives, but he would be completely free from any selfish desires, motives or preferences.
>
> (Matilal 2002: 130)

One might take this to mean that the impermissible class of desires are those that are excessively self-interested. Merely self-interested desires, however, might be permissible. The *karmayogin* may be thirsty, notice their thirst, and act to alleviate it. What they will not do, however, is privilege their own interests over others' in a way that is unjustified. This, the proponent might insist, is just what it means to "exercise unbiased reason."

Likewise Chatterjea explains that "[t]he *Gītā* is asking Arjuna to give up excessive self-centeredness" (Chatterjea 2002: 133). So the impermissible desires are not just those desires that are based on self-interest. They are those desires that are excessively self-interested. It is true, the proponent might admit, that *nirmama* and *nirahaṅkāra* do not entail the elimination of desires that are selfish in the first sense. It does entail the elimination of desires that are selfish in the second sense, however, and this is just the position that the No Selfish Desires Interpretation advances.

This version of the argument for the No Selfish Desires Interpretation faces a number of problems as well, however. For one thing, actions that are excessively self-interested are generally not motivated by desires that are excessively self-interested. Suppose that a child is given the job of dividing the last piece of cake in two, and distributing one part to their sibling and one part to themselves. The child desires cake and knows that their sibling also desires cake. The child believes that neither deserves more cake than the other. In the end the child decides to cut the cake so that one piece is half the size of the second, and takes the larger of the two.

It is uncontroversial to say that the child, at least at this moment, is neither *nirmama* nor *nirahaṅkāra*. The action is excessively self-interested. It is not excessively self-interested, however, because it is motivated by an excessively self-interested desire. The desire that motivates the action is the desire to eat cake, and this desire is not excessively self-interested. Outside of the present context, the child's desire for cake is permissible. Of course the child desires cake! Cake tastes good! The action is motivated by a desire for cake, so the excessive self-interest of the action is not due to the excessive self-interest of the desire that motivates it.

The child's excessive self-interest manifests in the way that the child counts their desire as an overriding reason to do what they do, when in fact it is not. The action is selfish, but not because it is motivated by a selfish desire. It is selfish because the child unjustifiedly privileges the satisfaction of their own desire to eat cake over the same desire of their sibling.

The proponent of the No Selfish Desires Interpretation might dispute this analysis and insist that the child's desire is not the desire to eat cake, but the desire to eat more cake than their sibling eats. Hence the desire is itself impermissible, and is inconsistent with *nirmama* and *nirahaṅkāra*. Even if this is right in this case, however, the proponent of this view must argue for the additional claim that every time one acts in an excessively self-interested way, the action is motivated by an excessively self-interested desire. This is implausible. Surely it might be that a child eats more cake than they should just because they want cake.

In most cases, actions turn out to be selfish because the agent's practical reasoning is not cogent in a certain way. The lack of justification is a characteristic not of the desires themselves, but of the reasoning that weighs the desires. Excessively self-interested actions are much more common than excessively self-interested desires. So the elimination of excessively self-interested desires does very little to preclude selfish actions.

The proponents of the No Selfish Desires Interpretation might concede this, and point out that the elimination of selfishness in general entails the elimination of selfish actions as well as selfish desires. So even if most selfish actions remain once all selfish desires are eliminated, the advice to eliminate selfishness forbids counting self-interested desires more heavily than one should. On the No Selfish Desires Interpretation, then, selfishness is still precluded. The No Selfish Desires Interpretation still counts the great range of excessively self-interested actions that survive the elimination of excessively self-interested desires as impermissible.

There is an additional problem, however. If the advice to eliminate desire is the advice to eliminate only those desires that are themselves excessively self-interested, the class of impermissible desires is extremely small, and much less relevant than expected. Not only are many of the desires of the typical agent permissible, but many of the desires that motivate excessively selfish actions are permissible.

The advice to eliminate desire occurs in almost every Indian text that discusses motivation. In each case, the author is careful to argue that their position is consistent with this advice, and there is usually some dispute over whether it in fact is.[27] If the advice covers only a small subset of desires responsible for only a small number of unacceptable actions, however, it is difficult to make sense of the intense preoccupation with the elimination of desire.

Additionally, this interpretation of the advice makes little sense in the context of some of the debates surrounding it. As I describe in Chapter 6, commentators on the *Nyāyasūtra* debate the Vedāntins over the role of desire in action. Much of the disagreement centers on whether the advice to eliminate desire covers the desire for *mokṣa*. TheVedāntins claim that the desire for *mokṣa* cannot be eliminated, because if it is, the attainment of *mokṣa* is impossible. The Naiyāyikas argue that since desire is an obstacle to liberation, even the desire for *mokṣa* must be eliminated. Surely this debate is not over whether an excessively self-interested desire for *mokṣa* is required to achieve liberation. (Although it makes sense to think that an excessively self-interested desire for *mokṣa* would preclude it.) An excessively self-interested desire for *mokṣa* is no more necessary to achieve *mokṣa* than an excessively self-interested desire to eat more cake than one's sibling without justification is a necessary condition of eating cake!

This debate and many like it suggest that the advice to eliminate desire cannot be the advice to eliminate only excessively self-interested desires. The class of desires to be eliminated must be broad enough that one might think that a desire of the impermissible sort could be a necessary condition of action.

The third version of the No Selfish Desires Interpretation

There is a third version of the No Selfish Desires Interpretation. It states that the advice to eliminate selfishness is the advice to eliminate excessively self-interested action, but that the advice also entails the elimination of all self-interested desires. The argument may be schematized in the following way:

(SA3)

Premise One: Kṛṣṇa advises Arjuna to act without some desires. He permits others.
Premise Two: The *Gītā* advises the elimination of excessive self-interest (*nirmama* and *nirahaṅkara*).
Conclusion: Hence Kṛṣṇa advises Arjuna to act without self-interested desires. He permits desires that are not self-interested.

Since excessively self-interested actions are motivated by self-interested desires, it is possible to eliminate excessively self-interested actions by eliminating self-interested desires, even when the desires themselves are not excessively self-interested. In the cake example above, if the child's desire for cake is eliminated, they will not take more cake than they should.

On this account, the impermissible class of desires is large – it includes all self-interested desires. This is consistent with the importance of the advice to act without desire in the Indian traditions.

There are two problems with this modified account however. The first is that the account entails the elimination of all self-interested actions, just because a self-interested action is an action motivated by a self-interested desire. So the account faces the same problem that faces the first account: the agent cannot count their own well-being as a reason in itself for acting.

The second problem is that if the inference from no excessively self-interested actions to no self-interested desires is justified, an inference from no excessively altruistic actions to no altruistic desires is justified. So long as the sage should count their own well-being as valuable, there will be cases in which they are justified to count their well-being as more valuable than someone else's, as when the degrees of well-being at stake diverge dramatically. If the fact that the sage is in a burning house justifies the action of exiting the house, surely exiting the burning house remains justified when the sage can only exit at the cost of breaking an upper-floor window that would otherwise survive the fire. If the sage thinks, "I could escape through this window, but I will have to break it, and since this section of the house might still be saved, and the home owner will not want to replace this window, I should perish in the fire" and actually stays in the house, they act in a way that is excessively altruistic. If the risk of excessively self-interested actions justifies the elimination of all self-interested desires, then the risk of excessively other-interested actions justifies the elimination of all other-interested desires. Neither inference is sensible.

A fourth version of the No Selfish Desires Interpretation

It seems to me that the most plausible version of the No Selfish Desires Interpretation is that the advice to eliminate selfishness amounts to the advice to eliminate all false beliefs about the self and all desires based on false beliefs about the self. If there is an inference from no selfishness to no selfish desires (as the proponents of the No Selfish Desires Interpretation claim), and if the absence of selfishness is, in part, the absence of false beliefs about the distinction between the empirical and real self (as I argue above), surely the sage does not have desires that are based on false beliefs about the self. The argument goes:

(SA4)

Premise One: Kṛṣṇa advises Arjuna to act without some desires. He permits others.
Premise Two: The *Gītā* advises the elimination of false beliefs about the nature of the self (*nirmama* and *nirahaṅkara*).
Conclusion: Hence Kṛṣṇa advises Arjuna to act without desires that are based on false beliefs about the self. He permits desires that are not based on false beliefs about the self.

On this interpretation, excessively self-interested desires like the child's desire to eat more cake than their sibling are impermissible on account of their dependence on false beliefs about the self. The view also has the benefit of permitting seemingly permissible self-interested desires. The sage can escape the burning building, tend to their wounds, and so on, so long as the sage knows that this body and psyche are transient, only as valuable as the bodies and psyches of others, much less valuable than usually thought, and much less valuable than the well-being of society at large. The sage can avoid physical pain because pain is bad, so long as they do not desire to avoid all pain for the rest of their life. This would be to misunderstand the nature of embodied existence, which is always subject to change, dissatisfaction, loneliness, sickness, and so on. When one has false beliefs about the self, one usually has impermissible desires, just because the desires are based on the false beliefs.

All of this is right, but we cannot infer from it that the advice to eliminate desire is the advice to eliminate selfish desires. The fourth version of the argument still faces the apparent problem of reducing the advice to eliminate desire to relative obscurity. Additionally, desires that result from mistaken beliefs about the nature of the self are not always selfish in any normal sense of the word. A parent might falsely believe that one of their children is more valuable than the others, or that their own mother will not succumb to old age. As a consequence, they desire to secure preferential treatment for their child, and desire that their mother live independently long after she is capable. They might also be excessively altruistic, as in the examples above, and go without food so that their child can have the most gratuitous creature comforts. These are unacceptable desires based on false beliefs about the self, but not necessarily beliefs about the agent's own self. They are desires based on false beliefs about the selves of others. They are certainly impermissible for the same reason that unacceptable self-interested desires are, but they are not self-interested. Hence they are not selfish. The advice to eliminate desire, then, must cover a wider class of desires than the class referred to by the word 'selfish' – no matter which of the two meanings of 'selfish' one has in mind.

Additionally, there is a wide range of desires based on false beliefs about things other than the self that are to be eliminated as well. I might believe that a student has cheated when they have not, and therefore desire to fail them. If my belief were correct, the desire would be permissible. Since it is not correct, the desire is impermissible. But it is not as if its lack of permissibility can be traced to a false belief about the nature of the self. I am wrong to fail the student no matter what metaphysical picture turns out to be true. Hence the desires that are impermissible are those that are based on false beliefs more broadly. As I said in Chapter 2, any desire that a fully knowledgeable agent would have is permissible. Any desire that a fully knowledgeable agent would not have is impermissible.

5 Desireless action in the *Manusmṛti*

In the last chapter I considered the No Selfish Desires Interpretation, according to which the advice to eliminate desire is the advice to eliminate selfish desires, and act on unselfish desires. I considered four versions of the No Selfish Desires Interpretation, and argued that none are plausible.

Desires that are based on false beliefs about the self are impermissible, but some desires that are based on false beliefs about the self are not selfish in any normal sense of the word. Additionally, there are desires that are not based on false beliefs about the self that are impermissible. Hence the advice to eliminate desires is not simply the advice to eliminate selfish desires. Instead, it is the advice to eliminate desires that are based on false beliefs. In other words, a desire is permissible if and only if it is a desire that a fully knowledgeable agent would have.

In this chapter, I consider the theory of motivation in the *Manusmṛti*. I begin by considering Wendy Doniger and Brian K. Smith's translation of the verses that outline the theory. I argue that they make two mistakes. First, they reverse the relationship between *kāma* and *saṅkalpa*. They take *Manu* 2.3 to say that *kāma* is the basis of *saṅkalpa*, when in fact it is the reverse. Second, they mistranslate *saṅkalpa* as 'intention'. In the present context, however, *saṅkalpa* means belief. Rather than saying, "desire is the basis of intention," the verse reads, "belief is the basis of desire." The theory of motivation in the *Manusmṛti* is that belief produces desire, and desire produces action.

The proponents of the Humean Theory of Motivation might raise two objections. First, desire cannot produce action without the help of an additional belief. Second, belief cannot produce desire without the help of an additional desire. The theory of motivation in the *Manusmṛti* must be shorthand, then, for the view that belief and desire produce desire, and belief and desire produce action. Hence the theory corresponds to (HTM2) from Chapter 2.

I argue that neither modification of the account is plausible. First, since the desire that plays a necessary role in motivating action is the desire to do what one does, the claim that an additional belief is also required is implausible. Since the desire takes the action as its content, no additional means–end belief is needed to explain the action. Second, commentators on the *Manusmṛti* explicitly deny that a desire for an end must combine with a belief in order to produce a desire for a means. They argue that at least in some cases, a desire for an end is impermissible. Hence the theory of motivation advanced in the *Manusmṛti* is importantly anti-Humean. It admits that action can have its origin in beliefs alone, and denies that an agent must desire that state of affairs that it is their purpose to bring about.

Finally, I consider whether this analysis can be applied to the *Gītā*. I argue that there is extensive textual evidence to support this view. The *Gītā* claims repeatedly that desires for *phala* should be eliminated. One should perform actions simply because they are to be done. The *Gītā*, however, does not restrict the advice to a narrow class of actions as the *Manusmṛti* does. In the *Gītā*, no action should be motivated by a desire for an end.

Motivation in the *Manusmṛti*

The *Manusmṛti's* theory of motivation is outlined in verses 2.2 through 2.5.[1] Wendy Doniger and Brian K. Smith translate the verses in the following way:

> Acting out of desire is not approved of, but here on earth there is no such thing as no desire; for even studying the Veda and engaging in the rituals enjoined in the Veda are based upon desire. //2.2//
>
> Desire is the very root of the conception of a definite intention, and sacrifices are the result of that intention; all the vows and the duties of restriction are traditionally said to come from the conception of a definite intention. //2.3//
>
> Not a single rite is ever performed here on earth by a man without desire; for each and every thing that he does is motivated by the desire for precisely that thing. //2.4//
>
> The man who is properly occupied in these (desires) goes to the world of the immortals, and here on earth he achieves all the desires for which he has conceived an intention. //2.5//
>
> (Doniger and Smith 1991: 17)

The passage begins by citing the problem of desirelessness. Acting from desire is not praised, but action without desire is impossible. Enjoined actions, like discouraged actions, are motivated by desire. The text's theory of motivation is articulated in 2.3, where the relationships between action, intention and desire are explained. Desire produces intention, and intention produces action. As I mentioned in Chapter 1, verse 2.2 in particular cites the problem of desireless action.

While the distinction between a desire and an intention is in some ways obvious, it is helpful to keep in mind two important distinctions between them. Michael Bratman gives the following example, which demonstrates both distinctions nicely:

> Suppose I desire a milk shake for lunch, recognize that the occasion is here, and am guilty of no irrationality. Still, I might not drink a milk shake; for my desire for a milk shake still needs to be weighed against conflicting desires – say, my desire to lose weight. My desire for a milk shake potentially influences what I do at lunchtime.
>
> In contrast, suppose that this morning I formed the intention to have a milk shake at lunch, lunchtime arrives, my intention remains, and nothing unexpected happens. In such a case I do not normally need yet again to tote up the pros and cons concerning milk shake drinking. Rather, in the normal course of events I will simply proceed to execute (or, anyway, try to execute) my intention and order a milk shake. My intention will not merely influence my conduct, it will control it.
>
> (Bratman 1987:15–16)

When we reason about what our course of action ought to be, we consider our desires. When deciding what I will do at lunchtime, I might consider the fact that I desire a milk shake, consider this desire against others – I also desire to lose weight – and come to a conclusion about whether I will have a milk shake or not. If I decide that I indeed will have a milk shake, then I have formed the intention to do so.[2]

So the difference between a desire and an intention is at least twofold. First, practical reasoning often begins with considerations of desires, and ends with intentions. Desires are inputs to deliberation, intentions are outputs. There are exceptions to this general rule, but they will not be important here.[3] Second, an intention suggests that the issue of what to do is settled – I have resolved, at least for the time being, to do that which I intend to do.[4] A desire does not have the same implication. As Bratman says, my desire for a milk shake must still be weighed against other goals.[5]

If Doniger and Smith's translation of verse 2.3 is correct, the theory of motivation in the *Manusmṛti* may be diagrammed as follows:

(MTM1)

desire	⇨	intention	⇨	action
(*kāma*)		(*saṅkalpa*)		(*karma*)

Doniger and Smith's translation of these verses is inaccurate in two essential ways, however. In Sanskrit, verse 2.3 reads:

> *saṅkalpamūlaḥ kāmo vai yajñāḥ saṅkalpasambhavāḥ* /
> *vratāni yamadharmāśca sarve saṅkalpajāḥ smṛtāḥ* //.
>
> (Dave 1972–1985: 157, lines 11–12)

Doniger and Smith's first mistake is that they get the relationship between desire and intention backwards.[6] They take *kāmaḥ* (*kāmo* with *sandhi*) and *saṅkalpamūlaḥ* (desire basis) as subject and predicate, but read *saṅkalpamūlaḥ* as a *tatpuruṣa* compound. Hence, "Desire (*kāmo*) is the very root (*mūlaḥ*) of the conception of a definite intention (*saṅkalpa*)." If that is the case, however, the compound should have the gender of its final element *mūlam*, which is neuter. Since, instead, the ending is masculine in gender – *mūlaḥ* – it must be a *bahuvrīhi* compound. The gender of *mūlam* is determined by the gender of *kāma*.[7] Hence the text is importantly different from Doniger and Smith's translation. Verse 2.3 instead ought to read: "Even desire has a definite intention as its basis. Sacrifices arise from particular intentions. The *smṛtis* state: 'All restraints and vows are born of a particular intention.' "

The claim in 2.3 is that a *saṅkalpa* produces *kāma*, and not vice versa. Hence,

(MTM2)

intention (*saṅkalpa*)	⇨	desire (*kāma*)	⇨	action (*karma*)

Action is produced by desire, and desire is produced by intention.

Doniger and Smith's second mistake is to translate the word *saṅkalpa* as 'intention'. As Bratman points out, the notion of an intention implies some kind of resolution. When it is true of me that I intend to have a milk shake, I have resolved to do so. My mind is made up – at least for the moment. If, however, we have a look at some of the commentaries on these verses, the analysis of *saṅkalpa* is quite different.

In his commentary to *Manu* 2.3, Medhātithi openly asks: "Then what is this [thing] called *saṅkalpa* that is the basis of all action?" He replies at some length, again stating that a *saṅkalpa* produces a desire, and not vice versa:[8]

> Then what is this [thing] [which is] called *saṅkalpa* that is the basis of all action? It is said: [*saṅkalpa* is] that [which is] called the beholding of the mind. It is the cause of that desire (*prārthana*) and purpose (*adhyavasāya*) that follow it. For these actions of the mind serve as the basis with regard to the performance of all actions. For no physical actions are possible without them. So first, [there is] the determining of the nature of a thing, for example, "this object is attained by this purposeful action." The cognition which is like this is considered a *saṅkalpa*.
>
> (Dave 1972–1985: 157, lines 18–22)[9]

A *saṅkalpa*, then, is not an intention, but a belief or cognition. Medhātithi offers the example of a means–end belief in particular – "this thing brings about this effect."[10] Kullūkabhaṭṭa, another commentator, describes *saṅkalpa* in the same way. "A *saṅkalpa* is a cognition which has this content: 'by [means of] this action this desirable end is attained' " (Dave 1972–1985: 158, lines 9–10).[11]

Elsewhere in his commentary to 2.3, however, Medhātithi offers an example in which *saṅkalpa* is not a means–end belief.

> In that way a hungry person sees (*paśyati*) the action of eating, [and] then desires (*icchati*) "I should eat." Then they form the purpose (*adhyavasyati*), "I [will] make food, having desisted from other actions." So they say to the superintendent of the place where the work occurs, "Get ready! Prepare the kitchen!"
>
> (Dave 1972–1985, 157: lines 24–27)[12]

Here the *saṅkalpa* is more like a perception or cognition – the person first sees others eating. As a result, they desire to eat. This desire produces the purpose of eating, which in turn motivates the action that is a means to satisfying the desire – ordering the cook to prepare food. Hence *saṅkalpa* is more accurately translated as 'belief' than 'means–end belief'.[13]

If we incorporate this change into the translation as well, we get:

> Even desire has belief as its basis. Sacrifices arise from beliefs.
> The *smṛtis* state: "All restraints and vows are born of a belief."

Hence,

(MTM3)

belief (*saṅkalpa*)	⇨	desire (*kāma*)	⇨	action (*karma*)

Action is the immediate result of desire, and desire is the product of belief.

Indeed, if intention or purpose plays a role in motivating action, it occupies a position between desire and action. As Medhātithi says, both *kāma* and *adhyavasāya* (purpose) – in that order – are the result of *saṅkalpa* (see below).

Two Humean objections

The Humeans will advance at least two objections to this account. First, they will object that a desire cannot produce action without the help of a belief. The required belief must connect the desire with the appropriate action, hence the belief that produces the desire itself cannot play this role. In the original coffee example, in order for my desire for coffee to move me to go to the café, I must believe that going to the café is a means to getting a coffee. (MTM3) should instead read:

(MTM3′)

belief	⇨	desire		
		+	⇨	action
		belief		

Second, the Humeans will object that a belief cannot produce desire without the help of some additional desire. If my desire for coffee is the result of a belief, then there must be some additional desire that combines with the belief to produce the desire for coffee. My belief that in order to finish this chapter tonight I must have coffee does not produce the desire for coffee without the desire to finish this chapter tonight. Indeed, in Medhātithi's own example of a person who resolves to eat, the agent is hungry to begin with. If they were not, the perception of people eating would not produce the action of ordering the preparation of food. Hence (MTM3′) should read:

(MTM3″)

belief				
+	⇨	desire		
desire		+	⇨	action
		belief		

Furthermore, the first desire in the series must be a desire for an end. Any desire that is derived from the first is a desire for a means. Hence,

(MTM3‴)

belief				
+	⇨	desire		
desire		(for means)		
(for end)		+	⇨	action
		belief		

At this point, the diagram is essentially equivalent to (HTM2) in Chapter 2.

Neither of these modifications is plausible, however. First, the desire that the *Manusmṛti* claims is a necessary condition of action is a desire to do what one does. *Manusmṛti* 2.4 states, "No action of [a person who is] desireless is ever seen here. For whatever a person does, [that] is the deed of someone who desires just that" (Dave 1972–1985: 159, lines 5–6).[14] Medhātithi explains, "here in this world, never at any time is any action possible, of a person in a waking state [who is] without the desire that it be carried out" (Dave 1972–1985: 159, lines 8–9).[15] So if I go to the café, the necessary desire is the desire to go to the café.

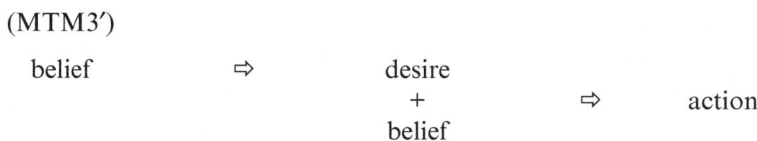

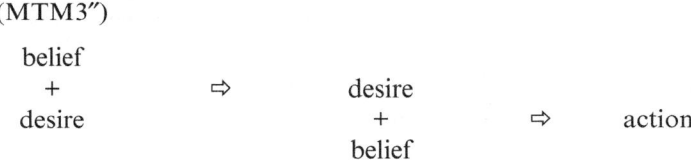

I mentioned in Chapter 2 that one way in which the theories of motivation in Indian texts explicitly diverge from the Humean view is that they typically

cite the desire to do what one does as the paradigmatic desire for a means. The *Manusmṛti* is in accord with this convention. If the desire for a means is a desire to do what one does, however, then it is at least less intuitively obvious that some additional belief is needed to motivate action. If the desire for a means that motivates my action of walking to the café is a desire to walk to the café, there is no explanatory gap that must be filled by an appropriate means–end belief, as there is when I walk to the café because I desire coffee.

Of course, there will always be some belief without which the agent will not act on their desire. In this case, if I do not believe that in order to go to the café I must move my legs, and so on, then I will not do it. From this it does not follow, however, that these beliefs must be mentioned in an explanation of my action. If this were necessary, then even the more standard, Humean explanation of my action of walking to the café, according to which I walk to the café motivated by a desire for coffee and a belief that the café has coffee, would be incomplete. It too must cite my belief that in order to walk, I must move my legs, and so on. Once we start citing trivial beliefs of this sort, however, the theory of motivation diverges dramatically from ordinary action explanations.

Another way to put this point is to say that when I explain that I walked to the café motivated by a desire to walk to the café, there is no more of an explanatory gap between my desire and my action than there is if I explain that I desired a coffee, and believed that by walking to the café I could have one.

Additionally, the claim that every action is immediately motivated by a desire and belief is disputed among contemporary philosophers. Rosalind Hursthouse, for example, argues that for some actions there is no appropriately ascribable means–end belief that explains them. She offers the following example: "Jane . . . in a wave of hatred for Joan, tears at Joan's photo with her nails, and gouges holes in the eyes" (Hursthouse 1991: 60). In this case, the only obvious candidates for means–end beliefs that connect Jane's desire with her action are beliefs like "the photo of Joan *is* Joan, or that scratching the photo will be causally efficacious in defacing its original" (Hursthouse 1991: 60). The problem is that Jane almost certainly does not believe these things.

Again, there will always be some belief without which the agent would not have done what they did. Hursthouse says,

> I can agree that she would not have torn at the photo if she had not believed that it was a photo of Joan; and if someone wants to say, "So those are the reasons for the action," I do not want to quarrel, for these "reasons" do *not* form the appropriate desire–belief pair assumed by the standard account.
>
> (Hursthouse 1991: 59–60)

These beliefs do not further explain the action, however. They do not connect the desire with the action in the right way. If they must be cited in the seemingly odd case in which no means–end belief combines with desire to produce action, then they must be cited in the more usual cases as well.

This is not to say that the desire to do that Medhātithi claims plays a necessary role in motivating action is always "arational." My point is that if there are cases in which a means–end belief is not necessary, the case for insisting that a means–end belief must combine with a desire to do what one does in order for action to arise is weak in the first place.

The second modification is implausible as well. Medhātithi explicitly claims that a desire for an end is not a necessary condition of action. Near the end of his commentary on verse 2.5, he concludes his own position by saying, "in the case of *nityakarmas* (ritual actions for which no result is mentioned in the Vedas), a desire (*abhilāṣa*) characterized by *phala* (a result) [is prohibited]" (Dave 1972–1985: 160, line 20).[16] That is, in the case of *nityakarmas*, a desire for some result or end of action is prohibited. If a desire for an end is prohibited in the case of *nityakarmas*, then a desire for an end cannot be a necessary condition of action more generally.

In order to explain this claim, it is necessary to explain the discussion that precedes it. In his commentary to verse 2.2, which I translate as "Essential desirefulness (*kāmātmatā*) is not praiseworthy (*praśashtā*), but never does desirelessness (*akāmatā*) exist here on Earth, since the study of the Vedas and the performance of Vedic actions are to be desired (*kāmya*)" (Dave 1972–1985: 154, lines 26–7),[17] Medhātithi explains that *kāmātmatā* refers to a person "whose reason (*hetu*) for performing action is the desire (*abhilāśa*) for *phala* (some end)" (Dave 1972–1985: 154, line 28).[18]

So Medhātithi immediately attempts to resolve the apparent tension cited in verse 2.2 between the advice to eliminate *kāmātmatā*, on the one hand, and the impossibility of *akāmatā*, on the other. He says that *kāmātmatā* in this context has to do with the agent's desire for an end, not desire more generally. This leaves open the possibility that the desireless agent is nonetheless motivated by a desire of some other sort – like a desire for a means. Hence the two claims are consistent. Desirefulness – in the sense of desiring the end of action – is to be avoided, even if desirefulness – in the sense of being motivated by a desire of some sort – is unavoidable.

The *pūrvapakṣin* (opponent) objects that if *kāmātmatā* is not to be done (*na kartavya*), then all actions are prohibited. "The performance of each and every action has the purpose of the attainment of *phala*. It is not for the sake of bringing about [its] own form!" (Dave 1972–1985: 155, lines 1–2).[19] To require that an action not be performed from a desire for an end is to insist that it be done for its own sake. This is absurd, however. A person does not go to work simply to walk down the street, but to receive money, provide for their family, and so on. Hence a prohibition on the desire for *phala* amounts to a prohibition on action. "This follows from that: Nothing is to be done by anyone. Sitting in silence is to be done by all beings" (Dave 1972–1985: 155, lines 10–11).[20]

Medhātithi replies that verse 2.1, which I translate as "That *dharma* which is fostered by the wise [and] favored by the good, [whose] hearts are always without *dveṣa* and *rāga*, that is [to be] known" (Dave 1972–1985: 151, lines 13–4),[21] states that the subject of the present chapter is *dharma*. Hence we should assume that Manu's claims are claims about ritual actions – Vedic actions – and not mundane actions. A desire for the end of mundane actions, then, is not covered by the injunction to avoid *kāmātmatā* in verse 2.2.

The *pūrvapakṣin* also objects that if *kāmātmatā* is not to be done, then *kāmyakarmas* (ritual actions performed for the sake of some *phala*) are prohibited.[22] This consequence is absurd as well, however, because *śruti* endorses *kāmyakarmas* for those who desire certain earthly and heavenly rewards. The *karmas* are often thought of as hypothetical imperatives: "If you desire such and such, then perform this certain ritual."

We might expect that Medhātithi will accept this consequence, and insist that even though *śruti* endorses *kāmyakarmas* for those who desire certain impermanent rewards, it does not endorse desires for these rewards. After all, the complete prohibition of *kāmyakarmas* is certainly consistent with the austere view endorsed by Vyāsa in his *Yogasūtrabhāṣya*. Kṛṣṇa, we might remember, advises Arjuna to be indifferent to the *guṇas*. Certainly everything that can be attained by means of the performance of *kāmyakarmas* is constituted by the *guṇas*.[23]

Instead, however, Medhātithi says that the advice to act without a desire for an end does not apply to *kāmyakarmas* either.[24]

> As for the claim [that] there is the consequence of a prohibition on *kāmyakarmas*, like the *saurya* (sun) [sacrifice] and so on, with regard to that [claim], he [namely Manu] will say [at verse 2.5], "And he attains all desires in this world as they are thought of (*saṅkalpitāṃ*)." Indeed, if there is a prohibition [on desire], how could there be a thought (*saṅkalpa*) [of that which is desired], and how could there be the fulfillment of desires?
>
> (Dave 1972–1985: 155, lines 12–14)[25]

Manu will say in verse 2.5 that a person who lives rightly with regard to their desires attains anything they think of.[26] If there were a complete prohibition on desire, however, this would be impossible. First, without desires, no desires could be thought of. Second, without desires, no desires could be fulfilled. So Manu does not prohibit the desires that are satisfied by and motivate *kāmyakarmas*.[27]

Medhātithi eventually specifies that the restriction mentioned in verse 2.1 applies only to the performance of *nityakarmas*.

> With regard to *nityakarmas*, since the *phala* is not mentioned [in *śruti*], [the end] is not to be intended . . . For since [its being] a means to an end

is not known from *pramāṇa*, it is not the case that from [the agent's] purpose alone, the end arises.

(Dave 1972–1985: 160, lines 2–3, 5)[28]

When *śruti* prescribes *nityakarmas*, no result is mentioned. Since no result is mentioned, no result arises.[29] So when a person performs a *nityakarma*, they should not desire some further end of the action. A result will not arise simply because the person intends it. So "in the case of *nityakarmas*, a desire (*abhilāṣa*) characterized by *phala* [is prohibited]" (Dave 1972–1985: 160, lines 19–20).[30]

In these cases, a desire for the means motivates the action. "The fulfillment of the means [to the agent's end], however, is certainly to be desired" (Dave 1972–1985: 160, line 20).[31] If we assume that the desire for a means in this context is the same as that mentioned in 2.4, then a desire to do what one does motivates *nityakarmas* without the help of a desire for an end.

Hence the advice to eliminate desire in verse 2.1 is limited in three ways. First, it does not apply to everyday actions in which *dharma* – taken rather narrowly to refer to ritual actions – is not an issue. Second, it does not apply to *kāmyakarmas*. Third, it amounts to the advice to eliminate only desires for ends, and act on desires to do.[32] So according to Medhātithi, desireless action in the *Manusmṛti* is the performance of *nityakarmas* without a desire for *phala*. Even in the case of *nityakarmas*, however, the agent can desire that which is a means to their end. Their action is motivated by a desire to do what they are doing.

While Medhātithi's claims about desireless action only apply to *nityakarmas*, from them we can infer claims about the *Manusmṛti's* theory of motivation in general. If, in the case of *nityakarmas*, a desire to do can motivate action without the help of a means–end belief that connects the desire to do with the action, and without the help of some additional desire that combines with *saṅkalpa* to produce the desire to do, then the only necessary conditions of action are *saṅkalpa* and the desire to do.[33] The basic theory of motivation in the *Manusmṛti*, then, may be diagrammed as follows:

(MTM4)

belief (*saṅkalpa*)	⇨	desire to do (*kāma*)	⇨	action (*karma*)

This is not to say that there will not be cases in which the desire to do is explained by some additional desire as well. Indeed, typically, actions will be motivated in this way. As I said above, Medhātithi's own example of a person who orders a cook to prepare food seems to cite a desire for the end of satisfying the agent's hunger as well. In these cases, the motivation may be diagrammed in the following way:

(MTM4′)

belief (*saṅkalpa*) + desire for end (*kāma*)	⇨	desire to do (*kāma*)	⇨	action (*karma*)

Nonetheless, (MTM4) is the most basic model of the theory of motivation in the *Manusmṛti*, since a desire for an end is not always necessary.

One objection from the *pūrvapakṣin* still lingers. At one point the *pūrvapakṣin* objected that action is never performed for its own sake. All action is done for some reason, and the action itself cannot be the reason that it is performed.[34] If an agent cannot have a desire for something other than the action, then the agent can have no reason for performing the action. So if (MTM4) is correct, action is performed without reason or purpose.

This objection, however, depends on the same equivocation that I accused some of the proponents of the Some Desires Interpretation of committing in Chapter 1. Just because the properly motivated agent does not desire some end of action, it does not follow that they have no end or purpose in doing what they do. It only means that they do not desire that which is their purpose.

As Medhātithi says in his commentary to *Manusmṛti* 2.2 above, the word *kāmātmatā* refers to an agent whose reason (*hetu*) for acting is a desire for *phala*. In contrast, "the [properly motivated agent's] reason (*prayojana*) [for acting] is the fulfillment of *vidhi* (Vedic injunction), or the non-production of demerit" (Dave 1972–1985: 160, lines 15–16).[35] This implies that the desireless agent's answer to the question "Why did you do such and such?" might simply be: "because it is enjoined by *vidhi*." The agent has a *prayojana/hetu* – a reason, or purpose, in acting – even though they do not desire that which is their purpose. Their *prayojana* is the state of affairs they intend to bring about by means of the action they perform.

There are two ways to interpret this claim. First, the agent's *prayojana/hetu* might simply be their *adhyavasāya* – the purpose that arises as a result of *saṅkalpa* and *kāma* (see above). If this is right, then the diagram reads:

(MTM5)

belief (*saṅkalpa*)	⇨	desire to do (*kāma*)	⇨	purpose (*adhyavasāya/prayojana/hetu*)	⇨	action (*karma*)

The problem with this interpretation is that the agent's purpose sets the end of their action, and the desire to do sets the means to it. In order for an agent to determine the means to their end, however, they must first establish their end! The alternative is that the agent's *prayojana/hetu* is distinct from their *adhyavasāya*. Hence,

(MTM6)

belief (*saṅkalpa*)	⇨	purpose (*prayojana/ hetu*)	⇨	desire to do (*kāma*)	⇨	purpose (*adhyavasāya*)	⇨	action (*karma*)

The *prayojana/hetu* sets the agent's end, and the *adhyavasāya* is the purpose of performing some particular action. The required *kāma* and the *adhyavasāya* take the same state of affairs as their object.[36]

An example of this might be that, first, the agent comes to know that the Vedas prescribe a certain *nityakarma*, like the agnihotra sacrifice.[37] Second, and as a result, they form the purpose of performing the agnihotra. As Medhātithi says, the agent's *prayojana* is the fulfillment of *vidhi* – this is the end that will be accomplished by the agent's action. Third, the agent comes to desire to perform some action that is a means – understood broadly – to the end of fulfilling *vidhi*, such as finding a priest to perform the sacrifice, and so on. Fourth, they form the purpose or intention of finding a priest, and finally they do so.

One apparent oddity of this account is the order of *kāma* and *adhyavasāya*. It seems strange to say that an agent comes to desire to do what they do before they have decided to do what they do. One explanation is that the desire to perform some particular action arises before the agent decides to perform that particular action, and then the agent assesses whether this is indeed the best means. As Bratman says, desires are inputs, purposes or intentions are outputs to deliberation. So I desire a cup of coffee, and decide to have one. I then desire to go to the café. Perhaps I also desire to go to my kitchen, go to the store, go to my neighbors, and so on, as well, all as a means to having a cup of coffee. I then decide which of these desires to act on – that is, I decide which desire will form my intention.

Now, of course, the Humeans will immediately object that if an agent performs some action because it is in accord with *śruti*, it follows that they desire to act in accord with *śruti*. Hence a desire for an end is still required. As I argued in Chapter 1, however, the entailment between action and desire – if there is one – is not so obviously true that it must serve as a constraint on the interpretations of Indian texts. Hence this kind of objection does not weigh against the interpretation per se.

The Humeans might instead object that the theory of motivation in the *Manusmṛti* is simply implausible. This depends, however, on whether the arguments for the Humean Theory of Motivation are convincing. I consider these arguments in detail in Chapter 7.

A reconsideration of the *Bhagavadgītā*

It is worth reconsidering the theory of motivation in the *Bhagavadgītā* in the context of the theory of motivation in the *Manusmṛti*. There is a great deal of textual evidence to suggest that the *Gītā* also considers at least some desires for ends impermissible.

First, the *Gītā* advocates performing ritual actions without the desire for *phala*. Kṛṣṇa contrasts two ways of offering a sacrifice.

> Sacrifice in accord with *vidhi* (injunction) by those not desiring *phala*, the mind having been focused only on [the thought] "[this] is to be sacrificed," that [sacrifice] is *sattvic*. That which is offered having intended (*abhisandhāya*) the *phala*, however, and also for [some] false purpose, O Arjuna, know that sacrifice to be *rajasic*!
>
> (17.11–12, Sadhale 1985c: 257–258, lines 2–3 and 1–2)[38]

This suggests that at the very least, Kṛṣṇa accepts that *nityakarmas* should be performed without a desire for *phala*. The claim that the agent should have their mind focused on the thought "this is to be sacrificed" parallels the *Manusmṛti's* claim that the agent should desire the means, but not the end. A similar claim is repeated in the final verses of Chapter 16:

> The person who, disregarding the *vidhis* of *śāstra*, [who] pursues the fulfillment of [their desires], they do not attain success, nor happiness, nor the ultimate goal. Hence *śāstra* is your standard for establishing what is to be done (*kārya*) and what is not to be done (*akārya*). Having known the *vidhis* declared by *śāstra*, you should perform [that] action in this world.
>
> (16.23–24, Sadhale 1985c: 231–232, lines 13–14 and 27–28)[39]

Again, rather than acting for the sake of fulfilling one's desires, the agent who is properly motivated acts for the sake of fulfilling the *vidhis* of *śāstra*. They perform a certain action because it is in accord with *śāstra*, rather than because they desire some end.

One important difference between the *Gītā* and the *Manusmṛti*, however, is that the *Gītā* does not restrict the advice to act without the desire for *phala* to *nityakarmas*. Kṛṣṇa repeatedly enjoins Arjuna to always act without desire.[40] "The right is to only the action, never to the *phala* [of action]. Let there be no [action] caused [by the desire for] the *phala* of action!" (2.47, Sadhale 1985a: 190, lines 34–35).[41] He describes those who are motivated by the desire for *phala* as ignorant and miserable:

> Seek refuge in discrimination! Those who are moved by *phala* are pitiable . . . The wise, joined with discrimination, having abandoned the *phala*

born of action, are freed from the bondage of birth. They go to the place [that is] free of pain.

(2.49 and 2.51, Sadhale 1985a: 196 and 205, lines 41 and 14–15)[42]

This sentiment is repeated throughout the *Gītā*, without the *Manusmṛti's* qualification that only ritual actions are to be done desirelessly. Verses 2.47, 2.49, 2.51, 4,14, 4.20, 5.12, 6.1, 12.11, 12.12, 17.11, 17.21, 18.2, 18.6, 18.9, 18.23 and 18.34 all qualify the desires to be eliminated as desires for *phala*, without this additional qualification. This suggests that the model of motivation that the *Manusmṛti* advises in the case of *nityakarmas* is applied more generally in the *Gītā*.

A number of influential contemporary authors have drawn the comparison between desireless action in the *Gītā* and the performance of *nityakarmas*. Arvind Sharma, for example, claims that Arjuna's action of fighting in the battle should be performed on the model of a *nityakarma*, rather than on the model of a *kāmyakarma*.

> Arjuna should look upon engaging in battle as obligatory duty or as *nitya-naimittika karma*.[43] If Arjuna fails to fight he would be remiss in the performance of duty and will therefore attract bad *karma*. If, however, Arjuna engaged in battle . . . out of a desire to gain some personal end then his action would fall within the category of *kāmya karma*, and again result in karmic entrapment. Hence the emphasis on *niṣkāma-karma* in the *Gītā*.
>
> (Sharma 1985: 192)

B. K. Matilal speculates that "the 'desireless' action of the *Gītā* was derived indirectly from such notions of the *nitya*-type of action" (Matilal 2002: 129). This suggestion is supported by the parallels between the two texts.

This suggests that Kṛṣṇa advises Arjuna to act without desire for *phala* in every case. If this is right, then he does indeed discourage all *kāmyakarmas*. This is consistent with a passage to which *Manusmṛti* 2.2 seems to allude.

> This flowery word which those who are ignorant recite, gratified in the word of the Veda, O Arjuna, thus saying, "nothing else exists," those who are essentially desirous (*kāmātmānaḥ*), [whose] goal is heaven, affecting rebirth as the *phala* of action, [performing] many various ritual actions (*kriyā*), [whose] end is enjoyment and power, of those who are attached to enjoyment an power, whose will is stolen, discrimination that is resolved in meditation is not found.
>
> (2.42–2.44, Sadhale 1985a: 177, lines 31–36)[44]

Heaven, enjoyment, and power are standard *phalas* of *kāmyakarmas*. Vyāsa mentions both heaven and power as states of affairs that the *vairāgin* does not desire (cf. *Yogasūtrabhāṣya* 1.15 and 1.16; see also Chapter 2, this volume).

Kṛṣṇa characterizes a person who is concerned with these things as ignorant, attached, and without their own will. They falsely believe that nothing greater than these impermanent enjoyments can be attained. This implies that unlike the *Manusmṛti*, the *Gītā* does not endorse the desires that motivate and are satisfied by *kāmyakarmas*.

This conclusion is also supported by Medhātithi's own assessment of the position of the *Gītā*. As I said above, in his commentary to *Manusmṛti* 2.5, Medhātithi limits desireless action to the performance of *nityakarmas* without a desire for *phala*. He then contrasts his position with that of the Brahmavādins – that is, Vedāntins: "The Brahmavādins, however, think that *kāmātmatā* means [that there is] a prohibition of the *saurya* [sacrifice], and so on [as well]. [They say,] '[any] acting for the sake of *phala* has the nature of bondage' " (Dave 1972–1985: 160, lines 21–22).[45] The Brahmavādins do not limit the prohibition on desire to the desire for the *phala* of *nityakarmas*. Any desire for *phala* is a fetter, hence all desires for ends are prohibited.

Medhātithi then cites the *Gītā* itself in support of ascribing this view to the Brahmavādins:

> This is said by the Venerable Kṛṣṇadvaipāyana [that is, Kṛṣṇa in the *Gītā*[46]]: "Let there be no [action] caused [by the desire for] the *phala* of action" [*Bhagavadgītā* 2.47]. Similarly, [Kṛṣṇa says,] "The performance of an action becomes useless from the incompleteness of the means, or from the intending of *phala*, or the *vidhi* imperfectly remembered."
>
> (Dave 1972–1985: 22–25)[47]

The first passage repeats the claim above: the prohibition on desire covers any desire for *phala*. The second passage states that a person's desire for the *phala* of their action is one of three mistakes that renders an action a failure.[48]

Rather than performing actions because they are means to some desired end, then, an agent ought to perform actions because they are to be done (*kārya*). "Always without attachment, perform the action that is to be done (*kāryaṃ*)!" (3.19, Sadhale 1985a: 309, lines 23–24).[49]

> The discriminative faculty (*buddhi*) that knows activity and inactivity, that which is to be done (*kārya*) and that which is not to be done (*akārya*), that which is to be feared, and that which is not to be feared, bondage and *mokṣa*, that [discrimination], O Arjuna, is *sattvic*.
>
> (18.30, Sadhale 1985c: 341, lines 16–17)[50]

This claim parallels Medhātithi's claim that *nityakarmas* should be performed because *vidhi* commands them. The phrase 'to be done' is consistent with the broader scope of the advice in the *Gītā*. That which is prescribed by the *vidhis* of *śāstra* are to be done, but there are a wide range of actions that are to be done that are not explicitly enjoined by *vidhi*. According to the *Gītā*, these actions are to be performed without a desire for *phala* as well.

If the *Gītā* advises the elimination of all desires for *phala*, but still admits that desire plays a necessary role in motivating action – as the Some Desires Interpretation claims – then presumably desires for means are permissible. More specifically, desires to do are permissible. This is consistent with one of the only passages in the *Gītā* in which Kṛṣṇa seems to endorse desire. The passage reads: "As the ignorant act attached in action, O Arjuna, so the wise should act without attachment, desiring (*cikīrṣur*) *lokasaṃgraha*" (3.25, Sadhale 1985a: 25–26).[51] The word *cikīrṣu* in this passage is a desiderative agentive adjective, formed from the root √ *kṛ* (to do). So it literally means *desiring to do* (*lokasaṃgraha*). Hence the desire that Kṛṣṇa advises Arjuna to act on is a desire to do what he does – just as it is in the *Manusmṛti*.

A related word, *cīkirṣā*, appears in Mohanty's diagram of the standard theory of motivation in the Indian systems. (Mohanty translates *cīkirṣā* as 'desire'.) As I said in Chapter 1, Viśvanātha Nyāya-Pañcānana uses the word *cīkirṣā* to describe the required desire in the *Bhāṣā-Pariccheda* as well. Roy W. Perrett, summarizing the standard Indian view, says, "a voluntary action requires the presence of a number of factors: agent, knowledge, *desire to act*, and effort" (Perrett 1998: 23, emphasis added). All of this is consistent with my analysis of both the *Manusmṛti* and the *Bhagavadgītā*.

This is a rather straightforward point, and is in accord with a widely held moral intuition. It would be strange to hear a parent explain that they saved their child from drowning because it was a means to some desire of their own. The expectation is that the parent acts rightly insofar as they save the child for the child's own sake – that is, because the child's life is valuable – regardless of their own desires.[52] In a case where a parent saves their own child rather than the child of a stranger (where they must choose between one or the other), it is the fact that the first is their child that justifies their action (if anything does), not the greater strength of their desire for the survival of their own child.

As far as I can tell, this is the sense of the extremely common, although not always clearly explained claim that Indian philosophy advocates performing "duty for duty's sake." Tara Chatterjea, for example, claims that "[a]ctions should spring from the sense of duty. It [that is, the sense of duty] replaces the desire for the fruits of action" (Chatterjea 2002: 140). Chatterjea implies that this view is found throughout the Hindu tradition: "[a]n important and influential part of Hindu ethics might be seen as a duty for duty's sake theory as we find in the *Bhagavadgītā*" (Chatterjea 2002: 151).[53]

This can only mean that the agent does what they do because it is what is to be done, not because in doing what they do, some desire of theirs is satisfied. In other words, the agent's purpose is the doing of what is right, not the satisfying of their own desire. As Chakrabarti says, the agent performs "individual acts prescribed by the scriptures *because* they are so prescribed and with no ulterior motive" (Chakrabarti 1988: 331, emphasis in original).[54]

A reconsideration of the *Yogasūtra*

This analysis is helpful in further analyzing the *Yogasūtra*. In one of the passages I cited above, Vyāsa describes the motivation of Īśvara. He says,

> [Īśvara has] the *prayojana* of the assistance of beings, even though there is no [possibility of the] promotion of his [own] self. At the dissolutions of the epochs and the great dissolutions, [he resolves,] 'I will remove [those] *puruṣas* [who are] *saṃsārins* by teaching knowledge and *dharma*' [see Chapter 2, this volume].

If Vyāsa's use of the word *prayojana*, rather than some word that might be translated as 'desire', is deliberate here – and presumably it is, since he only uses it in this one passage – perhaps he means to emphasize that Īśvara, unlike the ordinary person, is not motivated by a desire for that which is his end. Instead, Īśvara's end is established by his purpose.

I argued in Chapter 2 that if the Some Desires Interpretation is correct, Īśvara desires the assistance of beings, or that *saṃsārins* no longer suffer. If Īśvara does not desire that which is his end, however, then this cannot be right. Instead, if Īśvara has a desire at all – and remember, the *Yogasūtra* itself does not say this – it must be a desire for the means of teaching knowledge and *dharma*.

First, Īśvara comes to know – by means of *saṅkalpa* – that *saṃsārins* suffer, that the attainment of *kaivalya* is the means of ending this suffering, and so on. He then forms the purpose – *prayojana/hetu* – of helping these beings, even though he does not desire to do so. Next he comes to desire – *kāma* – to teach them, and forms the purpose – *adhyavasāya* – of doing so. This desire motivates his action of teaching *saṃsārins* knowledge and *dharma*, if any does. Likewise, the *jīvanmukta*, and even the ordinary person who manages to be motivated in the right way only occasionally, desire that which is a means to their end, without desiring the end itself. They form two intentions or purposes. The first establishes their end, and the second establishes the means to it. Hence both the *Manusmṛti* and the *Yogasūtra* deny that an agent must desire that which is their end in acting.

6 Desireless action in the *Nyāyasūtra* and *Brahmasiddhi*

In the last chapter I argued that according to the *Manusmṛti*, the only desire that plays a necessary role in motivating action is a desire to do what one does. Medhātithi analyzes the *Manusmṛti's* advice to eliminate desire as the advice to eliminate the desire for the *phala* of *nityakarmas*. Since *nityakarmas* do not produce results, an agent should not desire any result. They should perform *nityakarmas* motivated by a desire to perform that very action, because it is prescribed by the *vidhis* of *śāstra*.

Since an agent can act without a desire for *phala* in the case of *nityakarmas*, it follows that a desire for some end of action is not a necessary condition of action. When an agent acts without a desire for some end, it does not follow that they act without a *prayojana* (purpose), however. Their *prayojana* is established by beliefs about what *śāstra* requires.

I also argued that the *Bhagavadgītā* seems to advance a similar position. Unlike the *Manusmṛti*, however, the *Gītā* does not limit the advice to act without desire to a narrow class of ritual actions. The *Gītā's* advice to act without desire for ends extends to all actions. The text prescribes acting motivated by a desire to perform the very action that one performs, because it is to be done.

In Chapter 3 I argued that there is at least superficial evidence for three more specific versions of the Some Desires Interpretation. In chapters 3 and 4 I considered two of these interpretations – the *Mokṣa*-only Interpretation, and the No Selfish Desires Interpretation. In this chapter, I consider the last of these three views – the view that phenomenologically salient desires are impermissible.

Both the *Nyāyasūtra* and *Brahmasiddhi* seem to support this view. They state that neither *rāga* nor *dveṣa* is permissible, because *rāga* and *dveṣa* are inconsistent with what I call the 'equanimity requirement'. The standard interpretation of these texts is that *rāga* and *dveṣa* refer to phenomenologically salient desires. Hence the advice to act without desire is the advice to act without phenomenologically salient desires.

I argue that the class of desires that are impermissible according to the *Nyāyasūtra* and *Brahmasiddhi* is much broader than this. A desire, by definition, disposes the agent towards joy and disappointment, depending on whether the desire is satisfied or frustrated. Since desires that are inconsistent with the equanimity requirement are impermissible, all desires are impermissible. Hence not only desires for ends, but desires for means as well, are impermissible.

Since the second version of the Some Desires Interpretation claims that the *Gītā* must be consistent with the claim that desire is a necessary condition of action because the traditions more generally claim that desire is a necessary condition of action, the second version of the argument is not convincing. Indeed, some of the same evidence that weighs in favor of interpreting the *Nyāyasūtra* and *Brahmasiddhi* to advise the elimination of all desire may be found in the *Bhagavadgītā* as well. Hence the Some Desires Interpretation is implausible.

The basic Nyāya–Vedāntin debate

The debate between the Naiyāyikas and Vedāntins over whether all action is motivated by *rāga* occurs within the debate over how to characterize *mokṣa*. The Vedāntins argue that *mokṣa* is a state of pure, eternal bliss. The Naiyāyikas deny this, and argue that *mokṣa* is the complete absence of pain.[1]

In his commentary to *Nyāyasūtra* 1.1.22, Vātsyāyana summarizes the Vedāntin position: "Some think that in *mokṣa*, the eternal bliss of the true self, which is like an immensity of size, is manifested. By that manifestation [of eternal bliss], the completely liberated [person] is happy" (Thakur 1967: 453, lines 1–2).[2] Uddyotakara, a later Nyāya commentator, paraphrases the argument for this claim:

> Here [in] this world, [a person] acts for the sake of obtaining a desirable object. Likewise, those who are liberating themselves act [for this purpose]. Their activity also must be for the purpose of obtaining the desirable object. This very activity is purposeful for the sake of eternal bliss, not otherwise.
>
> (Thakur 1967: 456, lines 21–23)[3]

Since all actions are performed for the sake of attaining pleasure, the *mumukṣu* also acts for the sake of pleasure. If the goal of the *mumukṣu* is pleasure, then *mokṣa* must be pleasurable, because this is what the *mumukṣu* pursues.[4] The Vedāntin argument – at least as it is characterized by the Naiyāyikas – may be schematized as follows:

(V1)

Premise One: All action is for the sake of attaining pleasure.
Conclusion One: Hence the action of pursuing *mokṣa* is for the sake of attaining pleasure.
Conclusion Two: Hence *mokṣa* is pleasurable.

More needs to be said about why the Vedāntins claim that the bliss of *mokṣa* is eternal and pure, but the details can be filled in rather easily. All people seek only pleasure. The wiser one is, the better one is at succeeding in this fundamental human task; indeed, this is part of what it means to be wise. The *mumukṣus* are the wisest of all. Hence that which they pursue must be the most pleasurable state of affairs possible. Since they pursue *mokṣa*, *mokṣa* is the most pleasurable state of affairs possible.

The Naiyāyikas object to the Vedāntin view. Uddyotakara argues, "If this [person] is saying, 'in *mokṣa* there is eternal bliss', then they act [motivated] by the *rāga* for bliss, and are not liberated. Why? Because of the acknowledgement that *rāga* is a fetter" (Thakur 1967: 457, lines 2–3).[5] Maṇḍanamiśra, a Vedāntin, summarizes the Nyāya objection in this way: "Some [object]: If Brahman is the nature of bliss, then the action of the *mumukṣu* is due to the *rāga* for bliss, and since action based on *rāga* is a seed of *saṃsāra*, it would not liberate" (Vacaspati and Sastri 1984: 1, lines 16–17).[6]

If *mokṣa* is pure, eternal bliss, as the Vedāntins claim, then the *mumukṣu* is motivated by *rāga*. If the *mumukṣu* is motivated by *rāga*, then they are bound to continued rebirth. If the *mumukṣu* is bound to continued rebirth, then they cannot achieve *mokṣa*. So under the assumption that *mokṣa* is bliss, *mokṣa* is unattainable, which is absurd. So *mokṣa* is not blissful. The Nyāya objection to (V1) may be schematized as follows:

(OV1)

Premise One: *Mokṣa* is blissful.
Premise Two: If *mokṣa* is blissful, then the *mumukṣu* is motivated by *rāga*.
Premise Three: If the *mumukṣu* is motivated by *rāga*, then they are bound to rebirth.
Premise Four: If the *mumukṣu* is bound to rebirth, then they cannot attain *mokṣa*.
Conclusion One: If *mokṣa* is blissful, then it is unattainable, which is absurd.
Conclusion Two: *Mokṣa* is not blissful.

The Naiyāyikas avoid the conclusion that *mokṣa* is unattainable by drawing a distinction between acting for the sake of pleasure and acting for the sake of avoiding pain. Uddyotakara explains – in the form of an additional objection to (V1) – that "two kinds of action are known in the world: [that] for the sake of obtaining [what is] desirable, and [that] for the sake of eliminating [what is] undesirable" (Thakur 1967: 456, lines 23–24).[7] Since the pursuit of that which is pleasurable precludes *mokṣa*, it must be that the *mumukṣu* acts for the sake of avoiding pain. So *mokṣa* is the complete absence of pain. The Nyāya argument may be schematized as follows:

(N1)

Premise One: All action is either for the sake of attaining pleasure or for the sake of avoiding pain.
Premise Two: If an action is for the sake of attaining pleasure, then it is motivated by *rāga*.
Premise Three: *Rāga* precludes the attainment of *mokṣa*.
Conclusion One: Hence the successful *mumukṣu* is not motivated by *rāga*.
Conclusion Two: Hence the successful *mumukṣu* does not act for the sake of attaining pleasure.
Conclusion Three: Hence the successful *mumukṣu* acts for the sake of avoiding pain.
Conclusion Four: Hence *mokṣa* is the complete absence of pain.

The Vedāntins reply that the Nyāya objection to their view, if convincing, also refutes the Nyāya view. If all actions carried out for the sake of attaining pleasure are motivated by *rāga*, and if *rāga* precludes *mokṣa*, then likewise all actions carried out for the sake of avoiding pain are motivated by *dveṣa* (aversion), and *dveṣa* precludes *mokṣa* as well.

Uddyotakara paraphrases the objection: "Even if [a person] acts from *dveṣa*, saying, 'I will eliminate *duḥkha*', even then [that person] is not liberated, since there is the acknowledgment of *dveṣa* as a fetter [as well]. For it is said that *rāga* and *dveṣa* are fetters" (Thakur 1967: 457, lines 4–5).[8] So the Naiyāyikas face the same problem that the Vedāntins face, namely the problem of explaining how one can be motivated to pursue *mokṣa* without precluding *mokṣa*. The Vedāntin objection to (N1) may be schematized in the following way:

(ON1)

Premise One: *Mokṣa* is the complete absence of pain.
Premise Two: If *mokṣa* is the complete absence of pain, then the *mumukṣu* is motivated by *dveṣa*.
Premise Three: If the *mumukṣu* is motivated by *dveṣa*, then they are bound to rebirth.
Premise Four: If the *mumukṣu* is bound to rebirth, then they cannot attain *mokṣa*.
Conclusion One: If *mokṣa* is the complete absence of pain, then it is unattainable, which is absurd.
Conclusion Two: *Mokṣa* is not the complete absence of pain.

The Naiyāyikas reply to this objection by denying that the *mumukṣu* is motivated by *dveṣa*. Uddyotakara says,

This is not the case, since it is not counter-productive. The avoidance

> of pain is not counter-productive. Moreover, [this person, namely the *mumukṣu*] is not *dveṣṭi* (the adjective formed from *dveṣa*) towards *duḥkha*, and this [person who] acts without *dveṣa* attains the elimination of *duḥkha*, which is not counter-productive.
>
> (Thakur 1967: 457, lines 5–6)[9]

The successful *mumukṣu* is not motivated by *rāga*, because they conceive of *mokṣa* as the complete absence of pain, rather than a state of bliss. They do not act motivated by *dveṣa* either, however. Whatever motivates the action of eliminating all pain is not counter-productive in the way that both *rāga* and *dveṣa* are.[10]

Uddyotakara's response is unsatisfactory. If the successful *mumukṣu* is motivated to eliminate pain, but is not motivated by *rāga* or *dveṣa*, how are they motivated? Vācaspatimiśra, a later Nyāya commentator, explains that "[the words] *dveṣa*, *krodha* (anger), and *manyu* (rage) are not different in meaning.[11] For it [namely, *dveṣa*] has the nature of a blazing fire. *Vairāgya* is not like this" (Thakur 1967: 459, lines 25–26).[12] The successful *mumukṣu* is motivated by *vairāgya*, rather than *rāga* or *dveṣa*. Unlike *rāga* and *dveṣa*, *vairāgya* does not preclude the attainment of *mokṣa*. Hence Premise Two of the Vedāntin's objection to the Nyāya argument (ON1) is false – acting in order to eliminate pain does not entail *dveṣa*.

Maṇḍana's reply parallels the Nyāya reply. Acting for the sake of pleasure does not entail *rāga*.

> It is not [the case] that action [aimed at pleasure] is [necessarily] based on *rāga*, for it is not the case that mere *icchā* (*icchāmātraṃ*) is *rāga* . . . Indeed, the *prasāda* (equanimity), *abhiruci* (approval), or *abhīcchā* (purpose) of the mind . . . does not fall on the side of *rāga*.
>
> (Vacaspati and Sastri 1984: 3, lines 17–19)[13]

The successful *mumukṣu* is motivated by mere *icchā*, rather than by *rāga* or *dveṣa*. Unlike *rāga* and *dveṣa*, mere *icchā* does not preclude the attainment of *mokṣa*. Hence Premise Two of the Naiyāyika's objection to the Vedāntin argument (OV1) is false – acting in order to attain the bliss of *mokṣa* does not entail *rāga*.

The standard interpretation

The standard interpretation of this debate is that both the Nyāya distinction between *dveṣa* and *vairāgya* and the Vedāntin distinction between *rāga* and mere *icchā* amount to distinctions between phenomenologically salient and non-salient desires and aversions, respectively. Mere *icchā* is a phenomenologically non-salient desire, and *vairāgya* is a phenomenologically non-salient aversion. Hence according to the standard interpretation of both accounts, the distinction between permissible and impermissible desires is a distinction between desires that lack phenomenological saliency and those that are phenomenologically salient.

R. Balasubramanian, for example, claims that Maṇḍana's distinction between *icchā* and *rāga* is a distinction between the "desire for the highest bliss which arises from the tranquil mind of the seekers of truth" and an "intense and passionate longing," respectively (Balasubramanian 1976: 105). According to Balasubramanian, Maṇḍana admits that the pursuit of *mokṣa* is motivated by a desire for *mokṣa*, but denies that the required desire precludes *mokṣa*. The required desire is not *rāga*, because *rāga* is a desire that is phenomenologically salient; it is 'intense' and 'passionate.' As Maṇḍana says, mere *icchā* is *prasāda*. Since the endorsed motivation is not phenomenologically salient – it is consistent with a 'tranquil' mind – it is not *rāga*, and therefore need not preclude *mokṣa* in the way that *rāga* does. *Icchā*, on this reading, is a desire without phenomenological saliency.[14]

Balasubramanian paraphrases the Nyāya position in this way: "Realizing the futility of the things of the world, a person becomes detached," but this is "not *dveṣa*, which means hatred" (Balasubramanian 1976: 105). This is an allusion to the passage cited above, in which Vācaspati compares *dveṣa*, *krodha* (anger), and *manyu* (rage). Balasubramanian takes this passage to mean that it is the phenomenological feel – the blazing fire aspect – that is the essential criterion of impermissible aversions. Just as Maṇḍana permits desires that are not phenomenologically salient, the Naiyāyikas permit aversions that are not phenomenologically salient.

A. Chakrabarti seems to interpret the two positions in the same way. Having reviewed the disagreement between the Naiyāyikas and Vedāntins, he concludes that "neither a violent 'fiery' aversion towards the sufferings and evils of worldly existence, nor a passionate attachment to (however pure or permanent – or profound) pleasure, can be the right motive for *mokṣa*" (Chakrabarti 1988: 332). This suggests that it is the phenomenological saliency of certain desires that is problematic; any desire that is salient is impermissible.

Instead of acting from a violent, fiery aversion or desire, one should be motivated by "a state of 'colourlessness' " (Chakrabarti 1988: 333). Presumably these are states devoid of phenomenological feel. So according to Chakrabarti as well, the distinction between permissible and impermissible desires is a distinction between desires that lack phenomenological saliency and those that possess it.[15]

There is a great deal of textual evidence that supports this interpretation. The most obvious is the passage in which Vācaspati draws the distinction between *dveṣa* and *vairāgya* by saying that *dveṣa* has the nature of a blazing fire, and that *vairāgya* does not have this nature. *Dveṣa* is synonymous with *krodha* (hatred) and *manyu* (rage); *vairāgya* is not.

In addition, when Maṇḍana first paraphrases the Nyāya objection to the Vedāntin argument (OV1, above), he elaborates that, "for [someone who is] equanimous (*śānta*) and restrained (*dānta*), there is a seeing of the true self.

Acting from the *rāga* for bliss, [however,] one is not equanimous" (Vacaspati and Sastri 1984: 1, lines 18–10).[16] This suggests that Maṇḍana takes the basis of the Nyāya objection to be that since the properly motivated *mumukṣu* is equanimous, it cannot be that they are motivated by *rāga*, because *rāga* disrupts equanimity. Since Maṇḍana responds to this objection by drawing the distinction between mere *icchā* and *rāga*, he must mean that mere *icchā* does not disrupt equanimity in the way that *rāga* does, and is permissible for this reason. This conclusion also seems supported by Maṇḍana's claim that mere *icchā* is synonymous with *prasāda*.[17]

In his subcommentary on Maṇḍana's *Brahmasiddhi*, Śaṇkhapāni also characterizes mere *icchā* in terms of equanimity. As I point out in Appendix iii, after Maṇḍana offers the clarification mentioned above between mere *icchā* and *rāga*, he continues to use the word *rāga* to refer to the endorsed motivational state. Śaṇkhapāni explains this apparent inconsistency by saying that Maṇḍana proceeds as if his opponent does not accept the distinction. He says, "or else, let that [mere *icchā*] be *rāga*. Even then, that [so-called *rāga*] is not prohibited by the *śruti* on equanimity,[18] and so on" (Vacaspati and Sastri 1984: 12, lines 1–2).[19] The opponent can categorize the endorsed motivating state as *rāga* if they like. The point is that there is a subset of motivational states that are consistent with equanimity, and therefore permissible.

As I mentioned in Chapter 3, there are a number of passages in the *Gītā* that seem to support this interpretation as well. Kṛṣṇa says that blameworthy action is motivated by *kāma*, which is *krodha* (anger). He characterizes *kāma* as all-consuming, and compares it to an insatiable fire. The desireless person, in contrast, is unmoved (*acala*) by desire. "As the waters enter the sea, [which, although] filling, [remains] unmoved [and] tranquil, likewise desires enter the person whom [remains unmoved, tranquil]. That person attains equanimity, not the person who desires things" (2.70, Sadhale 1985a: 239, lines 33–34).[20] This suggests that the *Bhagavadgītā* draws the distinction between permissible and impermissible desires in the same way that the Naiyāyikas and Vedāntins do. Permissible desires are not phenomenologically salient. Impermissible desires are.

The argument for the "No Phenomenologically Salient Desires Interpretation" in the context of the *Gītā* may be schematized in the following way:

(NPSDI)

Premise One: Kṛṣṇa advises Arjuna to act without desire.
Premise Two: Desire is a necessary condition of action.
Conclusion One: Hence Kṛṣṇa's advice is a contradiction.
Conclusion Two: So this cannot be Kṛṣṇa's advice.
Conclusion Three: Kṛṣṇa advises Arjuna to act without some desires. He permits others.
Conclusion Four: Kṛṣṇa advises Arjuna to act motivated by phenomenologically non-salient desires.

Again, the first two premises and Conclusion One constitute the basic argument. Conclusions Two and Three are common to all Some Desire Interpretations. Only Conclusion Four is unique to the No Phenomenologically Salient Desires Interpretation.

Likewise, the *Yogasūtra* characterizes impermissible desires – *rāga* and *dveṣa* – with some of the same synonyms that Vācaspati and Maṇḍana use. *Rāga*, according to Vyāsa, is synonymous with *tṛṣṇa* (thirst) and *lobha* (greed), qualities opposed to the *prasāda* that characterizes Maṇḍana's mere *icchā*. Vyāsa, like Vācaspati, characterizes *dveṣa* in terms of *manyu* (rage) and *krodha* (anger) (see Chapter 2). Permissible desires, then, are those that are not phenomenologically salient. If a desire is phenomenologically salient, it is impermissible.

Objections to the standard account

There is a great deal of evidence for the claim that the Naiyāyikas and Vedāntins consider phenomenologically salient aversions and desires impermissible. Like most classical orthodox Indian texts that deal with motivation and action, the *Nyāyasūtra* and *Brahmasiddhi* – along with the *Yogasūtra* and *Bhagavadgītā* – are concerned with the preservation of equanimity. Desire sensations are inconsistent with equanimity. Since phenomenologically salient desires are accompanied by desire sensations by definition,[21] they are inconsistent with the equanimity requirement.

The problem with the standard account, however, is that it is not broad enough. If equanimity is to be preserved, then any desire that so much as disposes an agent to the sensations that are inconsistent with equanimity must be eliminated. My calm desire for a coffee later this afternoon lacks phenomenological saliency, but it disposes me to sensations that are inconsistent with the equanimity requirement, just because it makes me more likely to have those sensations under certain circumstances.

If, for example, I wait too long to go to the café, I begin to crave coffee. If I find the café is closed, I am frantic. If I discover then that the open sign was turned off by mistake, I am greatly relieved. None of this is consistent with equanimity. If the desireless person is eternally equanimous, then in addition to lacking any phenomenologically salient desire, they lack non-phenomenologically salient desires that dispose them to sensations that disrupt their equanimity. Otherwise their equanimity is tenuous and short-lived. Another way of putting this is that if the desireless person is eternally equanimous, it cannot be the case that they have mental states that dispose them to lose their equanimity, just because they are not disposed to lose their equanimity.

This more robust requirement is more explicit in the *Bhagavadgītā*. The *Gītā* repeatedly describes the wise person as unaffected by success and failure. "Free of attachment and excessive talk of the self, possessed of firmness and fortitude, unchanged (*nirvikāraḥ*) in success or failure, [this] agent is called *sattvic*" (18.26, Sadhale 1985c: 336, lines 29–30).[22] This suggests that the agent is not only equanimous before they act and while they act, but after they act as well (unlike me in my quest for coffee). Whatever motivates their action, it does not additionally dispose the agent to sensations that disrupt their equanimity. To be unchanged in success or failure is to feel no joy or disappointment as a consequence of the events of the world. "The person who is without desire towards all things, having attained this or that pleasant or painful [thing], neither rejoices nor dislikes (*na dveṣṭi*).[23] That person's wisdom is firm" (2.57, Sadhale 1985a: 219, lines 34–35).[24]

This, presumably, is why Vācaspati says that *dveṣa* has the *nature* of a blazing fire. To say that someone has an angry nature is not to say that they are constantly angry, or identical with anger. It is to say that they are often angry, or likely to become angry – that they are disposed towards anger.

I mentioned above that the *Gītā* seems to equate *kāma* and *krodha*. Arjuna asks, "moved by what, then, does a person act [in a way that is] blame-worthy?" (3.36, Sadhale 1985a: 337, line 17).[25] Kṛṣṇa responds, "this is desire (*kāma*). This is anger (*krodha*)" (3.37, Sadhale 1985a: 338, line 36).[26] In his commentary to this verse, Śaṅkara explains, however, that "this *kāma*, when impeded by something, is transformed into *krodha*" (Sadhale 1985a: 339, line 6).[27] That is, *kāma* only produces *krodha* when it is frustrated. *Kāma* is a disposition towards *krodha*; it is not identical with it. Elsewhere the *Gītā* itself claims that "from *kāma*, *krodha* arises" (2.62, Sadhale 1985a: 226, line 39).[28]

Likewise, Vācaspati's claim that *dveṣa*, *krodha*, and *manyu* (rage) are not different in meaning might be taken to mean that *dveṣa*, when impeded, becomes *krodha* and *manyu*. If the claim is not taken in this way, the account allows desires that dispose the agent to lose their equanimity, just because they are not presently phenomenologically salient. Likewise, Vyāsa's claims that *rāga* is *tṛṣṇa* (thirst) and *lobha* (greed), and that *dveṣa* is *manyu* and *jighāmsā* (the wish to destroy) might be taken to mean that *rāga* and *dveṣa* are those desires that dispose the agent towards phenomenological sensations, depending on whether the desires are satisfied or not. Otherwise even the saint can have desires that may cause them to erupt in anger, so long as they never happen to do so.

Some of Chakrabarti's claims reflect this broader interpretation of the advice. He claims that the desireless agent is motivated by a state "which guarantees its own peaceful effect" (Chakrabarti 1988: 333). The word 'guarantees' is important here. In order for the equanimity of the agent to be guaranteed, the agent must not only be without states that are inconsistent with equanimity. They must also be without states that dispose them towards the loss of equanimity. If the agent is disposed towards losing their equanimity, their equanimity is not guaranteed. This means that the class of desires that are impermissible is much broader than the standard interpretation allows. Any desire that either (1) is phenomenologically salient or (2) disposes the agent towards sensations that are inconsistent with equanimity is impermissible.

Of course, it is not enough that a desire not dispose the agent towards sensations that are inconsistent with equanimity. In addition, the desire must play a necessary role in motivating action and take as its object the most valuable state of affairs available to the agent for a desire of its type. Put simply, a desire must also be one that a fully knowledgeable agent would have under the circumstances. (Maṇḍana and Śaṅkhapāṇi make this additional conclusion explicit. See below.)

This dispositional quality is part of what it means to be a desire (or aversion), however, at least as the word 'desire' is ordinarily used in English. It would contradict our expectations from the standpoint of ordinary language if I claimed to desire a coffee but denied that the subtlest sensation of joy or disappointment could even possibly arise from my success or failure.[29] Indeed, one of the things that I typically do as a means of determining whether I desire something is to imagine having it or not having it, and imagine whether I would have phenomenological sensations in either case. If there is no scenario in which I would feel joy on achieving some end, then I just don't desire it. If there is no scenario in which I would feel disappointment on not achieving some end, then I do not have an aversion to it.[30]

Melinda Vadas claims that the type of desire that the Humean insists is a necessary condition of action disposes the agent towards affective states.

> I desire to eat pizza, have children, or run in a marathon. This is to say that I *feel, I am emotionally disposed toward*, my eating pizza, my having children, my running in a marathon. That I am disposed toward these activities or states of affairs is borne out by my emotional reaction when I accomplish, or fail to accomplish, the desired goal. Thus, if I desire to have children . . . and am for some reason unable to do so . . . I will feel perhaps disappointed, enraged, or sad.
>
> (Vadas 1984: 276)

If an agent is not disposed towards joy or disappointment, depending on whether the mental state is satisfied or not, then the mental state is not a desire (or aversion).

Another reason to reject the standard interpretation is that it is an implausible interpretation of the earlier part of the debate. If it were accurate, the original Nyāya objection to the Vedāntins would be that *mokṣa* cannot be bliss because, if it were, one would be motivated to pursue it by a phenomenologically salient desire for bliss. Since, when interpreted this way, the claim is so obviously false, it cannot be the sense of the Nyāya objection.

It is much more plausible to take the original formulation of the objection to be that *mokṣa* cannot be bliss because, if it were, one would be motivated to pursue it by a state that disposes an agent towards sensations that are inconsistent with equanimity. That is, if *mokṣa* is bliss, one would be motivated to pursue it by a desire for *mokṣa*. The advice to eliminate desire, then, amounts to the advice to eliminate all desire.

Desires for ends certainly dispose an agent towards joy and disappointment, based on whether the desired end arises or not. Indeed, this is part of what makes the *Manusmṛti's* advice to eliminate desires for ends sensible. If an agent is unmoved, whether or not they fulfill their purpose, then they do not desire that which is their purpose.

Desires for means, however, dispose an agent towards joy and disappointment as well. Arjuna's desire to fight in the battle – even if it is only a means to his end of doing what is morally required of him because it is morally required of him – disposes him to feel disappointed in the event that he is unable to fight. He might, after all, be struck down with appendicitis before he begins, and be crippled with physical pain. States that dispose the agent in this way are to be eliminated. Hence the liberated agent is without all desires. Desireless action, in this context, must be taken literally. The desireless agent has no desire whatever, but acts nonetheless. This means that neither mere *icchā* nor *vairāgya* can be translated as desires or aversions of a particular sort.

The revised account

The most plausible translation of the word *icchā* in this context is 'positive purpose'. When Maṇḍana claims that mere *icchā* is not necessarily *rāga*, he claims that not every positive purpose of an agent is accompanied by a desire that takes the same object. Just because the attainment of *mokṣa* is someone's purpose, it does not follow that they desire *mokṣa* as well. *Icchā*, then, refers to a broader class of states that can be further divided into *icchā* that is *rāga*, and mere *icchā* – that is, *icchā* that is not *rāga*.

It is clear from both Maṇḍana and Śaṅkhapāṇi that the distinction between *rāga* and *icchā* is easily missed. As I mentioned above, Maṇḍana reverts to calling the endorsed state *rāga*, even after he has clarified the distinction between *rāga* and mere *icchā*, presumably with the expectation that the opponent will either deny the distinction, or fail to comprehend it. As I argued in Chapter 1, the distinction between desire and purpose is easily missed as well.

In addition, there is already a precedent for defending the notion of desireless action by drawing the distinction between desire and purpose. As I argued in the last chapter, Medhātithi claims that an agent might have some purpose (*prayojana*/*hetu*) for acting, without desiring that which is their purpose. On this interpretation of the *Brahmasiddhi*, Maṇḍana offers the same basic claim: an agent might have some purpose (*icchā*) for acting, without desiring that which is their purpose.

Indeed, in his commentary to *Manusmṛti* 2.2, Kullūkabhaṭṭa uses the words *icchāmātra* – mere *icchā* – to characterize the motivating states that Manu does not mean to prohibit.

> But it is not the case that by this [verse] mere *icchā* is prohibited. For this reason, [Manu] says: "but never does desirelessness exist here on Earth."

> For the learning of the Veda and the totality of all Vedic *dharma* is an object of *icchā*.
>
> (Dave 1972–1985: 156, lines 15–16)[31]

This suggests that mere *icchā* and *prayojana/hetu* are equivalent, and that Kullūkabhaṭṭa uses the words *icchāmātra* to distinguish purpose from desire.

One difference between the *Manusmṛti* and the *Brahmasiddhi* is that the *Manusmṛti* only discourages desires for ends. The *Brahmasiddhi* considers both desires for ends and desires for means impermissible. Nonetheless, the same kind of distinction can be drawn between desires for means and purposes and desires for ends and purposes.

If I write this chapter as a means to my end of writing this book, there is nothing odd in saying that writing this chapter is my purpose. So on this interpretation, in those cases where it seems that a desire for a means is required, the *Brahmasiddhi* claims that an agent should have a purpose that takes the state of affairs that would ordinarily be the object of the desire for the means as its object, but that they should not also desire that means. (See below for a further elaboration.)

The verb root √ *iṣ* – from which the word *icchā* is derived – primarily refers quite generally to the pursuit of a goal. M. Monier-Williams defines √ *iṣ* as "to endeavour to obtain, strive, seek for" (Monier-Williams 1998: 169). The word 'goal' is synonymous with 'purpose'. Monier-Williams also lists 'intend' as a definition of √ *iṣ* (Ibid.) – another synonym of 'purpose' (see Chapter 1).

In addition, *icchā* must dispose the agent towards acting, without disposing the agent towards joy or disappointment depending on the outcome. When an agent has some purpose, they are disposed towards bringing about the state of affairs that is their purpose. A purpose by itself, however, does not obviously dispose the agent towards joy or disappointment depending on whether or not the purpose is satisfied.

Suppose, for example, that my neighbors go on vacation for a week, and need someone to water their tomato plants. They specify that I do not have to fertilize, weed around, or prune the plants. "Just make sure they don't die," they say. So I adopt the purpose of making sure the plants do not die. Suppose also that I neither desire that the plants don't die, nor desire that they do, nor desire any further end to which the plants living or dying is a means.

For the first three mornings of their vacation I dutifully water the tomato plants, and the plants do not die. On the fourth morning of their vacation I walk over to my neighbors' house, only to discover that the tomato plants are dead. I surmise that some animals have gotten into the garden – it looks as if it was some moose – and devoured and trampled the plants. There is nothing left of them. It seems plausible that in these circumstances the frustration of my purpose of keeping the tomato plants alive by itself does not produce disappointment in me.[32]

On the other hand, if I desire that the tomato plants survive – perhaps my neighbors always share their crop in the fall – it seems implausible that I would not experience at least some subtle disappointment with the situation. Not only my purpose, but my desire is frustrated. Likewise, if I desire that the plants die – perhaps because I care only about having the best tomatoes on the block, and my neighbors are my only competitors – it seems implausible that I would not experience at least some subtle happiness with the situation, because my desire has been satisfied.[33] Hence the term 'purpose' captures the dispositional qualities of mere *icchā*. A mere purpose – unconnected to any related desires – meets the equanimity requirement, and yet disposes the agent to act.[34]

The most plausible translation of *vairāgya* in this context is 'negative purpose'. The relationship between *vairāgya* and *dveṣa* in the *Nyāyasūtra* is different from the relationship between *icchā* and *rāga* in the *Brahmasiddhi*, however. *Icchā* is a broad category of motivating states that includes but is not exhausted by *icchā* that is *rāga*. Some *icchā* are mere *icchā*, others are *rāga*. *Vairāgya* and *dveṣa*, in contrast, are mutually exclusive. As Vācaspati says, *dveṣa* has the nature of a blazing fire, *vairāgya* does not. Hence no *vairāgya* is *dveṣa* and vice versa.

Again, it is clear from Vācaspati that the distinction between *dveṣa* and *vairāgya* is subtle. The distinction between an aversion and a negative purpose is similarly subtle. In addition, the *Manusmṛti* sets the precedent of drawing a distinction between *kāma* and *prayojana*. There is little reason to think that a *prayojana* might not establish an agent's end even when the end is some negative state of affairs – one in which the agent avoids something. Just as Īśvara acts to bring about the liberation of those trapped in *saṃsāra*, likewise he acts to avoid those lesser pleasures, the faults of which he perceives quite clearly. If *prayojana* can play the role that *kāma* plays, presumably it can also play the role that *dveṣa* plays.

Vācaspati explains *vairāgya* in the following way: *vairāgya* "is the thought 'enough [of this]' " (Thakur 1967: 459–60, lines 26–1).[35] While not perfectly explicit, this description at least implies the kind of resolution that is typical of a negative purpose. Yet it is clear from the word *pratyaya* (thought), among other things, that Vācaspati does not count *vairāgya* as a kind of *dveṣa*. This is consistent with the fact that *vairāgya* disposes an agent to act – it takes the place of *dveṣa* in the chain of states that produces action – without disposing the agent to joy or disappointment. Unlike *dveṣa, vairāgya* does not have the nature of a blazing fire. Since a purpose, by itself, does not obviously dispose an agent towards joy or disappointment depending on the outcome, 'negative purpose' seems to be a suitable translation of *vairāgya*.

Finally, it is clear that Maṇḍana takes the Nyāya distinction to parallel his own. He says,

> *rāga* is known as an attachment (*abhiniveśa*) to some non-existent quality brought about by ignorance.[36] Indeed, the *prasāda, abhiruci*, [or] *abīcchā* of the mind arising from the clarity of the seeing of reality does not fall

> on the side of *rāga*, as the *udvega* (aversion) arising from the seeing of the unreality and valuelessness of *saṃsāra* [does not fall] on the side of *dveṣa*.
>
> (Vacaspati and Sastri 1984: 3, lines 18–20)[37]

If Maṇḍana draws a distinction between a positive desire (*rāga*) and a positive purpose (*icchā*), then he takes the Naiyāyikas to draw a distinction between a negative desire (*dveṣa*) and a negative purpose – for which Maṇḍana uses the word *udvega*. This too supports my interpretation of the Nyāya account.

The relationship between *icchā, rāga*, and action in the *Brahmasiddhi*, then, may be schematized in the following way.

(BS1)

positive purpose (*icchā*)	⇨	(desire ⇨) (*rāga*)	action (*karma*)

Icchā is a necessary condition of action. An agent cannot act without some purpose. *Rāga*, however, does not play a necessary role in motivating action, although it might play some role.[38] Sometimes an agent desires that which is their purpose, but a desire of this sort is not required in order to act.

In the passage cited above, Maṇḍana says that in the case of the rightly motivated *mumukṣu*, the kind of mere *icchā* that he endorses arises from the seeing of reality. If this claim is generalized, (BS1) may be revised to read:

(BS2)

belief/ perception (*jñāna*)	⇨	positive purpose (*icchā*)	⇨	(desire ⇨) (*rāga*)	action (*karma*)

The relationship between *vairāgya, dveṣa*, and action in the *Nyāyasūtra*, in contrast, may be schematized as:

(NS1)

negative purpose (*vairāgya*) or aversion (*dveṣa*)	⇨	action (*karma*)

Either *vairāgya* or *dveṣa* motivates action, but not both. Hence in the *Nyāyasūtra*, there is no general term corresponding to purpose, as there is in both the *Manusmṛti* and *Brahmasiddhi* –

Just as Maṇḍana claims that the mere *icchā* that motivates the *mumukṣu* arises from the perceiving of reality, likewise, *vairāgya* arises from seeing the pain inherent in all things other than *mokṣa*. As Vātsyāyana says,

> There is nothing desired [that is, nothing pleasurable] that is not connected with something undesirable [that is, something painful]. Since there is a connection with the undesirable, even the desirable is undesirable. Acting to abandon the undesirable, one also abandons the desirable, because of the impossibility of abandoning [the undesirable] by means of discriminating [the desirable from the undesirable].
>
> (Thakur 1967: 454, lines 17–19)[39]

The *mumukṣu's* motivation has its source in beliefs about the presence of pain even in seemingly pleasurable items. If this explanation is generalized, (NS1) reads as follows:

(NS2)

belief/perception (*jñāna*)	⇨	negative purpose (*vairāgya*) or aversion (*dveṣa*)	⇨	action (*karma*)

Both Maṇḍana and the Naiyāyikas seem to admit that an agent might pursue either a positive or a negative state of affairs. As I mentioned above, the Nyāya commentators object to the Vedāntin claim that all action is the pursuit of pleasure by stating that action is also performed for the sake of avoiding what is painful. Likewise, Maṇḍana claims that the distinction between *icchā* and *rāga* parallels the distinction between *udvega* and *dveṣa*.[40] Hence neither (BS2) nor (NS2) represent a general model of motivation that applies to all cases. Instead, (BS2) should read:

(BS3)

belief/perception (*jñāna*)	⇨	purpose (*icchā/* *udvega*)	⇨	(desire ⇨) (*rāga/dveṣa*)	action (*karma*)

The agent's purpose might take a positive or negative state of affairs as its object, and might or might not be accompanied by desire or aversion.[41]

Similarly, (NS2) should instead read as follows:

(NS3)

belief/perception (*jñāna*)	⇨	negative purpose (*vairāgya*) or desire (*rāga/dveṣa*)	⇨	action (*karma*)

As I mentioned above, the Naiyāyikas claim that *vairāgya* and *dveṣa* are mutually exclusive. In addition, they deny that an agent might be motivated to pursue pleasure without being motivated by *rāga*. For this reason, I have not included 'positive purpose' in the diagram. This is not to say that they deny that there might be some positive state of affairs that is the object of an agent's action. It is only to say that in these cases the agent is simply motivated by *rāga*, rather than by some mental state that "does not fall on the side of *rāga*."

On both accounts, it is unclear whether the agent's purpose and/or desire takes the agent's end or the agent's means as its object. The broader dispute over whether *mokṣa* is a state of bliss, or simply the complete absence of pain, implies that mere *icchā* and *vairāgya* take the bliss of *mokṣa* or the complete painlessness of *mokṣa* as their objects, respectively. This need not be taken, however, to imply that *icchā* and *vairāgya* only take ends as their objects. Śaṅkhapāṇi, for example, says that "an ascetic whose *icchā* is *tapas* (the performance of austerities) is not called a *rāgin* (someone motivated by *rāga*) in the world" (Vacaspati and Sastri 1984: 11, lines 15–16).[42] If an ascetic is a properly motivated *mumukṣu*, however, then they also have an *icchā* for the end of *mokṣa*. The performance of *tapas* is simply a means to this end. This implies that *icchā* can take either ends or means as its object.

There is little reason to believe that *vairāgya* cannot take both ends and means as its object as well. As I mentioned above, Vācaspati explains *vairāgya* as the thought 'enough of this'. This might be understood as a very general statement, equivalent to the thought 'enough of everything in the world that consists at least in part of pain' (that is, everything). Under specific circumstances, however, the agent might think 'enough' with regard to those things in their immediate environment – 'enough wealth', 'enough fame', 'enough of family ties', and so on. These negative purposes are only a means, however, to the final end of the complete elimination of all pain.

Likewise, the desire that the improperly motivated person has might take the agent's end, means or both as their objects(s). Diagrams (BS2) and (NS3) are consistent with this: the desire and purpose represented in each diagram are intentionally ambiguous, so that it might serve as a desire or purpose for an end and/or means.

Despite these differences, the Naiyāyikas and Vedāntins both accept the same basic theory of motivation, according to which no desire of any sort – positive or negative – is a necessary condition of action. They allow that desires to acquire and desires to avoid sometimes motivate action, but deny that they must. In those cases in which no desire – for end or means – plays a role in motivating action, the agent is motivated by purposes that do not dispose them to joy or disappointment, depending on whether or not they are fulfilled.

A reconsideration of the second argument for the Some Desires Interpretation

Remember that the second argument for the Some Desires Interpretation of the *Gītā* goes as follows:

(SDI2)

Premise One: Kṛṣṇa advises Arjuna to act without desire.
Premise Two: Desire is a necessary condition of action in the Indian traditions more generally.
Conclusion One: Hence desire is a necessary condition of action in the *Gītā*.
Conclusion Two: Hence Kṛṣṇa's advice is a contradiction – at least prima facie.
Conclusion Three: So this cannot be Kṛṣṇa's advice.
Conclusion Four: Kṛṣṇa advises Arjuna to act without some desires. He permits others.

The conclusions of this chapter are inconsistent with Premise Two of (SDI2). Both the *Nyāyasūtra* and *Brahmasiddhi* explicitly deny that desire is a necessary condition of action. If Premise Two is false, then (SDI2) is unconvincing. If (SDI2) is unconvincing, then both arguments advanced in favor of the Some Desires Interpretation are unconvincing, and the Some Desires Interpretation is implausible. There is little reason, then, to think that the *Gītā's* advice to act without desire is the advice to act without some desires, while acting on others.

It is not just phenomenologically salient desires that are to be eliminated, but desires more generally. Hence it is not just desires for states of affairs other than *mokṣa* that are to be eliminated, but the desire for *mokṣa* as well. And it is not just selfish desires that are to be eliminated, but unselfish desires too.

Again, this is not to say that any purpose is acceptable. A purpose must also be in accord with knowledge, rather than based on ignorance. As Maṇḍana says, echoing the *Yogasūtra, rāga* is the "attachment (*abhiniveśa*) to some non-existent quality brought about by *avidyā*" (see above). In other words, a purpose is permissible if and only if it is a purpose that a fully knowledgeable agent would have under the circumstances.

Indeed, if the argument for the Some Desires Interpretation is unconvincing, there is little reason to think that the *Yogasūtra* claims that desire is a necessary condition of action either. As I pointed out in Chapter 2, neither Patañjali nor Vyāsa says anything to imply this. The only reason to believe that the *Yogasūtra* claims that desire is a necessary condition of action is the assumption that the Some Desires Interpretation is correct. Absent this assumption, the most plausible interpretation of the theory of motivation in the *Yogasūtra* is that in order to act, an agent must have some purpose, but need not have a desire.

7 A defense of desireless action

As I mentioned in Chapter 1, the Humean view of motivation is widely accepted among contemporary western philosophers. In Chapter 2 I outlined the Humean view in the following way. All action is motivated by a desire and a means–end belief. My desire for a coffee, for example, might combine with my belief that in order to have a coffee I must go to the café, and produce the action of walking to the café. In more complex cases, the desire that combines with a belief to produce action is a desire for a means, and is itself the product of an additional desire and means–end belief. My desire to remain alert, for example, might combine with my belief that in order to remain alert I must have a coffee, to produce my desire for a coffee. The Humean view, then, consists of at least two claims. First, all action is motivated by a desire. Second, any desire for a means is motivated by some additional desire.

In chapters 5 and 6 I argued that the theories of motivation in the *Bhagavadgītā, Yogasūtra, Manusmṛti, Nyāyasūtra*, and *Brahmasiddhi* contradict these claims. The most obvious objection at this point is that the theories of motivation in these texts are simply implausible, since the Humean view that they contradict is correct.

In this chapter I consider the most commonly cited argument for the Humean view. The direction of fit argument states that actions and desires for means are motivated by goal-directed states. All goal-directed states have world-to-mind direction of fit. If a state has world-to-mind direction of fit, then it disposes an agent to act and/or desire. Since only desires dispose an agent to act and/or desire, actions and desires for means are motivated by desires.

I argue that the direction of fit argument appears circular. One of the premises of the direction of fit argument states that only desires can dispose an agent to act and/or desire. This, however, is just the conclusion that the proponent of the Humean view means to prove. Hence some additional argument is needed.

One additional argument that is typically offered in support of this claim goes as follows. For any set of beliefs that supposedly motivate action without the help of desire, it is always possible to imagine a second agent who has all of and only those beliefs that supposedly motivate action in the first agent, but who is not motivated to act. The most straightforward explanation for this divergence is that the first agent has some additional state that the second agent does not, which plays a necessary role in motivating the action. The most obvious candidate for this additional state is a desire. A parallel argument may be constructed for the claim that desires for means are always motivated by some additional desire. Hence actions and desires for means are motivated by desires.

I argue that there are at least two problems with this argument. First, implicit in the argument is the more general principle that any time it is conceivable that some mental state does not perform one of its functions, it follows that it does not perform that function. I argue that this principle entails that no mental state performs any function. If the principle is rejected, however, then the additional argument is not convincing. Second, the functional roles that correspond with the two directions of fit are not roles that desires or beliefs typically perform.

I conclude that absent some additional argument for the Humean view, the theories of motivation that I have ascribed to the *Bhagavadgītā, Yogasūtra, Manusmṛti, Nyāyasūtra*, and *Brahmasiddhi* are plausible.

The direction of fit argument: a preliminary formulation

As I mentioned in Chapter 2, the Humean view claims that action is produced by a combination of a desire for some end and a means–end belief about how to bring about the desired end. In the simplest cases, action is motivated in the following way:

(HTM1)

desire (for end) + belief (about means to end)	⇨	action

In more complex cases, the desire that combines with a belief to produce action is a desire for a means.[1] It is itself produced by an additional desire and means–end belief. Hence,

(HTM2)

desire (for end) + belief (about means to end)	⇨	desire (for means) + belief (about means to means)	⇨	action

Hence the Humean view consists of at least two distinct claims:

1 Desire is a necessary condition of any action.
2 Some additional desire is a necessary condition of any desire for a means.

As I argued in Chapter 5, the *Manusmṛti, Bhagavadgītā*, and *Yogasūtra* deny claim 2. All three insist that an agent might come to desire some means to their end, without also desiring that which is their end. A person might come to desire to pour ghee into the sacrificial fires, for example, as a means to the end of performing a certain ritual, without having some further desire for the end of performing the ritual or for some *phala* that might arise as a result.

In Chapter 6 I argued that the *Nyāyasūtra, Brahmasiddhi, Bhagavadgītā* and *Yogasūtra* deny both claims. They insist that action might arise without any desire whatever. Not only the agent's end, but also the agent's means – if there is a means – might be established by purposes, rather than desires.

Someone sympathetic to the Humean view might object at this point that if the interpretations for which I have argued are correct, then the theories of motivation in these texts are simply implausible. In order to assess this objection, it is important to consider some of the standard arguments advanced for the Humean view.

Before considering these arguments, however, I want to point out an important difference between the account I have ascribed to the Indian texts that I have analyzed and the standard anti-Humean account. I have argued that the *Bhagavadgītā, Yogasūtra, Manusmṛti, Nyāyasūtra* and *Brahmasiddhi* deny that desire is a necessary condition of action and/or desire. Instead, they argue that a combination of purposes and beliefs alone might – in the sense that they sometimes do – motivate action.

The standard anti-Humean account, however, claims that beliefs alone might – in the sense that they sometimes do – motivate action. In particular, they tend to argue that an agent's normative belief – the belief that I should visit my grandmother, for example – can motivate action in the way that a desire can. As a consequence of this, contemporary proponents of the Humean view tend to direct their arguments against the standard anti-Humean account, rather than the anti-Humean account that I have ascribed to the *Bhagavadgītā, Yogasūtra, Manusmṛti, Nyāyasūtra* and *Brahmasiddhi*. They tend to argue that since beliefs alone cannot motivate action, desire is a necessary condition of action.

So even if the standard arguments for the Humean view succeed in demonstrating that beliefs alone cannot motivate action, it does not follow that beliefs and purposes cannot motivate action without the help of desires. On the other hand, if the standard arguments fail to demonstrate that beliefs alone cannot motivate action, then the views I attribute to the *Bhagavadgītā, Yogasūtra, Manusmṛti, Nyāyasūtra* and *Brahmasiddhi* are indeed plausible. If the claim that beliefs alone motivate action is plausible, surely the claim that beliefs and purposes motivate action is plausible as well. So in what follows, I will focus exclusively on the question of whether or not beliefs can motivate action without the help of desires. At the end of this chapter, I will reconsider the view I ascribe to the Indian texts in light of my conclusions.

One of the most well-known and widely accepted arguments in favor of the Humean view is Michael Smith's version of the direction of fit argument. Smith argues for claim 1 above in the following way:

> (DOF1)
>
> Premise One: Having a motivating reason is, *inter alia*, having a goal.
> Premise Two: Having a goal is being in a state with which the world must fit [that is, a state with world-to-mind direction of fit].
> Premise Three: Being in a state with which the world must fit is desiring.
> Conclusion: Having a motivating reason is desiring.
>
> (Smith 1994: 116)

To say that an agent has a motivating reason is to say that there are some mental states of the agent that might motivate the agent to act. As Smith says, "motivating reasons would seem to be *psychological states*, states that play a certain explanatory role in producing action" (Smith 1994: 96, italics in original).[2]

The notion of direction of fit is an elaboration of G. E. M. Anscombe's shopper-detective metaphor. Anscombe explains that if a person is shopping for groceries from a list, and puts an item in the basket that is not on the list, the act of putting the item in the basket is a mistake. If the detective – who is following the shopper and making a list of the items that the shopper puts in the basket – writes down some item that the shopper has not placed in the basket, however, then the mistake lies in the detective's list. This means that the shopper's list stands in a "different relation" to the world than the detective's list (Anscombe 1976: 56).

Smith applies this basic distinction to desires and beliefs. Like the two lists, desires and beliefs stand in different relations to the world. When the content of a belief does not accurately represent the world, it is mistaken, and should be discarded or changed. When the content of a desire does not match the world, however, it generally should not be discarded, and the agent should do something to make the world match their desire.[3]

In an attempt to make the distinction less metaphorical, Smith analyzes the two directions of fit in terms of functional roles. To say that a mental state has mind-to-world direction of fit is to say that the "belief that p tends to go out of existence in the presence of a perception with the content that not p" (Smith 1994: 115). My belief that my dog is in the car tends to go out of existence in light of the perception that my dog is not in the car.[4]

To say that desires have world-to-mind direction of fit is to say that the "desire that p tends to endure [the perception that not p], disposing the subject in that state to bring it about that p" (ibid.). My desire that my dog is in the car persists in the presence of a perception that my dog is not in the car, and disposes me to make it the case that my dog is in the car.[5]

Since Smith analyzes directions of fit in terms of their dispositional roles, (DOF1) is equivalent to (DOF1′):

> (DOF1′)
>
> Premise One: Having a motivating reason is, *inter alia*, having a goal.
> Premise Two: Having a goal is being disposed to act.
> Premise Three: Being disposed to act is desiring.
> Conclusion: Having a motivating reason is desiring.[6]

John Bricke ascribes a nearly identical argument to Hume himself:

> It is obvious, according to Hume, that someone with a reason for acting in a certain way is, at least in part, in what we have called a goal-directed, a practical, psychological state with respect to acting in that way . . . The individual has, we may say, a pro-attitude with respect to acting in the way in question. What could such a pro-attitude be but a desire?
>
> (Bricke 1996: 15–16)

If an agent is motivated to act, then they have some goal-directed mental state. If they have a goal-directed mental state, then they have a pro-attitude (that is, they are disposed towards some state of affairs). If they have a pro-attitude, then they have a desire. Hence if an agent is motivated to act, they have some desire.[7]

As Bricke points out, a similar argument can be constructed for claim 2:

> What of reasons for desire? On the assumption that reasons for desire must be, in part, practical or goal-setting states – an assumption common to both the conativist [that is, the Humean] and the cognitivist [that is, the anti-Humean] – conativism holds for reasons for desire just as for reasons for acting. In so far as they are goal-setting states they, just as the desires they help explain, must have the world-to-mind direction of fit.
>
> (Bricke 1996: 29)

For any desire for a means,[8] there must be some antecedent state or states that constitute a reason for desiring that which is the means. This reason must be goal-directed. If it is goal-directed, then it is constituted, at least in part, by a desire. The argument may be schematized as follows:

> (DOF2)
>
> Premise One: Having a reason for desiring is, *inter alia*, having a goal.
> Premise Two: Having a goal is being disposed to desire.
> Premise Three: Being disposed to desire is desiring.
> Conclusion: Having a reason for desiring is desiring.

As James Lenman says, "[b]ecause desires have a common direction of fit that beliefs do not share, it follows that not all the rational psychological antecedents of desire are strictly cognitive states: no beliefs can motivate any desire all by themselves" (Lenman 1996: 294).

Hence the direction of fit argument is advanced in support of both claims 1 and 2 of the Humean view.

An objection and reply

Understood this way, however, the argument is circular. It assumes in Premise Three that only desires can dispose an agent to act or desire. It is over this very claim, however, separated from all the talk of directions of fit, motivating reasons and goals, that the Humean and anti-Humean disagree in the first place. Hence some additional argument in support of Premise Three is required. As Bricke points out, "[o]n the face of it, Hume simply assumes . . . that practicality demands desire" (Bricke 1996: 19).

Smith replies with a second argument. If the belief that p has world-to-mind direction of fit, then it tends to endure the perception that not p, disposing the agent to make it the case that p. If the belief that p has mind-to-world direction of fit as well, then it tends to go out of existence in the presence of a perception with the content not p. Hence if a belief can dispose an agent to act, it both tends to endure the perception that not p and tends to go out of existence in the presence of the perception that not p. This, however, is a contradiction.

> A state with both directions of fit would therefore have to be such that, both, in the presence of such a perception [that not p] it tends to go out of existence, and, in the presence of such a perception, it tends to endure, leading the subject who has it to bring about that p. Taken quite literally, then, the idea that there may be a state having both directions of fit is just plain incoherent.
>
> (Smith 1994: 118)

Since this is a contradiction, it cannot be that beliefs have both directions of fit. Since few would argue that beliefs do not have mind-to-world direction of fit, beliefs do not have world-to-mind direction of fit. Hence beliefs cannot dispose an agent to act.

Bricke ascribes the same basic argument to Hume:

> As cognitive states, beliefs have the mind-to-world direction of fit. Their function is accurately to represent the way the world is. That being so, how can they serve the practical or goal-setting task that, as conativist [that is, Humean] and standard cognitivist [anti-Humean] agree, the major constituent in a reason for action must perform?
>
> (Bricke 1996: 27)

Smith admits, however, that without an additional argument, this kind of reply fails in the case of normative beliefs.[9] Suppose, for example, that I believe I should cut the lawn. If this belief is analyzed as a belief that p – where 'p' stands for 'I should cut the lawn' – then it seems right that it has the mind-to-world direction of fit, but not the world-to-mind direction of fit. If I perceive that 'I should cut the lawn' is false – perhaps I discover that my wife has already cut it – then my belief that I should cut the lawn will go out of existence. It will not endure the perception that not p, and it will not dispose me to make it the case that I cut the lawn.

Alternatively, however, the belief might be analyzed as a belief that p, where 'p' stands for 'that it should be the case that q', and where 'q' stands for 'I cut the lawn'. That is, the belief might be analyzed as a "unitary [state] having both directions of fit, though with respect to two different contents" (Smith 1994: 118).[10] In light of the perception that I do not cut the lawn (that is, I have not cut the lawn), my belief that it should be the case that I cut the lawn endures and disposes me to cut the lawn. Hence the belief has world-to-mind direction of fit with respect to content q. In light of the perception that it should not be the case that I cut the lawn, however, my belief that it should be the case that I cut the lawn goes out of existence. That is, the belief has mind-to-world direction of fit with respect to content p. This suggests that normative beliefs might have both directions of fit.

Hence Smith offers a third argument in support of his claim that beliefs cannot have both directions of fit:

> [I]t is always at least possible for agents who are in some particular belief-like state not to be in some particular desire-like state; that the two can always be pulled apart, at least modally. This, according to Humeans, is *why* they are distinct existences.
>
> (Smith 1994: 119)

Since, for normative beliefs like the one mentioned above, it is possible to imagine a person who has the normative belief – along with all of the other beliefs that supposedly produce the action, like any means–end beliefs, and so on – but who is not disposed to act, it cannot be that the normative belief constitutes or entails the disposition to act. Hence beliefs do not dispose an agent to act.[11]

This supplemental argument for Premise Three may be schematized as follows:

(S1)

Premise One: For any belief, or set of beliefs, that purportedly constitute a motivating reason to act, it is always possible to imagine a person who has the belief(s), but who is not motivated to act.

Conclusion One: Hence beliefs alone cannot motivate action. Something else is required.
Conclusion Two: The additional required state is a desire.
Conclusion Three: Hence desire is a necessary condition of any action.[12]

A parallel argument may be constructed in support of Premise Three of (DOF2) as well:

(S2)

Premise One: For any belief, or set of beliefs, that purportedly constitute a reason to desire, it is always possible to imagine a person who has the belief(s), but who does not have the desire.
Conclusion One: Hence beliefs alone cannot produce desire. Something else is required.
Conclusion Two: The additional required state is a desire.
Conclusion Three: Hence some additional desire is a necessary condition of any desire for a means.

If (S1) and (S2) are convincing, then belief can neither motivate action, nor motivate desire, without the help of some additional state – presumably a desire.

Additional objections

It is worth noting, at this point, that if (S1) and (S2) are convincing, arguments (DOF1) and (DOF2) are unnecessary. (S1) and (S2) conclude with the claims:

1 Desire is a necessary condition of any action.
2 Some additional desire is a necessary condition of any desire for a means.

Since these are the two basic claims that the typical Humean wants to establish, and since arguments (S1) and (S2) make no reference to arguments (DOF1) and (DOF2), (DOF1) and (DOF2) are simply red herrings. The plausibility of at least this version of the direction of fit argument depends entirely on the plausibility of (S1) and (S2).

There are at least two fundamental problems with any version of these arguments. Before considering these two problems, however, I want to mention an additional problem that arises for Smith's account in particular.

Smith offers a kind of hybrid Humean/anti-Humean account. According to Smith,

> [a]ll actions are indeed produced by desires, just as the Humean says; no

> actions are produced by beliefs alone . . . But, if what we have said here is right, some of these desires are themselves produced by the agent's beliefs about the reasons she has, beliefs she acquires through rational deliberation.
>
> (Smith 1994: 179)

Hence Smith accepts the claim that desire is a necessary condition of action (claim 1), but denies that some additional desire is a necessary condition of any desire for a means (claim 2). Under the right circumstances, an agent might come to have a desire for a means – like the desire to perform some action that they believe is right, or rational – without first desiring some additional end – like doing what is right, being praised, or some other.

It turns out that the details of Smith's argument against claim 2 are not important. Whether the argument is convincing or not, Smith's broader account appears inconsistent. As I said above, Smith offers argument (S1) in support of claim 1. Implicit in (S1) is a more general principle:

> (GP)
>
> For any mental state that appears to perform two or more functions, if it is possible/conceivable that the state does not perform one of the apparent functions, it follows that this function is performed by some other state.

If Smith is justified in inferring that one of the apparent functions of a normative belief – the function of disposing an agent to act – is actually performed by some other mental state – namely, a desire – from the fact that it is conceivable that the normative belief by itself does not dispose the agent to act, then this more general principle must be true.

If the general principle is true, however, then (S2) is convincing as well, and the second Humean claim – which Smith rejects – is also true. Just as it is possible to imagine a person who believes that they should perform some action – say, donate some percentage of their income to charity – without being motivated to do so, likewise, it is possible to imagine a person who believes that they should perform some action without being disposed to desire to do so.

Of course, the typical Humean can avoid this problem by simply denying that normative beliefs produce desires without the help of additional desires. They might admit the general principle above, and use it to prove that beliefs alone can produce neither desire nor action. Hence claims 1 and 2 are true.

Even this revised version of the account faces the two problems, however. The first problem is that if (S1) and (S2) are convincing, then the general principle is correct. If the general principle is correct, then no mental state can perform two functions. To say that a mental state performs a certain function is to say that the state plays a causal role in the context of other mental states, sensory inputs and behaviors. Jaegwon Kim gives a couple of examples that are helpful. An engine performs the function of producing force as output, given energy as input (Kim 1997: 75). A pain state performs the function of producing escape behavior, given the input of tissue damage (Kim 1997: 77). The functional analysis of the engine or the pain state, then, is just this specification of its role in producing certain outputs, given certain inputs.

Smith analyzes desire along these lines, citing a range of possible outputs given certain inputs.

> [W]e should think of desiring to ϕ as having a certain set of dispositions, the disposition to ψ in conditions C, the disposition to ψ in conditions C', and so on, where, in order for conditions C and C' to obtain, the subject must have, *inter alia*, certain other desires, and also certain means–end beliefs, beliefs concerning ϕ-ing by ψ-ing, ϕ-ing by χ-ing and so on.
> (Smith 1994: 113)

The desire to have an ice cream, then, produces the action of going to the freezer, given certain inputs – like the agent's belief that there is ice cream in the freezer, and so on. The same desire produces the action of going to the ice cream shop when the agent believes that there is no ice cream in the freezer, that the ice cream shop is still open, and so on.

Another way to put this is to say that the agent who desires to have ice cream is disposed to go to the freezer or the ice cream shop depending on what they believe about where the ice cream is, and so on, and that the desire is the locus of this disposition.

Likewise the agent's belief that they already have ice cream produces the action of refusing more ice cream, given their desire to avoid sickness, and so on. The same belief disposes the agent to believe that their sibling will be jealous, given their belief that when they have ice cream, their sibling is jealous. The agent who believes that they have ice cream is disposed both to refuse more ice cream and to believe that their sibling will be jealous, depending on their other desires and beliefs, and their belief that they have ice cream is the locus of these dispositions. This is a very basic overview of what it means to say that certain mental states have functional roles.

Hence it is ordinary to ascribe a range of functions to a single mental state. If the general principle on which Smith's direction of fit argument depends is true, however, then none of these states can perform all of the functions ascribed to them. After all, it is possible that an agent's desire for ice cream does not dispose them to go to the freezer, even when they believe that there is ice cream in the freezer, and so on. Perhaps, for example, they simply fail to connect the desire and belief in the right way and draw the conclusion that their desire can be satisfied by going to the freezer.

Given this possibility, it follows from the general principle that the agent's desire for ice cream does not dispose them to go to the freezer. If (S1) is convincing, then some additional mental state must be ascribed to the agent in order to explain their disposition to go to the freezer. Hence, even if it seems as if an agent's desire for ice cream disposes them to both go to the freezer and go to the ice cream shop, depending on their beliefs, perceptions, and so on, this is not the case. The two functions must be performed by different states, just because it is conceivable that the state might perform one function without the other.

Similarly, the agent's belief that they have ice cream cannot dispose them both to refuse more ice cream and to believe that their sibling will be jealous (given the appropriately related beliefs and desires), just because it is conceivable that they believe they have ice cream and believe that if they have ice cream, then their sibling will be jealous, but fail to derive the further belief that their sibling will be jealous. According to Smith's reasoning, this agent's dispositions to refuse more ice cream and believe that their sibling will be jealous cannot be explained by the single belief that they have ice cream. It must be explained by two distinct beliefs.

There is little reason to think that any example of a desire or belief will not face similar problems. If this is right, then it is not clear that a functionalist analysis of mind is tenable. At the very least, a functionalist analysis of mind would have to consist exclusively of mental states that perform single functions. This kind of analysis would wildly diverge from folk psychology, however, according to which single desires and beliefs can at least theoretically perform an infinite number of functions, depending on the circumstances.

Indeed, it is not clear how a functional analysis consistent with Smith's principle can ascribe any function at all to most mental states. Just as it is possible that the agent's belief that they have ice cream does not perform the function of generating the belief that their sibling will be jealous, given their belief that if they have ice cream, then the sibling will be jealous, it is also possible that the belief fails to perform the function of generating the action of refusing more ice cream, given their desire to avoid sickness, and so on. It follows that the agent's belief that they have ice cream cannot perform any function at all, just because it is conceivable that it fails to perform any function that it seems to perform. The same will be true for all beliefs.

Even desires will not perform any of the functions normally attributed to them if Smith's principle is true. Just as the agent might fail to connect their desire for ice cream with their belief that there is ice cream in the freezer, likewise the agent might fail to connect their desire for ice cream with their belief that there is ice cream at the ice cream shop. So if Smith's principle is correct, neither beliefs nor desires perform any input–output functions at all.

A second, related problem with these arguments is that if the directions of fit are understood in terms of functional roles, then neither beliefs nor desires have the directions of fit that Smith claims they do. Remember that Smith characterizes the direction of fit of a belief by saying, "a belief that p tends to go out of existence in the presence of a perception with the content that not p" (Smith 1994: 115).

If by 'functional roles' Smith means input–output functions, however – as the previous quotation says – it is not clear that a belief has the functional role that Smith assigns it. Presumably the input in this case is the perception with the content that not p, and the output is the elimination of the belief that p. If it is the belief that p that performs this function, then part of the function that the belief performs is the function of eliminating itself. Presumably desires perform a similar function: on the perception that p, the desire that p tends to eliminate itself.

This kind of view is very odd, however. Surely a rational agent is disposed to lose a belief that p in light of the perception that not p, and lose the desire that p in light of the perception that p, but it is not the belief or desire that p that is responsible for its own disappearance. Some additional element in the functional system – something like a concilience-preserving mechanism – does this job.[13]

After all, the functionalist already needs to posit this kind of mechanism in order to explain the production of beliefs and desires. Just as the belief that p will tend to go out of existence in light of the perception that not p, likewise the belief that not p will tend to come into existence in light of this perception. Surely it is not the belief that not p that performs the function of bringing itself into existence, however. Nor is it the belief that p that produces the belief that not p. Some other element in the system must perform this function. If some other mechanism performs this function, it is natural to assign to that element the functional roles associated with mind-to-world direction of fit in general. Not only does it perform the function of producing beliefs, it performs the function of eliminating beliefs as well.[14]

Likewise, some additional mechanism is responsible for the production and elimination of desires. If the world-to-mind direction of fit is in part the disposition to eliminate the desire that p in light of evidence that p and preserve the desire that p in light of evidence that not p, then this function is not performed by the desire itself, but by the mechanism that checks for concilience among desires and beliefs. So both the ascription of world-to-mind direction of fit to desire and the ascription of mind-to-world direction of fit to belief are unacceptable, because at least part of the functions that Smith analyzes the directions of fit in terms of is not performed by the desires and beliefs themselves.

There is some evidence that Smith is aware of the awkwardness of explaining directions of fit in terms of functions ascribed to single mental states. In the passage cited above, in which Smith explains the functions of a desire in terms of dispositions to act, he says nothing about the disposition to persist in light of the perception that not p. If he did, this third objection would be more obvious.[15]

In addition, there is no corresponding passage in which Smith fully elaborates the input–output functions of belief that correspond with the mind-to-world direction of fit. If the functional analysis is to map on to the mind-to-world direction of fit, it has to go something like this: "we should think of believing that p as having a certain disposition, the disposition to cease believing that p in light of the perception that not p." Put this way, however, it is obvious that beliefs do not have mind-to-world direction of fit.

The three arguments that I have ascribed to the proponent of the direction of fit argument are as follows. First, only desire has the right direction of fit to motivate action/desire. Hence desire is a necessary condition of action/desire (for a means). Since one of the premises in this argument states that to be disposed to act/desire is desiring, however, the argument is circular absent some additional argument in support of the premise.

Hence the second argument states that a belief cannot have both directions of fit, because if it did, it would both go out of existence in the presence of a perception that contradicts its content and endure a perception that contradicts its content. Since this argument does not apply to normative beliefs, however, some additional argument is needed for the claim that normative beliefs cannot have both directions of fit.

Hence the third argument states that since it is always possible to imagine that an individual is not motivated by their beliefs, it cannot be that beliefs motivate action. Since this argument leads to absurd consequences, however, it is not convincing. If the third argument is not convincing, then the first argument is not convincing. If the first argument is not convincing, then the most common argument advanced in favor of the Humean view is not convincing. Absent some additional argument for the Humean view, the Humean objection to the theories of motivation that I have ascribed to the *Bhagavadgītā, Yogasūtra, Manusmṛti, Nyāyasūtra* and *Brahmasiddhi* is not convincing.

As I pointed out above, there is an important difference between the view that I ascribe to these texts and the standard anti-Humean view. The view that I ascribe to these texts is that beliefs and purposes motivate action and/or desire without the help of desires. The standard anti-Humean view, however, claims that belief alone can motivate action and/or desire.

If the arguments against the standard anti-Humean view fail, however, then there is little reason to think that beliefs and purposes cannot motivate action. Indeed, quite ironically, the proponent of the standard anti-Humean view might deny the plausibility of the theories of motivation that I have ascribed to the Indian texts because they are not anti-Humean enough![16]

Hence the primary objection against the theories of motivation in the *Bhagavadgītā, Yogasūtra, Manusmṛti, Nyāyasūtra*, and *Brahmasiddhi* is not convincing. In addition, not only is the Humean view not so obviously true that it ought to serve as an interpretive constraint on the interpretation of Indian texts, but it is not even clear that the Humean view is more plausible than the anti-Humean view.

Conclusion

Neither of the arguments for the Some Desires Interpretation of desireless action in the *Bhagavadgītā* is convincing. The first argument depends on an equivocation. It states that since it is perfectly obvious that desire is entailed by action, it cannot be that the advice to act without desire is meant literally. It is false, however, that it is perfectly obvious that desire is entailed by action. Hence the first argument is unconvincing.

The second argument states that since the Indian traditions widely accept the claim that desire is a necessary condition of action, it follows that the *Gītā* must be consistent with the claim that desire is a necessary condition of action. It is false, however, that the Indian traditions widely accept the claim that desire is a necessary condition of action. The *Nyāyasūtra* and *Brahmasiddhi*, for example, explicitly deny this. Hence the second argument is unconvincing.

Since neither version of the argument for the Some Desires Interpretation is convincing, the advice to act without desire in the *Gītā* ought to be taken literally, as the advice to eliminate all desires. As I mentioned in Chapter 1, the Indian traditions insist that in order to abandon a literal interpretation of a text, it must be demonstrated that the literal reading leads to a contradiction of some kind. This condition is not met in this case. Likewise, the *Yogasūtra's* advice to act without desire ought to be taken literally. The *vairāgin* is entirely without desire, but acts nonetheless. Hence all four of these texts claim that an agent's end or means might be established by the agent's purpose, rather than the agent's desire.

At this point there are some remaining questions and objections to the account that I have defended, two of which I want to consider here.

Adaptations of the Some Desires Interpretations

In Chapter 2 I argued that any version of the Some Desires Interpretation must be consistent with the claims that permissible desires are those that a fully knowledgeable agent would have, and impermissible desires are those that a fully knowledgeable agent would not have. In Chapter 3 I pointed out that most proponents of the Some Desires Interpretation insist that all permissible desires must share some additional, more specific criterion. Hence they argue that all permissible desires are unselfish, or unimpassioned, or that the only permissible desire is the desire for *mokṣa*.

At this point I have concluded that permissible purposes are those that a fully knowledgeable agent would have, and impermissible purposes are those that a fully knowledgeable agent would not have. Permissible purposes are in accord with knowledge, impermissible purposes are the result of ignorance. Even if most proponents of the Some Desires Interpretation are convinced by my arguments, they may continue to insist that all permissible purposes – rather than desires – must share some additional, more specific criterion.

It should be clear that all permissible purposes share at least one additional criterion. All permissible purposes are not only phenomenologically nonsalient, but they do not so much as dispose the agent to joy or disappointment, depending on the outcome. This is a trivial criterion, however, since impermissible purposes do not dispose the agent to joy or disappointment either. If an agent is disposed to joy or disappointment depending on whether or not their purpose is fulfilled, it is because they also desire that which is their purpose, and the desire disposes them in this way. Hence an adapted version of the No Phenomenologically Salient Desires Interpretation – even when broadened to include not only desires that are phenomenologically salient, but also those that dispose the agent to joy or disappointment – cites only a necessary, but not a sufficient condition of permissible purposes.

All permissible purposes also share the additional criterion of being unselfish, in the sense that they are not based on false beliefs about the self. This too, however, is a trivial criterion. A purpose is permissible only if it is not based on false beliefs more generally, and there might be impermissible purposes that are based on false beliefs about things other than the self. So an adapted version of the No Selfish Desires Interpretation cites only a necessary, but not a sufficient condition of permissible purposes.

Nonetheless, this means that in the end there is something essentially right about both the No Phenomenologically Salient Desires Interpretation and the No Selfish Desires Interpretation. Proponents of these interpretations are correct to point out that permissible motivations are neither phenomenologically salient nor selfish. Their mistake is to think that either criterion is the sole or sufficient condition of permissible motives.

Lastly, the proponents of the *Mokṣa*-only Interpretation might offer an adapted version of their position, and claim that only the purpose of *mokṣa* is permissible. They might point out that some of the claims from both the Naiyāyikas and Vedāntins seem to support this view.

Maṇḍana, for example, says that just as a person who desires sovereignty over the world is advised to eliminate desires for anything inconsistent with this end, "likewise [in the case of the *mumukṣu*], there is a cessation of [any so-called *rāga*] other than the [so-called][1] *rāga* for the highest happiness [of *mokṣa*]" (Vacaspati and Sastri 1984: 3, line 24).[2] This suggests that *mokṣa* is the only permissible purpose an agent can have, and that all others are to be eliminated.

Śaṅkhapāṇi explains Maṇḍana's position in the following way: "[Maṇḍana] says the *icchā* for the true, eternal, unsurpassed bliss [of *mokṣa*] is not *rāga*" (Vacaspati and Sastri 1984: 11–12, lines 27 and 1).[3] This might be read to mean that only *icchā* that takes *mokṣa* as its object might be mere *icchā*. All other *icchā* is *rāga*.

Likewise, when Vācaspati explains *vairāgya* as the thought 'enough of this', the word 'this' refers to everything other than *mokṣa*. He says, "enough of this fleeting world, the pleasures of which are inevitably mixed with pain." This implies that the only thing a properly motivated agent pursues is the "complete cessation of pain" – another phrase repeated throughout the commentaries as a description of *mokṣa*.

There are a number of problems with this interpretation, however. First, Śaṅkhapāṇi himself offers the example of an ascetic, whose *icchā* is the performance of *tapas* (austerities), and who is not called a *rāgin*. This implies that it is possible to act without *rāga*, even when one's purpose is not *mokṣa*.

Elsewhere, Śaṅkhapāṇi says that the *icchā* that is prohibited is "the *icchā* for the happiness of a perishable object less than [the bliss of *mokṣa*] and opposed to [the bliss of *mokṣa*]" (Vacaspati and Sastri 1984: 12, lines 2–3).[4] This suggests that a purpose is impermissible only if it is inconsistent with the attainment of *mokṣa*, not that any purpose other than *mokṣa* is impermissible. As I argued in Chapter 3, since states of affairs other than *mokṣa* are valuable, there is little reason to think that an agent is never justified in pursuing states of affairs other than *mokṣa* – even for their own sake. It might be that all permissible purposes are a means to *mokṣa*, but from this it does not follow that the agent must pursue them because they are a means to *mokṣa*.

Second, the Naiyāyikas are careful to explain that the successful *mumukṣu* is motivated by the purpose of avoiding that which is painful. As Vātsyāyana says, "the teaching of liberation is for the sake of giving up the undesirable [that is, the painful]. Likewise the activity of the *mumukṣus* [is for the sake of giving up the painful]" (Thakur 1967: 154, lines 16–17).[5] If *mokṣa* is the only state of affairs that is perfectly devoid of pain, however, then it is the only state of affairs that should *not* be the object of the *mumukṣus* motivating states! If a person is finally liberated, they are liberated because they are motivated by the purpose of avoiding *saṃsāra*, not because they have the positive purpose of attaining *mokṣa*. To say that since the successful *mumukṣu* avoids the pain of *saṃsāra*, it follows that they pursue only the pleasure of *mokṣa*, is to make an error akin to that made by the Vedāntins of the *Nyāyasūtra*.

Hence the adapted version of the *Mokṣa*-only Interpretation is implausible. There is little doubt that the purpose of attaining *mokṣa* is typically permissible. It is a mistake, however, to limit the class of permissible purposes to the purpose of *mokṣa*, for all of the reasons I mentioned in Chapter 4, *mutatits mutandi*.

A final objection

Finally, I want to consider an objection to my analyses in Chapter 6. It might be argued that like a desire, a purpose disposes an agent towards joy and disappointment. Hence a purpose disposes the agent towards the loss of equanimity, just as desires do. Purposes, like desires, violate the equanimity requirement, and therefore ought to be eliminated.

Even if purposes dispose an agent towards joy and disappointment, and therefore violate the equanimity requirement, however, it does not follow that all purposes are to be eliminated. The argument for the Some Desires Interpretation is instructive here.

The proponent of the Some Desires Interpretation argues that since desire is a necessary condition of action, Kṛṣṇa's advice to act without desire cannot be taken literally, since Kṛṣṇa clearly advises action. Hence it must be that Kṛṣṇa advises Arjuna to eliminate some desires, and act on others. I have argued that this argument is not convincing. Nonetheless, a parallel argument may be offered in support of the position I have defended in this book. Since an agent's purpose is a necessary condition of action, Kṛṣṇa's advice to eliminate all purposes – because they dispose an agent to joy and disappointment – cannot be taken literally, since Kṛṣṇa clearly advises action. Hence it must be that Kṛṣṇa advises Arjuna to eliminate some purposes, and act on others. If an agent's purpose disposes them to lose their equanimity, then we must put up with it, for the same reasons that the proponents of the Some Desires Interpretation cite in favor of putting up with certain desires. In the case of purposes, however, the argument is convincing, because purposes, unlike desires, are indeed a necessary condition of action.

Appendix i

Manusmṛti 2.1–2.5 with Medhātithi's *Manubhāṣya* on 2.2–2.5[1]

Verse 2.1 [p. 151, line 1]:
That *dharma* which is fostered by the wise [and] favored by the good, [whose] hearts are always without *dveṣa* (aversion) and *rāga* (desire), that is [to be] known.

Verse 2.2 [p. 154, line 24]:
Essential desirefulness (*kāmātmatā*) is not praiseworthy (*praśasthā*), but never does desirelessness (*akāmatā*) exist here on Earth, since the study of the Vedas and the performance of Vedic actions are to be desired (*kāmya*).

> Taken literally, this verse seems to say that being dominated by desire is widely disparaged, but it is not possible to completely eliminate desire, because desire is a necessary condition of action.

Commentary to 2.2 (Medhātithi):
[p. 154, line 28] The person whose reason (*hetu*) for performing action is the desire (*abhilāśa*) for *phala* (result), that person is essentially desireful (*kāmātma*). That is the state of being (*bhāva*) that is essential desirefulness (*kāmātmatā*). By the word *ātma*, primacy (*pradhānatā*) of that [namely desirelfulness] is indicated. That [essential desirefulness] is not praiseworthy (*praśastā*). It is condemned (*ninditā*).

> This is Medhātithi's gloss on 2.2. He claims that *kāmātmatā* refers to a person who is motivated by a desire for the *phala* (consequence) of the action they are performing. The word *ātma* means primacy. Desire is primary because it is the origin, or basis of the action being performed. Hence *kāmātmatā* means having desire as the basis of one's action – being motivated by a desire for the *phala* of one's action.
>
> Medhātithi equates *abhilāśa* with *kāma*. I translate both as 'desire'. In what follows, Medhātithi also uses the words *prārthanā* and *icchā* as synonyms with *abhilāśa* and *kāma*. The words *abhisandi*, *hetu* and *prayojana*, in contrast, are used synonymously to refer to the agent's purpose. This supports the distinction that I draw in Chapter 5.

[The *pūrvapakṣin* (opponent) objects:] And so, since there is an inference (*anumāna*) of a prohibition (*pratiṣedha*) by this condemnation (*nindayā*), "not to be done" is concluded (*pratīyate*). Since [this] is the meaning, this is a prohibition of all *kāmyakarmas* (ritual actions performed for the sake of some desired *phala*), like the *saurya* (sun sacrifice), and so on [p. 155, line 1].

> The opponent begins a three-part objection. The first objection consists of three inferences. First, from the claim that being essentially desirous – as Medhātithi has just defined it – is condemned (*nindita*), it follows that being essentially desirous is prohibited (*pratiṣedha*). Second, from the claim that being essentially desirous is prohibited, it follows that essential desirousness is not to be done (*na kartavya*). Third, from the claim that essential desirousness is not to be done, it follows that *kāmyakarmas* – ritual actions that the Vedas prescribe to those who desire certain *phala* – are not to be done, since *kāmyakarmas* have a desire for *phala* as their basis. Hence according to the *pūrvapakṣin*, verse 2.2 prohibits *kāmyakarmas*.
>
> This consequence is absurd because scripture seems to endorse *kāmya-karmas* for those who desire certain earthly and heavenly rewards. So the more serious consequence of the account, according to the *pūrvapakṣin*, is that Medhātithi's account contradicts scripture.
>
> It is tempting to expect that Medhātithi will reply that *kāmyakarmas* should not really be performed, since even the attainment of heaven is not a means to *mokṣa*. This is not Medhātithi's (or Manu's) explicit view, however (see Chapter 5). In the end, Medhātithi avoids the present objection by admitting that it is permissible to perform *kāmyakarmas* motivated by a desire for *phala*. The injunction to avoid a desire for *phala* is directed at other kinds of actions (see below).

On top of that (*athavā*), why do we speak with the specification "of the *saurya* and so on"? The performance of each and every (*sarvameva*) action has the purpose (*artha*) of the attainment (*siddhi*) of *phala*. It is not for the sake of bringing about (*niṣpattaye*) [its] own form. And there is no action without *phala*.

> *Athavā* normally means 'otherwise' or 'either', but here it indicates an additional counter-intuitive consequence of Medhātithi's view, hence "on top of that". The *pūrvapakṣin*'s second objection is that Medhātithi's view entails that not only *kāmyakarmas*, but all *karmas* are prohibited, since all actions are motivated by a desire for *phala*. To require that an action not be performed from a desire for the action's *phala* is to insist that it be done for its own sake. This is absurd, however. A person does not go to work simply to walk down the street, but to receive money, provide for their family, and so on. Here the term *phala* is used broadly, to refer to any consequence of an action.

Implicit in the objection is the distinction drawn later by Medhātithi between a desire for the end of one's action – the *phala* of the action – and a desire for the means to one's end – which in this case is the desire to perform the action itself. If there is no desire for *phala*, then the action must be motivated by a desire to perform the action itself. This is absurd, however, because all actions are performed for the sake of something other than the action itself. Hence absent a desire for *phala*, no action occurs.

Even if [it is said] "one should not perform an effort (*ceṣṭā*) in vain (*vṛthā*)" [as at *Manusmṛti* 4.63], [or] "seeking news, and so on of the king of a country in a distant region is an offering in the ashes," even in this case, the *phala* of action is known. For [it is] due to the non-existence of the primary (*pradhāna*) *phala* – namely heaven, a village, and so on – which is useful to people in seen or unseen [realms], [that] it is called "an effort in vain."

The *pūrvapakṣin* considers a possible reply. Medhātithi might say that there are common phrases that imply that some actions are without *phala*. One might say, for example, that certain foolish actions that are unlikely to succeed are "actions in vain." To say that an action is in vain is to say that it is without *phala*. If some actions are without *phala*, then presumably a person can perform these actions without a desire for *phala*.

The *pūrvapakṣin* replies that an action of this kind is *aphala* (without consequence) only in the sense that the main purpose for which the action was performed is unfulfilled. There is still *phala*, even if it is unintended. A person who seeks information about a distant king, for example, may become exhausted and frustrated in the attempt. These consequences – exhaustion and frustration – are the *phala* of the action, even if the news is never learned.

The word *pradhāna* is used again here to mean primary. In the previous passage, Medhātithi says that in the phrase *kāmātmatā, ātma* means *pradhāna* – primary. *Kāma* is primary in the sense that it is the foundation of the action. The action is motivated by a desire for *phala*. This sense is reinforced here, because Medhātithi uses the phrase *pradhāna-phala* (primary *phala*) to refer to the *phala* for the sake of which the agent acts.

Otherwise it is said: "Let the action be *phalavat* (fruitful)!" With regard to that object [namely *phala*], desire (*abhilāśa*) is not to be done. The *phala* will arise from the *svabhāva* [inherent nature] of the thing [namely the action].

The *pūrvapakṣin* considers a further reply. Medhātithi might concede that all actions have *phala*, as the *pūrvapakṣin* argues. He might then insist that the *phala* is not counter-productive in itself, so long as the agent does not also desire it. So the fact that all action has *phala* does not entail that all action is motivated by a desire for *phala*.

This reply does not obviously deal with the additional problem of the apparent absurdity of performing an action for its own sake. If an action has *phala*, but the agent does not desire it, then the agent is motivated by the desire to perform the action itself, which is absurd.

Once Medhātithi elaborates his position more fully, however, he offers a reply to this objection as well (see below).

[The *pūrvapakṣin* continues:] even in that case, however, the *saurya* and so on are without fruition. [As Kumārila says,] "The desired (*kāmyamānaṃ*) *phala* which is known [from scripture], that will not arise for the person not desirous [of it]."

The problem with this response is that a *kāmyakarma* such as the *saurya* sacrifice is effective only if the agent desires its *phala*. The *pūrvapakṣin* cites Kumārila in support of this claim. In the absence of a desire for the *phala* of the *kāmyakarma*, the *phala* will not arise. If the *phala* does not arise, the *karma* is useless. So Medhātithi faces a dilemma. Either his position prohibits *kāmyakarmas* (along with all other actions), because they cannot be performed without a desire for their *phala*, or it prohibits effective *kāmyakarmas*, because they cannot succeed without a desire for their *phala*. Either way, it seems to nullify a portion of the Vedic injunctions.

In addition, the performance of worldly [action] without the purpose (*abhisandhi*) of *phala* is not seen. Also with regard to this, there is no distinction in *śruti*, [such as] "the *phala* of Vedic actions is not to be intended (*na abhisandheyam*)."

The *pūrvapakṣin* continues the earlier objection, according to which performing an action motivated only by a desire to perform the action is absurd. All action is performed with the purpose of, or desire for, *phala*. Hence if a desire for *phala* is prohibited, no action is possible, which is absurd.

It will be of no use to limit the prohibition on desire to Vedic actions, because there is no textual evidence to support this. Absent any support, we should assume that the *phala* of mundane actions is not to be desired either, and that the absurd consequence of prohibiting all action follows.

With regard to that, since [some] scripturally enjoined actions (*śruteṣu*) are *phala*-bearing, from the prohibition on desire there is the non-performance [of scripturally enjoined actions]. This is a contradiction of *śruti*.

> The Vedas enjoin actions that are *phala*-bearing. If a desire for the *phala* of action is prohibited, then there is a de facto prohibition on certain Vedic injunctions, which is absurd.
>
> It is obvious in what follows – in particular, the objection that immediately follows – that the *pūrvapakṣin* means to say that some scripturally enjoined actions – namely *kāmyakarmas* – are *phala* bearing, not that all scripturally enjoined actions are.

In the case of *nityakarmas* [daily obligatory rituals], however, the attainment [of *phala*] never occurs.

> The *pūrvapakṣin* offers a third objection, the sense of which only becomes clear in Medhātithi's reply. Vedic injunctions do not mention any *phala* that arise from the performance of *nityakarmas*. Hence no *phala* arise from the performance of *nityakarmas*. If *nityakarmas* have no *phala*, then a desire for the *phala* of an action of this sort is impossible. If a desire for the *phala* of an action of this sort is impossible, then the prohibition on the desire for *phala* is redundant in the case of *nityakarmas*.
>
> Taken in isolation, the *pūrvapakṣin* seems to admit that *nityakarmas* can be performed without desire for *phala*. Hence this objection is not consistent with the earlier objection that without a desire for *phala*, action is impossible.

And since there is no mention of a distinction [between worldly and Vedic action], there would be a cessation of worldly action. This contradicts experience. This follows (*āpatitam*): Nothing is to be done by anyone. Sitting in silence is to be done by all beings.

> Here the *pūrvapakṣin* returns to what seems like the most damaging objection. No action is possible if the desire for *phala* is prohibited. Since Medhātithi claims that the desire for *phala* is prohibited, he implies that all action is prohibited. This is an absurd consequence.

[Medhātithi replies:] [p. 155, line 12] As for the claim [that] "there is the consequence (*prasaṅga*) of a prohibition (*niṣedha*) on *kāmyakarmas*, like *saurya*, and so on," – with regard to that [claim], he [namely Manu] will say [at 2.5] "And he attains all desires in this world as they are thought of (*saṅkalpitāṃ*)." Indeed, if there is a prohibition (*niṣedha*) [on desire], how could there be a thought (*saṅkalpa*) [of that which is desired], and how could there be the fulfillment of desires?

> Medhātithi answers the three objections of the *pūrvapakṣin*. The *pūrvapakṣin's* first objection was that Medhātithi's account entails a prohibition on all *kāmyakarmas*. In response, Medhātithi points out that Manu

> claims in verse 2.5 that the person who performs actions rightly satisfies every desire that comes to mind. Hence it cannot be that he means to prohibit desire. If desire is prohibited, then it is not possible to think of that which is desired without violating the prohibition, because in order to think of that which I desire, I must desire it. Similarly, if desire is prohibited, then it is not possible to satisfy a desire without violating the prohibition, since in order to satisfy a desire, I must have a desire. Hence Medhātithi does not prohibit desire, and therefore does not prohibit *kāmyakarmas*. Hence the *pūrvapakṣin's* first objection is unconvincing.

Medhātithi continues,

As for [the claim that] "from the non-mentioning of a distinction, [a prohibition on] mundane actions also follows (*prasakta*)," with regard to that, a distinction [was] just stated: "That which is *dharma*, let you understand that." For the subject of *dharma* is the topic of the present discussion.

> The *pūrvapakṣin's* second objection was that Medhātithi's position entails a prohibition on all actions. Part of the objection was that since the Vedas do not mention a distinction between Vedic and non-Vedic acts, Medhātithi has no textual basis for drawing a distinction between Vedic actions, which are to be done without a desire for *phala*, and non-Vedic actions, to which the prohibition does not apply. Hence if Vedic actions are to be done without a desire for *phala*, so are ordinary actions. Just as it is impossible to perform Vedic actions without a desire for *phala*, likewise it is impossible to perform non-Vedic actions without a desire for *phala*. Hence neither Vedic nor non-Vedic actions are ever performed on Medhātithi's view, and all actions are prohibited.
>
> Medhātithi claims that a distinction is indeed drawn between Vedic and non-Vedic actions. This chapter begins by specifying (in verse 2.1) that the subject of the chapter is *dharma*. Hence we should assume that Manu's claims are claims about ritual actions – Vedic actions – and not mundane actions. Hence the *pūrvapakṣin's* second objection is unconvincing as well.

As for the claim, "with regard to *nityakarmas*, since there is no hearing of *phala*, there is never the attaining of the purpose (*abhisandhi*) of *phala*, [and] what [is] with the prohibition (*niṣedha*) [on that]?" With regard to that as well, it is said: since there is the absence [of the mention] of *phala*, someone [who is a] non-knower of the correct (*samyak*) meaning of the *śāstra* does not act. And [when this happens, a typical person] having seen previous activity [performed] for the purpose (*abhisandhi*) of *phala*, in the case of the *saurya*, and so on, with regard to which *phala* is heard of (*śruta*), [reasoning] by inductive generalization (*sāmānyatodṛṣṭa*), [thinking] "that which is to be done, that is done for the purpose (*hetu*) of *phala*" [concludes] that likewise [those cases in which *phala* is] not heard (*aśruta*), the purpose (*abhisandhi*) is *phala*. This is stated (*ārabhyate*) in order to avoid (*nivṛtti*) this [conclusion].

The *pūrvapakṣin's* third objection was that the prohibition on a desire for *phala* is redundant in the case of *nityakarmas*, because *nityakarmas* have no *phala*. It is only if someone believes that some consequence is possible that they might desire it. Suppose someone knows, for example, that no matter how hard they train, they will never qualify for the Boston Marathon. It makes little sense to warn such a person, as they walk out of the door to go for a run, not to desire to qualify for the Boston Marathon by means of this training. So the *pūrvapakṣin* asks, "Why do you allow the prohibition on desire for phala to cover *nityakarmas*, when *nityakarmas* have no *phala* in the first place?"

Medhātithi explains that Manu's prohibition covers *nityakarmas* as well, because the typical, uninformed person mistakenly infers that *nityakarmas* have *phala*, even though the Vedas do not mention *phala*. He explains that at first, an uninformed person, noting that the Vedas do not mention *phala* in the case of *nityakarmas*, and being motivated only by *phala*, simply does not perform *nityakarmas*. Eventually, however, they might infer from other cases – like *kāmyakarma* cases, or mundane cases – that *nityakarmas* are also performed for the sake of *phala*, even though there is no mention of *phala*. Having seen that people are generally motivated by a desire for the result of action, and having drawn the conclusion that people are only motivated by a desire for the result of action, the person assumes that some *phala* must be desired in order to act, and that therefore they should be motivated to perform *nityakarmas* by a desire for *phala*.

No exception is made for *nityakarmas*, because if it were said "do not desire the *phala* of actions, except in the case of *nityakarmas*" as a means of avoiding the redundancy of prohibiting a desire that will not arise for the informed person, the uninformed person might think that a desire for the *phala* of *nityakarmas* is acceptable.

It is worth noting that the words *hetu* and *abhisandhi* are synonymous. They mean purpose rather than desire. Later in the commentary to this verse, Medhātithi says that *kāma*, *icchā* and *abhilāṣa* are synonymous. This too implies that *abhisandhi* does not mean desire.

Although there is the [basic] rule that (1) that which is heard (in *śruti*) as possessed of *phala* [that is, *kāmyakarmas* for which *phala* is stated], that is to be done in just that manner, while (2) [that which is heard in *śruti*] as not possessing *phala*, [and which is] made known by *śāstra* as to be done without the postulation of *phala* by means of the Viśvajit rule, due to the words 'as long as life' and so on, when that [action] is performed otherwise, there is no incongruity. He who is not able to grasp this rule, he is instructed by this explicit statement.

Here Medhātithi continues to defend the wording of the text by further explaining the potential for misunderstanding. The rules for determining whether or not a Vedic *vidhi* (injunction) has *phala* are complex. There are two basic rules. First, if the Vedas mention that a particular *karma* has *phala*, then the *karma* is a *kāmyakarma*, and desire for the *phala* is permissible. Second, if the Vedas do not mention that a particular *karma* has *phala*, and includes the words 'as long as life' – indicating the action's obligatoriness – then the *karma* is a *nityakarma*, and desire for the *phala* is prohibited.

Implicit in the second rule, however, is a third. If the Vedas do not mention that a particular *karma* has *phala*, but does not include the words 'as long as life', then the *phala* of the action can be inferred, in accord with the Viśvajit rule. The Viśvajit rule states that when no *phala* is mentioned, heaven can be assumed to be the *phala*. The words 'as long as life', however, block the application of this rule.[2]

Rather than elaborating these rules, Manu simply states "essential desirefulness (*kāmātmatā*) is not praiseworthy (*praśasthā*)" with the intention of conveying the advice to avoid desiring the *phala* of action in the case of *nityakarmas* (see below). Medhātithi explains this strategy further:

For with regard to understanding in accord with the rule, it is [exegetically] heavy. From the direct statement, there is an easy understanding. This is lighter. Having been good-hearted, [Manu] explains [that this is the] meaning, as established by *pramāṇa* [namely *śruti*].

Manu could avoid the objection posed by the *pūrvapakṣin* that the prohibition on desiring the *phala* of *nityakarmas* is redundant by elaborating the rule mentioned above. The rule is complex, however, and some people will be unable to understand it. It is lighter – that is, simpler – in terms of expectations on the reader – to simply advise against desiring *phala*. Since Manu is compassionate, he chooses to teach in the simplest way possible, so as to be understood by as many people as possible.

Even though the word *kāma* is understood (*dṛṣṭa*) [as synonymous with] the word *hṛcchaya* (lust), nonetheless, because of the impossibility of that here, this therefore is not its meaning. In this context, [*kāma* simply means] *icchā* (desire) and *abhilāṣa* (desire). With regard to that, by reflection on [that which is] being said, [namely] "not in every case [is action] to be performed [motivated] by a desire (*abhilāṣa*) for *phala*." This meaning will be established [in what follows].

Medhātithi invokes the principle of charity (see Chapter 1), and points out that it cannot be that Manu uses the word *kāma* in its primary meaning, to refer to lust. Manu's point is not limited to the claim that certain actions should be performed without a lust for *phala*. If it were, the advice would be relatively easy to follow. In addition, Manu's claim that "never does desirelessness exist here on Earth" cannot mean that the complete absence of lust is impossible, since obviously the complete absence of lust is possible.

Instead, the word *kāma* should be understood in its secondary meaning, to refer to desire, broadly construed, for *phala*.

But the other [namely, the *pūrvapakṣin*], thinking [that] the meaning of the word *kāmātmatā* [implies] any connection to any *icchā* at all, also says [citing Manu 2.2], "Nor, however, does desirelessness exist here on Earth." This means that here in this world there is no activity of any non-desirer. That child himself, who is caused to recite the Veda by his father and others, being struck [otherwise], that also does not occur without desire. As much, farming, trade, and so on, done by [one whose] mind is experienced. For reading has the form of the enunciation of words, and without desire, enunciation does not, like thunder without a storm, persist. "If [he] desires [to read], then why is he beaten?" [you ask]. That very desire is born in this way. Indeed, with regard to an object that is desired, it arises by itself. So to this extent there is a difference. And that which is enjoined by the Veda – such as the performance of the ritual *darśapūrṇamāsa, karmayoga*, and so on – which is known to be obligatory, that also is not attained [without desire]. For without desire, there is no production of [the action of] forsaking one's wealth/substance by means of an indication of a deity. Hence since there is a prohibition on *kāmātmatā*, a prohibition on all actions relating to *śruti* and *smṛti* follows.

Medhātithi's commentary to this verse ends with the *pūrvapakṣin's* objection that desirelessness of the sort that Manu seems to endorse is impossible, since all action is motivated by desire. The *pūrvapakṣin* offers a range of examples: the student studies motivated by desire, the farmer plows motivated by desire, the merchant trades motivated by desire, and the performance of ritual actions are motivated by desire. Even if one wants to forsake the merit that arises from performing meritorious deeds, one cannot do this without desiring to forsake one's merit.

Medhātithi does not formally reply at this point, but his characterization of the *pūrvapakṣin's* position is instructive. He says that the *pūrvapakṣin* takes Manu's discussion of *kāma* to refer to any desire whatever, rather than a desire for *phala* in particular. This, it turns out, is the *pūrvapakṣin's* fundamental mistake. If *kāma* refers to any desire whatever, then the *pūrvapakṣin* is right that desireless action is impossible, and that the verse is a contradiction. If, however, *kāma* refers to the desire for *phala*, as Medhātithi specifies immediately in his commentary to 2.2, then the advice is consistent – as Medhātithi argues below. So the

> important mistake here is not taking the word *kāma* to refer to lust, but taking it to refer to all desires.

Verse 2.3 [p. 157, line 11]:
Even desire has belief (*saṅkalpa*) as its basis. Sacrifices arise from *saṅkalpa*. The *smṛtis* state: "All restraints and vows are born of belief."

Commentary to 2.3 (Medhātithi) [p. 157, line 13]:
And so, when it is said that there is no bringing about of the own form of the sacrifice without *kāma*, that is explained more clearly by this [verse]. *Saṅkalpa* is the basis of sacrifice, and so on, and of desire. [A person] wanting (*cikīrṣa*) to perform a sacrifice, and so on, inevitably forms [a corresponding] *saṅkalpa*, and the *saṅkalpa* being made, it [the *saṅkalpa*] is to be directed by *kāma* as its cause, even if unwanted, as from a person who makes a fire with the purpose of cooking, smoke arises, even though [it is] unwanted, having the same cause as that [fire]. With regard to that, it is not possible that sacrifices and so on will be done, but *kāma* will not exist.

> Medhātithi explains that according to verse 2.3, action is produced by *kāma*, and *kāma* is produced by *saṅkalpa*. At this point the account is somewhat obscure, but it is explained in detail in what follows. Medhātithi draws an analogy with a person who builds a fire, and as an unintended result, also produces smoke. In the same way, a person who acts produces *kāma*, even if unintentionally.

Then what is this [thing], [which is] called *saṅkalpa* that is the basis of all action? It is said: [*saṅkalpa* is] that [which is] called the beholding of the mind. It is the cause of that desire (*prārthana*) and purpose (*adhyavasāya*) that follow it. For these actions of the mind serve as the basis with regard to the performance of all actions. For no physical actions are produced without them. So first, [there is] the determining of the nature of a thing, for example, "this object is attained by this purposeful action." The cognition which is like this is considered a *saṅkalpa*. Then there is *prārthanā* – an *icchā* (desire). This is *kāma*. There being the *icchā* [of the form] "By means of what do I bring this about?" He genuinely resolves – that is, decides – "I [will] act." This is *adhyavasāya* (purpose). Then [the agent] acts to take up the means to [that which is] the goal of external activity.

> Medhātithi defines *saṅkalpa* as a belief or cognition. He offers a means–end belief as an example: by means of this action, this end can be attained. He offers an example of the entire chain of causes and effects:

In that way a hungry person sees (*paśyati*) the action of eating, [and] then desires (*icchati*), "I should eat." Then they form the purpose (*adhyavasyati*), "I [will] make food, having desisted from other actions." So they say to the superintendent of the place where the work occurs, "Get ready! Prepare the kitchen!"

> In the example, the *saṅkalpa* is not mentioned explicitly. Medhātithi says that the first step is the seeing of others eating. It might be that the *saṅkalpa* is this perception. The *saṅkalpa* produces the desire to eat, which in turn produces the purpose or intention to eat (see Chapter 5).

[The *pūrvapakṣin* objects:] is it not, then, that sacrifice, and so on is not from *saṅkalpa* alone, but from *saṅkalpa*, *prārthana* and *adhyavasāya*? Then why is it said that sacrifice and so on arises from *saṅkalpa*?

> The *pūrvapakṣin* objects that it is misleading to say that actions like the performance of sacrifice, and so on, arise from saṅkalpa, because *saṅkalpa*, *prārthana/kāma*, and *adhyavasāya* are all necessary conditions of action. Medhātithi replies that,

On account of *saṅkalpa* being the first cause, this is not a problem.

> *Prārthanā* and *adhyavasāya* arise from *saṅkalpa*, hence *saṅkalpa* is the first cause of action. That is why Manu says that actions arise from *saṅkalpa*.

Thus he [Manu] will say [in verse 2.4]: "No action of [one who is] desireless is seen." Vows [for example] – a vow is a mental resolution (*adhyavasāya*) which is conveyed [in a form such as] "this is to be done by me as long as I live," like the vows of *snātakas* (those who have undertaken vows such as fasting, celibacy, and so on). Restraints [on the other hand], such as non-harm, and so on, have the form of prohibitions. Neither acting with regard to what is to be done, nor abstaining from that which is prohibited occurs without *saṅkalpa*.

> Both vows – which are firm intentions or promises to do something – nor restraints – which are firm intentions or promises not to do something – can occur without *adhyavasāya*, and therefore *kāma*, and therefore *saṅkalpa*. This is the position that Manu endorses.

Verse 2.4 [p. 159, line 5]:
No action of [a person who is] desireless is ever seen here. For whatever a person does, [that] is the deed of someone who desires just that.

Commentary to 2.4 (Medhātithi):
[p. 159, line 7] By the preceding [verse, namely Manu 2.3], it is said that action and inaction in accord with scripture are based on *saṅkalpa*. By this verse, it is said that worldly actions are based on that [namely *saṅkalpa*] as well. This is the difference [between the two claims].

Here Medhātithi generalizes the theory of motivation to include all actions. The model he has described for ritual and *dharmic* actions also applies to mundane actions. The difference between the verses is that 2.3 discusses scriptural actions, whereas 2.4 discusses all actions.

Here in this world, never at any time is any action possible of a person in a waking state [who is] without the desire that it be carried out. That worldly or Vedic action which one does, [be it] a permitted or prohibited action, [that is] the action of one desirous of that. Since [desire] is the cause, it is said, "action is from desire."

Medhātithi specifies that the desire that plays a necessary role in motivating action is a desire for that which one does. If a person walks to work in order to receive a paycheck, it follows that they desire to walk to work.

The *pūrvapakṣin* objects,

This is absurd – *kāmātmatā* is not praiseworthy [as verse 2.2 says] – and [yet] without this nothing is to be done.

The *pūrvapakṣin* insists that this is a contradiction. Desire is to be avoided, yet desire cannot be avoided. Medhātithi responds in his commentary to the following verse.

Verse 2.5 [p. 159, line 29]:
The person living rightly with regard to these [desires] goes to the state of being in the immortal world. Additionally they attain all desires in this world as they are thought [of] (*saṅkalpitāṃ*).

Commentary to 2.5 (Medhātithi) [p. 160, line 1]:
With regard to this, he [Manu] replies [as follows]. With regard to these desires, [action] is to be done rightly. But what is the right action? That [action] is to be done just as it is stated [in scripture].

Right action is action in accord with scripture.

With regard to *nityakarmas*, since the *phala* is not mentioned, [*phala*] is not to be intended. With regard to *kāmyakarmas*, however, since they are stated thus, there is no prohibition. These [*kāmyakarmas*] are known according to the *vidhis* (injunctions) to be a means to *phala*. The person who does them without a desire (*icchā*) for *phala* would do what is not heard [in *śruti*]. With regard to *nityakarmas* [however], the intention (*abhisandhi*) of *phala* is an error. For since [its being] a means to *phala* is not known from *pramāṇa*, it is not the case that from [the agent's] purpose alone, *phala* arises.

The advice to act without desire is advice to act without desire for *phala*, and only applies to *nityakarmas*. Since *nityakarmas* have no *phala*, it is a mistake to perform *nityakarmas* motivated by a desire for *phala*. Since *kāmyakarmas* do have a *phala*, and since *kāmyakarmas* are understood in *śruti* as actions which are a means to *phala*, it is permissible to perform these actions with *icchā/kāma*. Indeed, to perform them without *icchā/kāma* is a mistake.

Acting in this way, [a person] goes to – that is, attains – the state of being of the immortal world – *amaraloka*. Immortals (*amarāḥ*) are gods; their world is heaven (*svarga*). From their dwelling there, the word *loka* (world) is used to refer to the immortals [themselves], since there is no distinction between the place and [its] dwellers, as [when it is said,] "the platforms [on which the priests sit] wail." By this, [it is understood that] this [compound, namely *amaraloka*] is a [*karmadhāraya*] compound. And those immortals and those worlds, that is the state of being that is *amaraloka*. The meaning is: the person attains god-hood. It is said in this way due to compliance with *vṛtta* (cadence).

Performing *kāmyakarmas* motivated by a desire for *phala*, and performing *nityakarmas* without a desire for *phala*, a person reaches the immortal world. The word *loka* refers to both the place where the immortals dwell, and the immortals themselves, in the same way that one would say that the platforms wail, when in fact the priests who stand on the platforms wail. For the sake of cadence, the six-syllabled *amaralokatām* is added to the end of the verse rather than the three-syllabled *devatām*.

Or else someone who sees the gods is *amaraloka*. That person becomes a seer of the gods. Also in this way, the attainment of heaven is stated. Or else [it means]: that person is seen as an immortal in the world.

All of this explains what is meant by the compound *amaralokatām*. It basically means the world of the gods, but may be understood in the variety of ways just mentioned as well – to refer to someone who sees the gods, and so on.

This is *arthavāda* (an elaboration). With regard to this, heaven is not enjoined as a *phala*, since there is no *phala* of *nityakarmas*, and since there is a hearing of many *phala* from *kāmyakarmas*. So by the attainment of heaven, the completion of the carrying out of [the dictates of] *śāstra* is stated. Indirectly, that which is the purpose of the carrying out of action, that is attained. This is the meaning.

In the case of *nityakarmas*, one should not understand heaven as the unmentioned *phala*, since *nityakarmas* do not have *phala*. Nor should one understand heaven as the *phala* of *kāmyakarmas*, since *kāmyakarmas*

> have many *phalas* – whatever the *kāmyakarma* is performed for the sake of. They do not have a single *phala*, as would be the case if heaven were the *phala* of *kāmyakarmas*.

With regard to this, of the *nityakarmas*, the motive is the fulfillment of *vidhi* (injunction) or the non-production of demerit.

> Here, finally, Medhātithi explains how the person who does not desire the *phala* of their action nonetheless acts. They have the purpose of fulfilling *vidhi*, but desire neither the *phala* of the performance of *vidhi*, nor the fulfillment of *vidhi*. This may be taken as Medhātithi's response to the *pūrvapakṣin's* objection that without desire for *phala*, action is impossible.
>
> The disjunction 'the fulfillment of *vidhi* or the non-production of merit' implies that either end might be the agent's purpose. It does no good to object, then, that an agent performs *nityakarmas* only for the sake of avoiding demerit, and hence motivated by *dveṣa*.

With regard to *kāmyakarmas*, however, [they attain all desires in this world] "as they are thought [of]" [in the present verse, means] "as they are thought [of] in accord with *śruti*." At the time of the undertaking, having thought of, or having intended, or having desired with the mind that *phala* which is of that action which is heard [in scripture], that [person thinks] thus: "I will attain this *phala*." In this way, all desires are attained – that is, the person attains all objects to be desired. In this way, the problem is avoided, since it is not the case that a desire for any object is prohibited.

> In the case of *kāmyakarmas*, an agent attains whatever *phala* it is that they desire, so long as their actions are in accord with *śruti*. So there is no problem of Manu's prohibition on desire entailing a prohibition on *kāmyakarmas*, as the *pūrvapakṣin* claims.

Then which [desire] is prohibited?

> The *pūrvapakṣin* asks, if a desire for the *phala* of *kāmyakarmas* are permissible, then what does Manu mean when he claims that desire is to be eliminated? Medhātithi replies,

In the case of *nityakarmas*, a desire (*abhilāṣa*) characterized by *phala* [is prohibited]. The fulfillment of the means, however, is certainly to be desired.

> At this point Medhātithi clarifies his position fully. The advice to eliminate desire is limited to the advice to eliminate the desire for *phala*, but only in the case of *nityakarmas*. For cases other than *nityakarmas*, a desire for *phala* is permissible. In addition, in the case of *nityakarmas*, a

desire for the means to the agent's end is permissible as well. The end, then, is established by *vidhi*, as was said above.

The Brahmavādins, however, think that *kāmātmatā* means [that there is] a prohibition of the *saurya* [sacrifice], and so on [as well].

Medhātithi contrasts his position with that of the Vedāntins, who claim that the desire for the *phala* of *kāmyakarmas* – and hence the performance of *kāmyakarmas* – is prohibited.

[The Brahmavādins say:] "any acting for the sake of *phala* has the nature of bondage." [The person who is] desireless (*niṣkāma*), acting with the manner of an offering to Brahman is liberated. This is said by the Venerable Kṛṣṇadvaipāyana [that is, Kṛṣṇa in the *Gītā*[3]]: "Let there be no [action] caused [by the desire for] the *phala* of action" [*Bhagavadgītā* 2.47]. Similarly, [Kṛṣṇa says,] "The performance of an action becomes useless from the incompleteness of the means, or from the intending of *phala*, or the *vidhi* imperfectly remembered."

The Brahmavādins do not limit the prohibition on desire to the desire for *phala* of *nityakarmas*. On their account, all desires are prohibited. Intending *phala* in the case of a *nityakarma* is one of three mistakes that render the *nityakarma* useless, where "useless" presumably means that the action does not fulfill the *vidhi*, and possibly does not avoid the demerit that results from failing to perform the *nityakarma*.

Appendix ii

Nyāyasūtra 1.1.22 with Vātsyāyana's *Nyāyadarśanabhāṣya*, and selected passages from Uddyotakara's *Nyāyabhāṣyavārttika*, and Vācaspatimiśra's *Nyāyavārttikatātparyaṭīkā*[1]

Nyāyasūtra 1.1.22 [p. 452, line 22]:
When there is completion (*niṣṭhā*), when there is an end (*paryavasānaṃ*), that [end] is this [*apavarga*]. *Apavarga* is the complete release from that [pain, and so on.]

Vātsyāyana's commentary [p. 452, line 24]:
Apavarga is the complete release from suffering and birth. How? From the abandonment of the received birth and the non-acquisition of another. The knowers of *apavarga* know that *apavarga* is this endless state. That state [which is] fearless, ageless, and deathless, which is Brahman, is called the attainment of peace.

> Vātsyāyana begins by offering a definition of *apavarga*, or *mokṣa*. He defines it as the complete elimination of pain, which is the standard Nyāya view.[2] It is attained by completing one's present birth, and avoiding a subsequent birth. He contrasts this account of *mokṣa* with the account offered by the Vedāntins:

[p. 453, line 1] Some [namely the Vedāntins] think, "in *mokṣa*, the eternal bliss of the true self, which is like an immensity [of size], is manifested. By that manifestation [of eternal bliss], the completely liberated [person] is happy." [But] since there is the absence of *pramāṇa* (means of valid knowing) of that, there is no proof. There is no perception, inference, or testimony known [in support of the claim that] in *mokṣa*, the eternal bliss of the true self, which is like an immensity [of size], is manifested.

> The Vedāntins say that *mokṣa* is pure bliss, the immensity of which can only be understood by analogy with immense size. Since *mokṣa* is bliss of this sort, the person who attains *mokṣa* is immensely happy. Vātsyāyana objects that there is no evidence for this position. It is not possible to have

a first-hand experience of the eternal bliss of *mokṣa* – at least not before it is achieved permanently. There is no convincing argument to this effect. Nor does *śruti* testify to this (although this is another point of contention dealt with below). Indeed, there are strong arguments against this view.

The manifestation of what is eternal is the awareness [of it]. The cause of that [manifestation] [is to be] stated. The manifestation of eternal happiness is considered awareness, knowledge [of eternal happiness]. The cause of that [awareness], from which that [awareness] arises is to be stated.

The Vedāntin states that in *mokṣa* the eternal bliss of the true self is manifested. This means that the agent becomes aware of the eternal bliss of the true self. If this is the Vedāntins' view, then they must explain what it is that causes this awareness to arise.

If it is said that it [the awareness of eternal bliss] is eternal, like bliss [itself], then there is no difference between the liberated person and the person who exists in *saṃsāra*. As the liberated [person] is endowed with bliss and with the awareness of that [bliss], which is in fact eternal, likewise [the person who is existing] in *saṃsāra* [will be endowed with both] as well. It follows that there is no difference, since both [the bliss and the awareness of it] are eternal.

One option is to say that the awareness of the eternal bliss of *mokṣa* has no cause, and is therefore eternal like the bliss itself. This cannot be right, however. If the awareness of eternal bliss were eternal, then everyone would always experience the bliss of *mokṣa*. If everyone were always aware of the immense bliss of *mokṣa*, then there would be no difference between the person who is liberated and the person who is not. This would mean that for all intents and purposes, everyone is already liberated. This, however, contradicts the expectation that some people are liberated and others are not.

And if [this claim that the awareness of the bliss of liberation is eternal is] assented to, then the simultaneous association [of eternal bliss] with the *phala* (result) of *dharma* and *adharma* would be experienced. Pleasure and pain [which is the] *phala* of *dharma* and *adharma* [respectively] in states of birth are perceived with succession, and the co-existence of that [successive pleasure and pain] and the eternal awareness [of the bliss of *mokṣa*] would be grasped simultaneously. There is no non-existence of bliss nor non-manifestation [of the awareness of bliss] because of the eternality of both.

In addition, if the awareness of the immense bliss of *mokṣa* is itself eternal, then people simultaneously experience both the eternal bliss of *mokṣa* and the succession of the mundane pleasure and pain that results from *dharma* and *adharma*. It would be possible for a given person to

> suffer pain as a result of demeritorious actions in the past while at the same time experiencing perfect bliss. This is counter-intuitive. Hence the awareness of the bliss of *mokṣa* is not eternal.

If it [namely, the awareness of bliss] is not eternal, the cause [of the awareness] is [to be] stated. So if in *mokṣa* there is a non-eternal awareness of eternal bliss, the cause from which that [awareness] arises should be stated. [The Vedāntin replies:] There is causation between the true self and the mind, connected with another cause [which causes the awareness of eternal bliss]. [Vātsyāyana objects:] [Then there should be a] mentioning of the other cooperating cause of that. If it is said, "the cause is the contact between the true self and the mind," even then, another cooperating cause of that has to be stated.

> If the Vedāntin admits that the awareness of the bliss of *mokṣa* is not eternal, then they must cite the cause of the arising of the awareness. The Vedāntin might say that its cause is the contact between the true self and the mind. If this is their position, they must cite some third element as well, since the connection between the true self and the mind cannot be sufficient for producing this awareness. If it were, the awareness would exist for all embodied beings, and the same problems that result from claiming that the awareness is eternal arise. So the Vedāntin must cite a cooperating cause.

[Suppose] the cause of merit (*dharma*) is stated. If merit is the other cause, then you should state the cause of that [merit] – [that] from which it arises. [Suppose one answers: *yogic samādhi* (concentration) is the cause of merit.] When there is an end of that [merit] born of *yogic samādhi*, there [would be] the cessation of the awareness [of bliss], since there is a contradiction in the non-ending of an effect. If the cause is merit born of *yogic samādhi*, when there is an end of that [merit], the awareness [of the bliss of *mokṣa*] completely ceases, since there is a contradiction in the non-ending of an effect.

> The Vedāntin might say that merit, together with the connection between the true self and the mind, is the cooperating cause of the arising of the awareness of the bliss of *mokṣa*. The difference between a person who experiences the eternal bliss of *mokṣa* and one who does not is that the person who experiences it has accumulated sufficient merit, by means of *yogic samādhi*. If this is the Vedāntin's position, however, there is the problem that the merit that results from *yogic samādhi* – or anything else – is an effect, and therefore impermanent, since anything caused is impermanent. Hence the merit that supposedly causes the awareness of bliss is not eternal. If merit is not eternal, then it ends. When it ends, its effect – namely, the awareness of bliss – ends. This is inconsistent,

> however, with the claim that the awareness of the bliss of *mokṣa* is permanent.

And if there is no awareness [of bliss], it is not different from the absence [of bliss itself]. If from the destruction of merit there is a cessation of the awareness [of bliss], then eternal happiness is not experienced. Whether something existent or non-existent is not experienced, there is no inference to determine this.

> If the awareness of bliss can end, then there is no reason to think that the bliss itself does not end, since the experience of the non-awareness of bliss is no different from the experience of the absence of bliss itself. The point here is that if there is no awareness of bliss, there is no reason to think that the bliss is there, unexperienced, rather than simply not there at all. So not only does the Vedāntin fail to make a case for the permanence of the awareness of bliss (once it is attained), it also fails to make a case for the permanence of bliss itself!

[p. 454, line 1:] And there is no inference of indestructible merit, on account of the non-eternality of that which has the quality of being arisen. [If one says] the merit from *yogic samādhi* does not end, there is no proof of this. Rather, there is the inference of the opposite: whatever has the quality of arising is impermanent. Indeed, of the person [for whom] there is no cessation of the awareness [of bliss], of that person, it is to be assented that the cause of the sensation is [itself] eternal.

> The Vedāntin cannot simply assert that there is some special sort of merit – namely the eternal merit that arises from *yogic samādhi* – that is permanent. Not only is there no argument for this, but there is a convincing argument to the contrary. Ordinary experience testifies to the fact that all effects are impermanent. If all effects are impermanent, then the effects of *yogic samādhi* are impermanent as well. Hence the merit that results from *yogic samādhi* is impermanent, and does not explain the permanence of the awareness of the bliss of *mokṣa*.

And if [merit] were eternal, then there [would be] no difference between the two states of *mokṣa* and *saṃsāra*. And that being so, a concomitance [of the experience of the eternal bliss of *mokṣa*] with the *phala* of *dharma* and *adharma* in the form of the sensations of pleasure and pain [respectively] would be seen.

> Vātsyāyana seems to say that if the merit that arises from *yogic samādhi* is eternal, the same two problems that were mentioned above arise. First, *mokṣa* and *saṃsāra* are qualitatively identical – both are characterized by the experience of the eternal bliss of *mokṣa*. This violates the expectation

that there is something to be achieved by attaining *mokṣa*. Second, the person who is in *saṃsāra* will experience both the alternating mundane pleasures and pains that result from moral and immoral actions at the same time that they experience the perfect bliss of *mokṣa*. This seems impossible.

It is not clear, however, why Vātsyāyana thinks these consequences follow. If the awareness of the bliss of *mokṣa* arises as a result of *yogic samādhi*, then there is no reason to think that everyone experiences it. Some people have not performed *yogic samādhi* enough to achieve this awareness. For them, the awareness of eternal bliss is absent. Since they do not experience the bliss of *mokṣa*, there is no reason to think that they experience the mundane pains and pleasures at the same time that they experience the bliss of *mokṣa*.

One explanation may be that Vātsyāyana does not draw the distinction between 'permanent' and 'eternal'. If the awareness of bliss is permanent once it is achieved, it is eternal, but only henceforth. It may be that Vātsyāyana takes the word 'eternal' to imply eternal in the past and future. Then his objections are sensible. They can be avoided, however, with this distinction.

Even if these last two objections fail, however, the previous objection seems sufficient. The merit that produces the awareness is not permanent, because it is caused. Hence the awareness cannot be permanent.

If [instead, it is claimed that] the union of the body, and so on is the cause of an obstruction [of the sensation], this is false [also], since the purpose of the body, and so on is enjoyment, and since there is no inferential proof of the opposite [being the case]. It might be thought that the union of body, and so on of someone in the state of *saṃsāra* is an obstruction to the cause of the awareness of eternal happiness. Therefore there is no non-distinction with that [awareness of bliss]. But this is incorrect. The body, and so on have the purpose of experience. [That] they will be an obstacle to experience is unproved. Additionally, there is no inference that there is any experience of the true self that is not embodied.

Another reply might be that the awareness of the bliss of *mokṣa* is blocked by the body, the sense capacities,[3] and cognitions. This seems to avoid the problem of the non-eternality of causes, since the elimination of some obstacle might be eternal, even if that which causes the elimination is not. If a bulldozer destroys a home, the home remains destroyed even after the bulldozer is destroyed. If this is right, then it is false that there is no distinction between the experience of the person in *saṃsāra* and the experience of the person who has attained *mokṣa*. Only the person in *saṃsāra* is embodied, and unable to experience the eternal bliss of *mokṣa*. The liberated person, however, has no body. There is therefore no obstruction to the experience of the bliss of *mokṣa* for the liberated person.

The problem with this reply is that there is no argument for the claim that the body is an obstacle to this experience. Indeed, the primary purpose of the body, the sense organs, and cognitions is the experience of pleasure and pain. It is not even clear how a disembodied self could have these experiences. So while there is no clear evidence in favor of this reply, there is strong evidence against it.

One might claim that activity only has the purpose (*artha*) of obtaining what is desired. This is false [however], since [we also act] from the purpose of avoiding what is undesirable. There is this inference: the teaching with regard to *mokṣa* is for the purpose of obtaining what is desired. Likewise [the activity] of *mumukṣus*. Neither [agent's action] is without purpose (*anarthakam*). But this is mistaken. The teaching of liberation is for the sake of giving up the undesirable. Likewise the activity of *mumukṣus*.

The Vedāntin might argue as follows. Since all action is for the sake of the attainment of pleasure, it must be that the actions of *mumukṣus* are for the sake of the attainment of pleasure. If the actions of the *mumukṣus* are for the sake of the attainment of pleasure, then *mokṣa* must be pleasurable.

Vātsyāyana objects that it is false that all action is for the sake of the attainment of pleasure. Actions are also for the sake of avoiding pain. Just as I might go to the café in pursuit of the pleasure of a coffee, likewise I might go to the café in flight from a threatening dog. The actions of the *mumukṣu* are for the sake of avoiding pain, rather than a desire for pleasure.

At this point, Vātsyāyana does not argue for his position. He simply asserts it. He has, however, already argued for the untenability of the Vedāntin position. He continues to do this in what follows.

[Moreover], there is nothing desired that is not connected with something undesirable. Since there is a connection with the undesirable, even the desirable is undesirable. Acting to abandon the undesirable, one also abandons the desirable, because of the impossibility of abandoning [the undesirable] by means of discriminating [the desirable from the undesirable].

Another problem with the Vedāntin position is that pleasure is always mixed with pain. If *mokṣa* is blissful, then it is also painful. This contradicts ordinary expectations, however. In addition, knowing that pleasure is mixed with pain, and knowing that liberation is pleasureable and therefore painful, the wise would avoid liberation, which is absurd.

One problem with this objection is that the Vedāntin does not accept the Naiyāyikas' claim that all pleasure is mixed with pain. Without this assumption the argument is unconvincing.

And the abandoning of the seen is the same in the case of the body, and so on. Just as having abandoned the impermanent happiness of the seen, eternal happiness is desired, likewise, having overcome the visible body, senses, and cognitions which are impermanent, an eternal body, senses, and mind are to be postulated for the liberated person. And so it is [the case that] the certainty of the isolation of the liberated person is inferred [by you].

> Vātsyāyana adds that if it is justified to infer the permanent pleasure of *mokṣa* from the fact that human beings abandon the fleeting pleasures of the world in order to pursue *mokṣa*, then it is also justified to infer that in *mokṣa* there is an eternal body, sense capacities, and cognitions from the fact that human beings abandon the impermanent body, sense capacities, and cognitions of the world in order to attain *mokṣa*.

If [you, the Vedāntin, say,] there is a contradiction with evidence [in the case of inferring the eternal body], [we reply:] the same [goes for inferring eternal bliss]. [If one says] it is impossible to postulate the eternality of the body, and so on, which is contradicted by the *pramāṇas*, [then] the same [goes for your view]. Then the eternality of bliss as well, which is contradicted by the *pramāṇas*, cannot be postulated.

> The Vedāntin might object that the conclusion that there is a permanent body, and so on in the state of *mokṣa* is contradicted by *pramāṇa*. *Śruti* denies that any such things exist. Likewise, however, the conclusion that *mokṣa* is eternal bliss is contradicted by the *pramāṇa* of *anumāna* (inference). As Vātsyāyana argues above and below, there are a number of arguments that seem to disprove the claim that *mokṣa* is a state of eternal bliss. Hence both the conclusion that there is no eternal body, and so on, and the conclusion that there is eternal bliss in *mokṣa* should be abandoned.

Since there is a stating of [the word] *sukha* [to refer] to the complete absence of the pain of *saṃsāra*, even though an *āgama* (scripture) [says otherwise], there is no contradiction. Even though a certain *āgama* states that the happiness of the liberated is unsurpassed, the word *sukha* is spoken [with reference] to the complete absence of pain. Thus [the Nyāya position] is valid. Indeed, frequently in the world there is the use of the word *sukha* in regard to the absence of *duḥkha*.

> One might object to the Nyāya position by pointing out that *mokṣa* is typically characterized as *sukha* or *ānanda*, the primary meaning of which is bliss. This implies that *mokṣa* is bliss (see Appendix iii). Vātsyāyana responds that *sukha* might also mean the avoidance or cessation of pain. Uddyotakara (below) gives a nice example: when a person is

ill and their fever breaks, they say, "I feel happy," even though they feel no positive joy. Recovering from a hangover is often like this.

If there is not an abandoning of the desire for eternal happiness, then there is no attainment of *mokṣa*, since there is the acknowledgement of *rāga* as a fetter. If in *mokṣa* eternal happiness is manifested, then acting for [the attainment of] *mokṣa* [motivated] by the desire for eternal bliss, one would not attain *mokṣa* – one would not be able to attain it. For *rāga* is acknowledged to be a fetter. And it is not valid that someone could be liberated if there is a fetter.

Vātsyāyana then argues that if *mokṣa* is bliss, the *mumukṣu* will pursue it motivated by *rāga* – a desire for pleasure. *Rāga*, however, is known to preclude the attainment of *mokṣa*, because it is a fetter. Hence *mokṣa* is not bliss (see below).

For one whose desire for eternal happiness is eliminated, [however,] there is no obstacle. Instead, [this person's] desire for eternal bliss is eliminated. When that is eliminated, there is of that person no *rāga* for eternal happiness that is an obstacle [to attaining *mokṣa*]. So whether there is eternal happiness of the liberated [person] or not, on either view, the attainment of *mokṣa* is not in doubt.

Here Vātsyāyana seems to say that even if there is some chance that *mokṣa* is blissful, it is important that the *mumukṣu* not think of it in this way. If the *mumukṣu* instead thinks of *mokṣa* as the complete absence of pain, they avoid *rāga*, and can attain *mokṣa*. Whatever *mokṣa* is like – whether it is pure pleasure or the complete absence of pain – the *mumukṣu* is guaranteed to reach it eventually, so long as the obstacle of *rāga* does not arise.

Uddyotakara's commentary [p. 456, line 21]:
Since the purpose [of human beings] is attaining a desirable object. Here [in] this world, [a person who] acts acts for the sake of attaining a desirable object. Likewise, those who are liberating themselves [that is, *mumukṣus*] act [for this purpose]. Their activity also must be for the purpose of obtaining a desirable object. This very activity is purposeful for the sake of eternal happiness, not otherwise.

Uddyotakara restates the Vedāntin argument that Vātsyāyana mentions. All action is done for the sake of attaining some desirable end. A *mumukṣu* is no exception. They act with the purpose of attaining the eternal bliss of *mokṣa*.

[Uddyotakara replies:] This is not the case, since action is known to be of two kinds. Two kinds of action are known in the world: [that] for the sake of obtaining [what is] desirable, and [that] for the sake of eliminating [what is] undesirable. With regard to that, it is said, "is this renunciation [of the *mumukṣu*] for the sake of attaining [that which is] desirable, or for the sake of eliminating [that which is] undesirable? This is uncertain."

> Like Vātsyāyana, Uddyotakara disputes the premise in the Vedāntin argument which states that all action is performed for the sake of attaining pleasure. Human beings may also act for the sake of eliminating some undesired end. So it does not follow that *mokṣa* must be blissful. It might just as well be the complete absence of pain. Either way, the motivation of the *mumukṣu* can be explained in a straightforward way.

One might say, "[It is known] from scripture . . ." From scripture [it is understood that] the eternal bliss (*sukha*) of the self for the liberated is gone to. It is heard [in scripture] that the liberated person becomes happy.

> Here the Vedāntin objects that *mokṣa* is described as *sukha* in scripture. The word *sukha* means pleasure or bliss. Hence *mokṣa* is bliss.

[Uddyotakara replies:] scripture also should be pondered [in the following way]: Does it state a connection with eternal bliss, or does it state a complete disconnection from pain [by means of the word *sukha*]? [p. 457, line 1:] After all, frequently in the world the use of the word *sukha* to refer to the absence of pain is seen. And so, when there is the getting rid of a fever, common people are wont to declare, "We have become happy!"

> Since the word *sukha* is ambiguous – it can mean either pleasure or the elimination of pain – the fact that scripture describes *mokṣa* as *sukha* does not settle the disagreement between the Naiyāyikas and Vedāntins.

But if this [person] is saying, "In *mokṣa* there is eternal bliss," then they act [motivated by] the *rāga* for bliss and are not liberated. Why? Because of the acknowledgement that *rāga* is a fetter. Certainly *rāga* is acknowledged as a fetter.

> So while an appeal to ordinary language does not settle the issue, there are additional reasons for taking the word *sukha* to mean the absence of pain. If it means pleasure, then the *mumukṣu* pursues *mokṣa* motivated by *rāga*, and this precludes their attainment of *mokṣa*. Hence *sukha* must refer to the absence of pain, and *mokṣa* must be the complete absence of pain.

Even if [a person] acts from *dveṣa*, saying, "I will eliminate *duḥkha*," even then [that person] is not liberated. Since there is the acknowledgment of *dveṣa* as a fetter [as well]. For it is said that *rāga* and *dveṣa* are fetters.

> Here the Vedāntin offers an additional objection that is not contained in Vātsyāyana's commentary. The Naiyāyika says that *mokṣa* cannot be blissful, because if it is, an agent will pursue it motivated by *rāga*, and *rāga* precludes the attainment of *mokṣa*, because it is a fetter. Likewise, however, if an agent pursues *mokṣa* motivated by *dveṣa*, they too are precluded from attaining *mokṣa*, because *dveṣa* is a fetter just as *rāga* is. So if the argument against *mokṣa* is bliss is convincing, then *mokṣa* is not the complete absence of pain either.

[Uddyotakara replies:] this is not the case, since this [the avoidance of pain] is not counter-productive. The avoidance of pain is not counter-productive. Moreover this [person, namely the *mumukṣu*] is not *dveṣṭi* (the adjective formed from *dveṣa*) towards *duḥkha*, and [this person] who acts without *dveṣa* attains the elimination of *duḥkha*, which is not counter-productive.

> First, Uddyotakara denies that avoiding pain is counter-productive to the attainment of *mokṣa*. Second, he denies that the *mumukṣu* is motivated by *dveṣa*. Presumably the claims are related: the avoidance of pain is not counter-productive because it is not motivated by *dveṣa*. In other words, Uddyotakara denies that if someone acts to avoid pain, it follows that they are motivated by *dveṣa*. At least in the case of the successful *mumukṣu*, the action of avoiding pain is motivated in some other way. Uddyotakara does not, however, explain this any further.

Vācaspati's commentary [p. 459, line 14]:
One might [say] that only if the primary (*mukhya*) [meaning] is inconsistent is the secondary (*gauṇa*) [meaning] reverted to. And the word *sukha* is primary in regard to bliss and is secondary in regard to the cessation of pain. So *mokṣa* is just eternal bliss.

> Both Vātsyāyana and Uddyotakara consider the objection that the word *sukha* means bliss, not the complete absence of pain. Since *mokṣa* is described as *sukha, mokṣa* is bliss. They both reply that the word *sukha* might also mean the elimination of pain. Hence the Nyāya claim that *mokṣa* is not bliss, but the complete absence of pain, is consistent with scripture.
>
> Vācaspati elaborates the objection. Even if in ordinary language the word *sukha* is used to refer to both bliss and the elimination of pain, its primary meaning is bliss. Since there is an exegetical principle – the principle of *lakṣaṇā* (see Chapter 1) – according to which the secondary meaning of a term can only be adopted if the primary meaning leads to a contradiction – either of common sense, or of other claims made in the

text – it must be assumed that the word *sukha* in scripture refers to bliss. If *sukha* refers to bliss, then *mokṣa* is a state of perfect bliss, and not the mere absence of pain as the Naiyāyikas claim.

For that person, attached, enjoying this or that object that they have acquired, and acquiring this or that thing that they have abandoned, is not delivered from *saṃsāra*. Thus it is acknowledged that *rāga* is a fetter. And activity based on a fetter is to be avoided. Otherwise, the demoness of desire, produced by the imagining of eternal happiness, having gained momentum and moving a person towards proximate pleasurable objects, takes them far away from liberation. Therefore, one should not give to this [*rāga*] even a little momentum.

Here Vācaspati elaborates the problem with *rāga* that both Vātsyāyana and Uddyotakara cite. If a person aims at the eternal bliss of *mokṣa*, then they have it in their mind that bliss is the ultimate goal of human life. If the pursuit of bliss is the person's guiding motive, however, they are inevitably tempted into indulging in more immediate pleasures. If the experience of bliss is the whole point anyway, why not get bliss while one can in sex, food, and so on? Since rāga has the tendency to undermine the *mumukṣu's* pursuit of *mokṣa*, it cannot constitute part of the *mumukṣu's* motivation. Hence the primary meaning of *sukha* should be abandoned, and its secondary meaning – the elimination of pain – adopted.

Of course, there is an answer to the question 'Why not simply pursue more immediate pleasures?' The answer is that indulgence in these fleeting pleasures precludes one from attaining the ultimate pleasure. The typical person, however, is not so prudent as to avoid all immediate bliss for some far-off bliss. There are two different attitudes that the *mumukṣu* might adopt. The first is that pleasure is the ultimate goal of human life, but that the immediate pleasures are to be avoided. The second is that all pleasure is to be avoided, because it is mixed with pain. Vācaspati's claim is that the *mumukṣu* who adopts the second attitude might succeed. The *mumukṣu* who adopts the first attitude cannot succeed.

Imagine, for example, advising a cocaine addict that they should not desire any of the cocaine that is actually available to them, because there is some superior cocaine that might be had if all other cocaine is avoided. Perhaps if the person saves all of the money they would otherwise spend on the less than optimum cocaine, they will have enough to afford the superior cocaine when they find it.

Contrast this advice with the advice that all cocaine is bad – it is addictive, life-threatening, and destructive to relationships – and therefore to be avoided. The latter advice, it seems, is more likely to keep the person from using cocaine than the former, at least in part because following the latter advice means coming to believe that cocaine is no good, period, whereas the first maintains the thought that using cocaine is fundamentally acceptable. (Although of course good advice is never sufficient for ending addictions.)

So the *śruti* that teaches [that *mokṣa* is] eternal *sukha* has a secondary [meaning]. It refers to the complete elimination of *duḥkha*.

This is just the kind of inconsistency that the principle of *lakṣaṇā* demands. Hence reverting to the secondary meaning of *sukha* is justified in this context.

And [if one] infers, saying "yes, but . . ." like *rāga*, momentum is not to be given to *dveṣa* either, and momentum is given by you to it. So the fault is the same.

The Vedāntin may try to argue by analogy that *dveṣa* is equally an obstacle. If a person aims at the complete absence of *duḥkha*, and has it in mind that the avoidance of *duḥkha* is the ultimate goal, they are likely to avoid more fleeting pains, even at the cost of attaining the complete elimination of pain, just as the person who takes bliss to be the highest goal might indulge in fleeting pleasures at the cost of attaining the ultimate pleasure.

Suppose, for example, that a person who believes that *mokṣa* is the complete elimination of *duḥkha*, must, in order to attain *mokṣa*, study with a teacher. Suppose also that studying with a teacher is the source of some pain on a given day, because the *mumukṣu* would rather do something else. Surely this person is just as disposed towards indulging in short-term pain avoidance as the Vedāntin is disposed towards indulging in short-term pleasures. If imprudence is the problem, it arises no matter what one pursues.

The Naiyāyika argues that if *mokṣa* is bliss, then the *mumukṣu* pursues bliss. If the *mumukṣu* pursues bliss, then they are motivated by *rāga*. If they are motivated by *rāga*, they cannot attain *mokṣa*. Likewise, however, if the *mumukṣu* pursues the avoidance of pain, they are motivated by *dveṣa*. If they are motivated by *dveṣa*, then they cannot attain *mokṣa*. (For a schematization of these arguments, see Chapter 6.)

[Vācaspati] answers, "No, because [the pursuit of the complete elimination of pain] is not counter-productive." Since pursuing eternal bliss is counter-productive, [because it is motivated] by attachment, which is counter-productive to [the attainment of] *mokṣa*, [therefore] the complete elimination of suffering is not attended by *dveṣa*.

Vācaspati argues that there is a disanalogy. The pursuit of *mokṣa* conceived as the complete elimination of pain is not motivated by *dveṣa*. The pursuit of *mokṣa* conceived as bliss, however, is invariably motivated by *rāga*. This is the point at which Uddyotakara's argument ends rather unsatisfactorily. Vācaspati, however, elaborates the distinction between *dveṣa* and the motivating state that he endorses.

[The words] *dveṣa, krodha* (anger), and *manyu* (rage) are not different in meaning. For it [namely, *dveṣa*] has the nature of a blazing fire. *Vairāgya* is not like this. For it [namely *vairāgya*] is the thought, "enough [of this]" (*alaṃ pratyāyaḥ*). Therefore the elimination of *duḥkha* is not counter-productive. This is the meaning.

The distinction is between acting to avoid *duḥkha* motivated by *dveṣa* – which is comparable to hatred, and is intense by its very nature – and acting to avoid *duḥkha* motivated simply by the thought "I have had enough of the impermanent world of suffering."

As I argue in Chapter 6, there are two ways to understand this distinction. On the one hand, it might mean that *dveṣa* refers to aversions that are phenomenologically salient – those that the agent can feel. On the other hand, it might mean that *dveṣa* refers to aversions that might become phenomenologically salient under the right circumstances – for example, under circumstances in which the painful state of affairs to which one is averse cannot be avoided (see Chapter 6).

Appendix iii

Maṇḍanamiśra's *Brahmasiddhi* and selections from Śaṅkhapāṇi's *Brahmasiddhivyākhyā*[1]

Verse 1 [p. 1, line 5]:
We will bow to Prajāpati, [who is] bliss, one, immortal, unborn, consciousness, unchanging, all [of this] and other than all [of this].

Maṇḍana's commentary [p. 1, line 7]:
The wise diverge in opinion with regard to the Vedānta texts [that is, the *Upaniṣads*]. Some think [they are] not a *pramāṇa*, on account of their [mere] repetition, since there is the establishment of the *ātman* by means of other *pramāṇas*. Or if it [the *ātman*] is not established [by other *pramāṇas*], there is no comprehension of a connection [between the word *ātman* and its referent]. Since it is not something corresponding to the meaning of a word, therefore it cannot be the object of a sentence.

Some argue that the *Upaniṣads* are not a *pramāṇa* (a valid means of knowing). They offer the following argument. Either the *ātman*, which is the subject of the *Upaniṣads*, is already known by means of other *pramāṇas*, or it is not. If the *ātman* is already known by means of other *pramāṇas*, then the *Upaniṣads* are redundant – they only state what is already known. If they are redundant, then they are not a *pramāṇa*, because *pramāṇas* are not merely redundant; they are informative.

If, however, the *ātman* is not known by means of other *pramāṇas*, then the word *ātman* makes no sense, because we are unable to connect the word with whatever it is that the word is supposed to refer to. If the word cannot be connected to some referent, then it cannot be the subject of a meaningful sentence, and nothing meaningful can be said about it. If nothing meaningful can be said about it, then the *Upaniṣads* say nothing meaningful about the *ātman*. Hence whether or not the *ātman* is already known by other *pramāṇas*, the *Upaniṣads* are not a *pramāṇa*.

This seems to be a clear case of a false dichotomy. It could be that we have some knowledge of the *ātman* – we have a vague sense of what the word refers to – but that only the *Upaniṣads* provide complete and accurate knowledge of it. Indeed, if convincing, the sort of objection that Maṇḍana considers here seems to prove that there are no *pramāṇas*.

And since, [in the *Upaniṣads*,] there is no instruction regarding activity or inactivity, they lack a purpose for human beings.

> A second objection is that since the *Upaniṣads* do not tell us what to do, they are not practically useful. They are simply metaphysical treatises, with no consequence for real life.

Indeed, others say [the *Upaniṣads*] are not a *pramāṇa*, [but] have [only] the false appearance of a *pramāṇa* relating to the apprehension of what is to be done.

> Others say that while the *Upaniṣads* seem to talk about what it is that one should do and not do, this is a mere appearance. It may be that this objection is related to the subsequent objection: given the ultimate metaphysical view advocated by the texts, action is impossible (for the reasons cited below). If action is impossible according to the *Upaniṣads*, then the *Upaniṣads* do not tell us what to do. They are practically irrelevant.

Indeed, others think that since, when there is a grasping of [their] primary meaning, there is a contradiction of the *vidhis* [of *śāstra*], and since there is a contradiction with perception, and so on, they are [to be taken] in [their] secondary meaning only.

> The Vedas offer injunctions (*vidhis*), and injunctions, in order to be sensible, require a distinction between agent, action, and so on. The *Upaniṣads*, however, state that all distinctions are illusory. Hence they contradict the Vedas, which are authoritative. They also contradict perception, since we can perceive distinctions with our own eyes. The *Upaniṣads*, however, insist that there are no distinctions, and therefore no actions.
>
> It is not entirely clear what the objection is here. If the point is simply that the primary meaning of the *Upaniṣads* contradicts the *pramāṇas* of *śabda* (scripture) and *pratyakṣa* (perception), and that therefore the *Upaniṣads* must be understood less literally, it seems that Maṇḍana can simply concede this. Even if he wants to resist this for other reasons, conceding that the *Upaniṣads* should be taken non-literally does not entail that they are not *pramāṇa*. As I point out throughout this book, Śaṅkara and others often claim that passages in the *Gītā* must not be taken literally. From this it does not follow that the *Gītā*, or even these specific passages of the *Gītā*, are not authoritative.

For the refutation of this [that is, these objections], this [treatise] is begun with the word *ānanda* (bliss).

> The purpose of this treatise is to refute the foregoing objections. The word *ānanda* is the first word of the treatise, translated as 'bliss' in verse 1 above.

[The author, namely Maṇḍana] worships the Highest Divinity with praise, characterized by the naming of [his] qualities, and by obeisance, characterized by the bowing down of body, speech, and mind. Also, [the author] describes the purpose of the treatise: since the establishment of the validity of the *Upaniṣads* with regard to this kind of object [namely Brahman], by means of repudiating the contrary opinion, is also the purpose of the treatise.

> In verse 1 above, Maṇḍana does two things. He worships Brahman by means of listing his superior qualities (bliss, one, immortal, and so on), and he mentions the subject of the *Brahmasiddhi*, namely Brahman. The purpose of the treatise is to show that the *Upaniṣads* are authoritative on the subject of Brahman. The word Brahman alludes to this purpose.

With regard to this, some [namely the Naiyāyikas] [object]: If Brahman is the nature of bliss, then the action of the *mumukṣu* is due to the *rāga* (desire) for bliss, and since action based on *rāga* is a seed of *saṃsāra*, [action motivated by it] would not liberate.

> Here we see the objection raised by Vātsyāyana in his commentary to *Nyāyasūtra* 1.1.22. If liberation is blissful, then the *mumukṣu's* pursuit of *mokṣa* is motivated by *rāga*. If the *mumukṣu* is motivated by *rāga*, then they cannot attain *mokṣa*, because *rāga* precludes it. The Nyāya objection continues,

It is said that for [someone who is] equanimous and restrained, there is a seeing of the true self. Acting from the *rāga* for bliss, [however,] one is not equanimous.

> Here Maṇḍana refers to what I call the 'equanimity requirement' in Chapter 6. In order to attain *mokṣa*, a person must realize the true self. In order to realize the true self, a person must be equanimous. When a person is motivated by *rāga*, however, they are not equanimous. Hence anyone motivated by *rāga* cannot realize the true self.
>
> This is also the sense of *Bhagavadgītā* 3.36–3.41, which states that *kāma* obscures knowledge as dust covers a mirror (cf. *Gītā* 2.67). In contrast, the discriminative faculty of the person established in equanimity (*prasāda*) is steady (2.65).
>
> Kṛṣṇa also compares *kāma* to *krodha* (anger) (3.37). He explains that *kāma* produces *krodha*, the loss of memory (*smṛti*) and discrimination (*buddhi*), and finally moral ruin (2.62–2.63). See Chapter 6 for a detailed comparison of these passages.

So if the reality of Brahman is the overcoming of all pain, [the person who] acts fearful (*udvignaḥ*) of pains and without desire for pleasure, [that person] is released. And the *śrutis* [that mention] *sukha* declare the overcoming of all pain, for it is seen that when there is the elimination of pain, like hunger, and so on, the word *sukha* [is used]. Additionally, others say that this alone [namely, the cessation of *duḥkha* (pain)] is *sukha*.

> The Naiyāyika *pūrvapakṣin* concludes that *sukha* must refer to the elimination of pain. If it does not, then *mokṣa* is unattainable (see Chapter 6 for a schematization of the argument).
>
> It is worth noting that Maṇḍana has already begun to set up his reply to the Nyāya position by attributing to the Naiyāyikas the claim that one should be motivated by fear (*udvigna*) of pain. If one of the central problems with *rāga* is that it disrupts equanimity, as Maṇḍana takes the Naiyāyikas to claim, then fear will be equally problematic, as Maṇḍana says below.
>
> There is a parallel here with the discussion within the commentaries on *Nyāyasūtra* 1.1.22. Vātsyāyana never says that a person should be motivated by *dveṣa*, rather than *rāga*. In Uddyotakara's commentary, however, the *pūrvapakṣin* assumes that if *rāga* does not motivate action, then *dveṣa* must. Both Uddyotakara and Vācaspati deny this. In what follows, Maṇḍana reviews the Nyāya response.

And there is not the unwanted consequence with regard to a stone, and so on, because happiness is the perception of an inner activity, or the perception of the self qualified by that [inner activity].

> The Naiyāyika considers a possible objection: If *sukha* is simply the absence of pain, then *sukha* is a characteristic of inanimate objects like stones. It is strange, however, to say "the stone is *sukha*."
>
> This consequence is avoided, however, because *sukha* is not simply the absence of pain. It is the experience of the absence of pain. Both a person who is *sukha* and a stone are without pain, but only a person without pain can experience their absence of pain. Hence a person, but not a stone, can be *sukha*.

To these [objections], [Maṇḍana] replies: *sukha*. *Sukha* is not just the cessation of pain, since there is a seeing of simultaneous pain and pleasure, [as in the case] of [a person] afflicted by heat, half of whose body is submerged in a cool pond.

> Maṇḍana begins with the first word of the verse – *sukha*. He replies to the Nyāya objections by pointing out that a person can experience *sukha* at the same time that they experience *duḥkha* (pain). Someone might feel *duḥkha* in the upper half of their body as a result of being burned – say, from the sun – while at the same time experiencing *sukha* in the lower half of their body, which is also burned, but which is submerged in cool water. If a person can experience *sukha* at the same time that they

experience *duḥkha*, however, then *sukha* is not the elimination of *duḥkha*, because the person who is *sukha* is not entirely without *duḥkha*.

[The Naiyāyikas might reply,] but it is also true that while there is pain in the half of the body not submerged, since [there is] an absence [of pain] in the other, [it is called] *sukha*.

The Naiyāyika seems to have a plausible response. The person is *sukha* in relation to the bottom half of their body, but not the top. The person simultaneously experiences *sukha* and *duḥkha*, but there is no *duḥkha* where there is *sukha*. Hence *sukha* can be the complete elimination of *duḥkha*.

[Maṇḍana replies:] then there is the [unwanted] consequence of [someone] being cooked in the hell in which people are cooked like the contents of a cooking pot being *sukha* on account of the absence of pain in another hell, and the [unwanted] consequence of the happiness of [a person] experiencing pain in one sense organ because there is the absence of pain in another sense organ.

Maṇḍana replies that if *sukha* and *duḥkha* are to be qualified as *sukha* or *duḥkha* in relation to some specific part of the body, then it is perfectly sensible to call a person who experiences a horrible earache *sukha*, so long as they do not have pain in their eyes. This seems absurd, however. If a person is *sukha*, then they cannot be experiencing excruciating *duḥkha*. They must be happy more generally. A person is called *sukha* when they are happy overall.

The two hells objection in this passage is less persuasive. The point seems to be that if *sukha* and *duḥkha* are always qualified in relation to some specific absence of pain, a person who is suffering in a specific hell might even be called *sukha*, just because they are without *duḥkha* in relation to some other hell. This is like saying, "sure you are suffering as a result of the death of a close friend, but you are nonetheless happy, because you are not suffering from the death of a parent." This is not consistent with the way the words *sukha* and *duḥkha* are typically used.

For this reason as well [pleasure is not just the absence of pain]: for [someone] without pain, there is the arising of an experienceable joy due to contact with a particular object. Also, wherever there is the cessation of pain, there is not also pleasure consisting in that alone, since there is the attaining of specific food and drink; for the cessation of pain is established by whatever food and drink.

There are additional reasons to reject the Naiyāyikas' analysis of *sukha*. First, sometimes a person is not in any pain at all, but feels *sukha* as a result of some pleasant object. I might be in no pain at all, but become happy as a result of eating ice cream, for example.

> Second, if *sukha* were nothing but the elimination of pain, then people would be completely impartial to which types of foods they ate, because any food, no matter how bland or positively repulsive, eliminates the pain of hunger. In fact, however, we see that people pursue specific types of food, and prefer the tasty to the bland. The best explanation of this is that the savory foods are more pleasing than the bland. Hence *sukha* is not simply the elimination of pain.

And it is not that [that is, *sukha* is not the cessation of pain], because there is a distinction [between levels of *sukha*]. For the distinction of that [that is, the levels of *sukha*], a distinction among means to that is required. Since, in regard to *sukha*, there is the possibility of an increase to the ultimate degree, there is a requirement of the ultimate means to that.

> As the food example demonstrates, there are different degrees of *sukha*. This is easily explained on the Vedāntin view: some objects produce greater pleasure than others. According to Maṇḍana, the Naiyāyikas cannot explain the degrees of *sukha*. If *sukha* is the elimination of pain, then one is either *sukha* or not.
>
> It might be thought that the Naiyāyika can reply that there are degrees of the elimination of pain – that a lower degree of *sukha* is achieved when some pain is eliminated, and that the ultimate level of *sukha* is achieved when all pain is eliminated.
>
> To this, presumably Maṇḍana would reply, as above, that a person cannot both be in pain and be *sukha*. If I have a broken arm that is causing me a great deal of pain, and I take an aspirin, which results in eliminating 20 percent of the pain, it seems strange to say that I am *sukha*. If I am not *sukha* in this case, however, then it is not clear how degrees of *sukha* can be explained on the Nyāya view.

As for [those who] think – and when there is no other pain to be eliminated, then, since desire has the nature of *duḥkha*, pleasure has the form of the destruction of that [that is, desire], [Maṇḍana replies:] in that case, however, someone without desire would not be possessed of *sukha*, [even] when enjoying a particular object [that is the source of pleasure]. But even the impartial person is pleased when there is contact with a pleasurable object.

> In order to avoid the objection that in some cases *sukha* arises even though there is no perceptible *duḥkha* to be eliminated, someone might reply that even in these cases, the person has a desire for the object, and the desire itself is painful, so long as it is not satisfied. So contrary to experiences, *duḥkha* is eliminated in these cases as well.
>
> Maṇḍana objects that the elimination of desire cannot explain all of those cases in which a person experiences *sukha* without first experiencing *duḥkha*. Sometimes a person who has no desire at all feels *sukha* as a result

of some pleasant object. I might not desire ice cream, but nonetheless feel *sukha* when I am handed an ice cream cone. This suggests that *sukha* might arise in the absence of both obvious *duḥkha* and unobvious *duḥkha* in the form of desire. Hence *sukha* is not merely the elimination of desire.

Perhaps this [is the case] – that for which there is a desire, that object alone pleases, not any other [object]. Hence objects are pleasing only by the elimination of desire. Otherwise the pleasure of one would be [the pleasure] of everyone. If, however, happiness is due to the elimination of desire, with regard to that which the desire of that person is pleased [by], the pleasure of that person is connected with that alone.

The Naiyāyika points out that there is a tight connection between what a person desires and what produces *sukha* for that person. This implies that the satisfaction of desire produces *sukha*.

If this were not the case, then the same things would be pleasing to everyone. If we say that a person is only pleased by what they desire, however, then there is a straightforward explanation for why some but not all people are pleased by fish, cilantro, dark chocolate, and so on. The explanation is that only some people desire these things. Those that desire them are pleased by them, those that do not desire them are not pleased by them.

If the satisfaction of desire produces *sukha*, then *sukha* is the elimination of desire. Since desire is painful, *sukha* is the elimination of *duḥkha*. The Naiyāyika continues,

With regard to that, even for someone [who is] desireless, from the enjoyment of specific objects, while there is a manifestation of desire, when there is the elimination of that desire [because it is satisfied by the object], there is *sukha* as a result of that.

The Naiyāyika explains that if this is right, then even the seemingly desireless person, in order to enjoy some object, must first have a desire, and then eliminate it. So if the seemingly desireless person enjoys a piece of chocolate, for example, it follows that a desire for chocolate arose and was satiated.

[Maṇḍana says,] that [view that pleasure is the elimination of desire] is also false. Since the enjoyments of objects do not necessarily [cause] the destruction of desire. For it is said, "Desire is never calmed by the enjoyment of desire" [*Manusmṛti* 2.94]. Likewise, [*Yogasūtrabhāṣya* 2.15 states,] "when there is repeated enjoyment, desires and the sensitivities of the senses grow."

In addition, it cannot be that the satisfaction of desire eliminates it, because, as many seminal texts say, satisfying desires only increases their strength. It may be that my desire for a morning coffee disappears when I drink coffee, but in the long run the desire is only strengthened by my repeated indulgence.

And the elimination of desire is from seeing the defect of the object [not from satisfying the object].

Desire is only eliminated by means of seeing the defect in that which is desired. If I see, for example, that coffee tends to make me jittery, that it maintains the uncomfortable craving with which I wake up every morning, that it is expensive, and so on, my desire for it might cease. It will not cease, however, simply by indulging in it. If desire does not cease by indulging in it, then the *sukha* that arises from getting what one wants cannot be explained by the elimination of desire, because the desire is not eliminated.

There seems to be an important ambiguity here. The Naiyāyika argues that whenever there is *sukha*, there is the elimination of *duḥkha* – sometimes in the form of desire. Hence *sukha* is the elimination of *duḥkha*. Maṇḍana objects that it is false that whenever there is *sukha*, there is the elimination of *duḥkha* – sometimes in the form of desire – by pointing out that the mere satisfaction of a desire does not eliminate desire permanently. Hence *sukha* is not the elimination of *duḥkha*, because *sukha* arises even when desires are eliminated only temporarily.

The Naiyāyika might simply reply, however, that when they claim that whenever there is *sukha*, there is the elimination of *duḥkha* – sometimes in the form of desire – they mean that whenever there is *sukha*, there is the elimination of *duḥkha*, albeit often only temporarily, in the form of desire. Hence *sukha* is the elimination of *duḥkha* – sometimes in the form of desire.

On this view, pleasure would be equivalent to enjoyment. And if the attainment of the desired object is the same, there would be no distinction of pleasure, because there would be no difference [in degrees] in the elimination of desire.

In addition, if, in these cases, *sukha* is the result of the elimination of the pain of desire by means of satisfying the desire, there is no explanation for the degrees of pleasure – it makes mere pleasure and full-blown enjoyment equivalent. If the elimination of desire produces pleasure, then there is only one level of pleasure – that which occurs when the desire is completely satisfied. If the desire is only partially satisfied, then the agent remains in pain and cannot be said to be *sukha*, as was argued above.

[The Naiyāyika replies:] Perhaps this [is the case] – when there is a high level of desire, when there is the elimination of that [intense desire], there is the erroneous conception of a superior *sukha*. In another case, it is not like this.

> The Naiyāyika argues that the experience of different levels of *sukha* is merely apparent. There really is only one degree of *sukha*. It seems as if some *sukha* is greater than others, but this is only because the desire that is eliminated by means of being satisfied is more intense, and thereby stands in greater contrast to the *sukha* that results from its satisfaction. In reality, however, the degrees of *sukha* are the same. The fact that the account of *sukha* as the elimination of desire cannot explain actual levels of *sukha* is not a genuine problem, then, since there are no actual degrees of *sukha*.

[Maṇḍana says:] But that is not the case [either]. An object that is attained by someone who strives for it out of an excess of desire is not as pleasing as an undesired object attained without effort. For the object that is attained from toil, a person is not pleased by it as they are by [that object which is] unexpectedly attained.

> This cannot be right either, however. The apparent difference in degrees of *sukha* is not explained by the intensity of the desire that is satisfied, because sometimes the *sukha* that arises as a result of the satisfaction of desire is not correlated with the desire's intensity. A person might be happier, for example, to unexpectedly win the lottery than to earn the same amount of money by hard work, motivated by a consuming desire for wealth. Yet the desire is more intense in the latter case, and hence ought – according to the Nyāya argument – to produce a greater apparent sensation of *sukha*.

And if happiness is only the absence of desire, then when there is pleasure when there is enjoyment of an undesired object, the states before and after would not be distinguished from the state of enjoyment.

> In cases like these, in which a person experiences pleasure as a result of attaining some undesired object, there is no explanation for the difference between the agent's states before, during, and after the undesired object is attained. If *sukha* is simply the absence of desire, then the agent should experience the same *sukha* before the undesired object is attained – because they do not desire it – and when it is attained – because they do not desire it – and after the desire is attained – because they do not desire it. This is not how things are, however. A person who attains some pleasurable but unsought end is happier when the end is attained than they were before it was attained.

Additionally, when there is the destruction of desire, the following state should not be different.

> In addition, if the Nyāya view is correct, and the *sukha* that one

> experiences on satisfying a desire is simply the elimination of the *duḥkha* of the unsatisfied desire, then the *sukha* should not dissipate in time, since the desire remains satisfied. Yet we see that the *sukha* that results from the attainment of some object does dissipate. Hence *sukha* is not merely the absence of pain.

If [one were to say] "in a state of enjoyment, there is a desire awakened and perished" [p. 3, line 1], then one is happy in the two states before and after. Otherwise [that is, in the state of enjoyment] one is pained. This leads to a contradiction of experience.

> Another possible response is that in those cases in which it does not seem that the agent desires some object that they later enjoy, a desire for the enjoyed object arises and perishes instantaneously at the moment of enjoyment, often without notice.
>
> Maṇḍana replies that if this is right, then the agent is *sukha* before and after the state of enjoyment, because there is no desire before it arises, and no desire once it perishes, but the agent is *duḥkha* at the moment at which the enjoyment of the object occurs, because a desire for the enjoyed object has arisen. Typically, however, the experience of enjoying either a desired object or a seemingly undesired object is not like this. The moment of enjoyment is one of *sukha*.

Additionally, the unattained object [which] wanders in one's memory awakens desire. [The object being] attained, it causes [the desire] to cease. If there is a state of aroused-ness [of desire] for an attained object, then the elimination [of desire] from that [attainment] would not occur.

> Typically, the desire for some object does not awaken and perish instantaneously just as the desire is satisfied. Instead, the agent has a memory in their mind that is the fundamental source of the desire that arises, and the desire is not satisfied until the desired object is attained. During this time, however, the agent does not necessarily feel pain.
>
> In addition, in some cases a desire persists even when the desired object is attained. Here too, however, the feeling of pain is not apparent.

And it is not the case that when there is *kāma* [satisfaction], there is *sukha*. Since it is seen that there is *duḥkha* for someone who suffers even with the enjoyment of [something] desired by a hundred wishes.

> It is false that wherever there is desire satisfaction, there is pleasure. It might be, for example, that a person looks forward to retiring for thirty years, only to become depressed soon after accomplishing this goal. Hence *sukha* cannot be the elimination of desire. If it were, there would be no counter-examples like this.

On the contrary, *kāma* is preceded by *sukha*, because it is seen in regard to that having the nature of that which has been experienced before.

> A present desire is explained by pleasure experienced in the past. As *Yogasūtrabhāṣya* 2.7 explains, a person has a memory of some past experience as pleasurable, and comes to desire some aspect of the past experience in the present. I remember coffee being pleasurable, and therefore desire coffee now.
>
> The point here is not that pleasure is not also a consequence of desire satisfaction. It is that if there is any inviolable law regarding the connection of desire and *sukha*, it is that *sukha* precedes desire, not that the satisfaction of desire produces *sukha*.

And that activity which is based on *kāma*, even with regard to some unexperienced [object] among things of a specific type, that [action] also is based on experience [of previous pleasure] in a previous birth. And as a certain desire of someone is based on a specific type, [having experienced the same type before,] likewise there is some pleasure for someone [for that particular type of thing]. There are no irregularities.

> In those cases where a person desires something that they have not experienced as pleasurable in this life, the desire is explained by an experience of the desired object as pleasurable in a previous life. The item that is desired in the present need not be identical with the object of experience in a previous life. It need only be an item of the same type as that experienced as pleasurable in a previous life. There are no exceptions to this rule: if an agent desires some item, they must have experienced an item of a similar type as pleasurable in the past. Hence this relationship between desire and *sukha* is exceptionless.

And also, some are pained even by the elimination of *kāma*, because there is an absence of the capacity for enjoyment of the object when that [desire] is absent.

> Another reason to believe that the elimination of desire does not inevitably produce *sukha* is that some people experience *duḥkha* when desire is eliminated. I realize now that I no longer desire to go sledding when it snows, and I sometimes feel sad that the hours of enjoyment I once experienced while sledding as a boy are now unavailable to me. Even if I did go sledding, it would not be very much fun. This demonstrates that the elimination of desire does not always produce *sukha*.

[*Pūrvapakṣin*;] then they are not [those whose] desires have ceased.

> The opponent might insist that in these cases, the desire has not really

ceased. The only way to explain sadness over not wanting to go sledding is that, at some level, the person does want to go sledding!

[Maṇḍana has said:] those whose desires have ceased towards objects are so [that is, they are desireless] because of the state of that [object] being unenjoyable for some reason.

Desires are eliminated as a result of seeing the faults in their objects.

[The *pūrvapakṣin* objects:] Why, then, are they [whose desires have ceased] pained [when desire ceases]?

If the person does not desire something because they see that it is not worth desiring, why would their lack of desire for this unworthy object produce *duḥkha*? If Maṇḍana is correct, and desires cease as a result of realizing the faults in the objects of desire, I should not feel sad as a result of not desiring to go sledding, because I see the overwhelming faults in sledding which make it an action not worth engaging in.

[Maṇḍana answers:] Because of the not attaining of the pleasure born of that [object] which had been formerly experienced [as pleasurable]. Just as those whose senses are afflicted by bile, and so on cease to have *kāma* for certain food and drink, likewise, with the cessation of *kāma*, they are tormented. [With regard to that,] there is no other reason than the cessation of the pleasure born from that [object which was] previously experienced.

Even if an agent realizes that some previously desired state of affairs has faults that make it not worth pursuing, they might still feel sadness as a result of no longer experiencing the pleasurable aspects of the previously desired state of affairs. A person might quit smoking, for example, and still miss smoking, even though they are convinced that smoking is a terrible habit.

So the rejection of the *sukha* known by everyone is illogical.

Everyone knows that there is positive *sukha*, apart from the elimination of pain in the form of desire or otherwise. To reduce *sukha* to the elimination of pain is implausible, because it contradicts common sense.

We see, however, that it [namely *sukha*,] is explained by you [as the elimination of pain] for the persuasion of people [who are] attached to *sukha*.

Analyzing *sukha* as the elimination of pain is simply a rhetorical tool to dissuade people from their obsession with *sukha*. If they believe that *sukha* is just the absence of *duḥkha*, they will be less attached to it. Your characterization of *sukha* as the absence of *duḥkha* is a pedagogical tool, and nothing more. You yourself do not really think that there is no positive pleasure distinct from the relief of pain.

Thus *sukha* is other than the elimination of *duḥkha*. And that is the primary meaning (*mukhyo 'rthaḥ*) of the word *ānanda*.

Maṇḍana concludes that *sukha* and *ānanda* refer to happiness primarily, and only secondarily to the elimination of *duḥkha*. Absent any convincing argument for reverting to a less literal reading, then, *śruti* states that *mokṣa* is bliss.

It is important to keep in mind here that while Maṇḍana has made a convincing case for the claim that *sukha* cannot be reduced to the elimination of *duḥkha*, this is not enough. He really must demonstrate that the translation of *sukha* as the elimination of pain in the present context is implausible.

One way to do this would be to show that the word *sukha* never refers to the elimination of pain. Maṇḍana has not made a compelling case for this stronger conclusion, however. Thus it is not yet clear that Maṇḍana's position is superior to the Nyāya view. In order to resolve this, a reply to the Nyāya arguments for reverting to a less literal reading of those passages that describe *mokṣa* as *sukha* is necessary. In what follows, Maṇḍana considers some of these arguments, and offers additional arguments for his position.

And with regard to that which is known by scripture, knowledge [that is] in accord with scripture is correct.

Śruti is the only authority on the nature of Brahman. Since *śruti* states that Brahman is bliss, Brahman is indeed bliss. It cannot be that a non-literal reading is justified by citing a contradiction with some other source – like *anumāna* (inference) – because only those sources that are in accord with *śruti* on this matter are correct.

And with regard to that, it is not [the case] that action [aimed at pleasure] is [necessarily] based on *rāga* (*na ca rāganibandhanā tatra*), for it is not the case that mere *icchā* (purpose) is *rāga* (*na hīcchāmātraṃ rāgaḥ*). *Rāga* is known as an attachment (*abhiniveśa*) to some non-existent quality brought about by ignorance.

The relationship between *rāga* and *icchā* is not entirely clear from Maṇḍana's explanation. Either the two classes are mutually exclusive – *rāga* is never *icchā* and vice versa – or the two classes overlap in some way. For this reason, my translation of *icchā* as 'purpose' is not yet clearly justified (see Śaṅkhapāṇi's subcommentary below).

Whatever their relationship to one another, the nature of the distinction between mere *icchā* and *rāga* is clear. *Rāga* is based on ignorance, and mere *icchā* is not. Hence there is a parallel between Maṇḍana's analysis of *rāga* here, and Vyāsa's analysis of *rāga* in the *Yogasūtrabhāṣya*. In both texts, *rāga* is based on *avidyā* (see Chapter 2 and Conclusion).

Indeed, the *prasāda* (equanimity), *abhiruci* (approval), [or] *abhīcchā* (purpose) of the mind arising from the clarity of the seeing of reality does not fall on the side of *rāga*.

Another difference between *rāga* and mere *icchā*, then, is that mere *icchā* is tranquil (see Chapter 6 for an analysis of this claim).

As the *udvega* (aversion) arising from the seeing of the unreality and valuelessness of *saṃsāra* [does not fall] on the side of *dveṣa* of that [*saṃsāra*].

Here Maṇḍana defends the distinction between mere *icchā* and *rāga* by pointing out that the Naiyāyika needs a similar distinction between *udvega* and *dveṣa*. The terminology becomes complicated here, because Uddyotakara simply denies that the motivational state he advocates is *dveṣa*. He does not say what it is. Vācaspati says that *vairāgya* motivates the desireless agent. If Maṇḍana understands the Nyāya position accurately, presumably *udvega* has the same referent as *vairāgya*, and mere *icchā* parallels *vairāgya*. Otherwise *udvega* refers to a broader category of mental states that includes (at least some) *dveṣa* (see Appendix ii and Chapter 6).

Maṇḍana also specifies that on the Nyāya account, the world of *saṃsāra* is without value. This implies that only that which is valuable is worth pursuing (see Chapter 2).

Otherwise [that is, if there were no distinction between *udvega* and *dveṣa*], although reality is beyond all pain, activity based on *dveṣa* to that [namely, the pain of *saṃsāra*], would have the consequence of *saṃsāra*.

If the Naiyāyika denies the distinction between *icchā* and *rāga*, then they must abandon the distinction between *udvega* and *dveṣa*. Without the latter distinction, however, their own account implies that acting to avoid the pain of *saṃsāra* is inevitably counter-productive, and on the Nyāya view, *mokṣa* is simply unattainable.

Śaṅkhapāṇi's subcommentary (on the immediately preceding) [p. 11, line 15]: For an ascetic whose *icchā* is *tapas* (the performance of austerities) is not called a *rāgin* (someone motivated by *rāga*) in the world.

There must be a distinction between *rāga* and some other motivational

> state – like mere *icchā* – because a renunciate performs *tapas*, but is not called a *rāgin*. If they are not called a *rāgin*, then we must understand their action to be motivated by something other than *rāga*.

What is that [namely, *rāga*]? [Maṇḍana says:] "[it is brought about by] *avidyā*." *Avidyā*, then, is the cognition of the true self with regard to that which is not the true self, the notion of the real with regard to what is unreal. Likewise, the wise say *rāga* to mean attachment (*abhiniveśa*) to the untranquil (*aśānta*) qualities of color, taste, and so on, brought about by that [namely *avidyā*]. This is the meaning [of the term *rāga*].

> Śaṅkhapāṇi cites both of the criteria that Maṇḍana mentions. *Rāga* is both based on *avidyā* and untranquil in some way. It is "attachment." An ascetic is not *rāga*, because an ascetic's motivations are neither based on ignorance nor restless.
>
> It is worth noting that Śaṅkhapāṇi's analysis of *avidyā* parallels Patañjali's analysis at *Yogasūtra* 2.5 (see Chapter 2).

This is said: Not all *icchā* is *rāga* (*na sarvaivecchā rāgaḥ*). Rather, [*rāga*] is an [*icchā*] that has a non-existent object.

> Śaṅkhapāṇi specifies here – unlike Maṇḍana – that *rāga* is a subset of *icchā*. Some *icchā* is *rāga*, but some is not. In order to capture this term and its relationship to *rāga* in English, it should be translated as something like 'purpose' or 'reason' (see Chapter 6). Hence Maṇḍana's claim that mere *icchā* is not *rāga* (*na hīcchāmātraṃ rāgaḥ*) amounts to the claim that mere purpose is not desire. In other words, to say that someone has a purpose in doing what they do does not entail that they have some desire. Śaṅkhapāṇi's claim that not all *icchā* is *rāga* (*na sarvaivecchā rāgaḥ*) amounts to the claim that not all purposes are desires (see Chapter 6 for a thorough analysis of the possible translations of *icchā*).

"*Prasāda* (equanimity), *abhiruci* (approval), and *abhīcchā* (purpose)" – this is an indication of synonymy.

> When Maṇḍana compares *icchā* to *prasāda, abhiruci*, and *abhīcchā*, he means to say that these terms are synonyms. To say that a person acts motivated by *icchā* is to say that they act motivated by tranquility, approval, and purpose.

That [mere *icchā*] [is known] by words of these sorts in the world, not by the word *rāga*. That is the meaning of the clarification. As [on] your [account], *dveṣa* is not mere *udvega* . . . Again, if mere *udvega* were *dveṣa*, then there would be no liberation on your [account] either . . . Thus [Maṇḍana] says the *icchā* for the true, eternal, unsurpassed bliss of *mokṣa* is not *rāga*.

Just as a person can act from *udvega* (or *vairāgya*) without acting on *dveṣa*, likewise a person can act from *icchā* without acting on *rāga*. Maṇḍana adopts the Nyāya strategy here. The advantage, however, is that *śruti* seems to support Maṇḍana's contention that *mokṣa* is blissful, and hence the object of *icchā*, rather than *udvega*.

Maṇḍana's commentary continued [p. 3, line 21]:
And also, to those who desire the highest excellence that has been seen, also a control of the senses is taught, consisting in the nature of renunciation of desire, and so on as a means. So here it will be.

Maṇḍana draws a parallel between advising the *mumukṣu* to eliminate *rāga* and advising someone who desires earthly goals, like kingship, to eliminate *rāga* for things other than kingship. Just as a *mumukṣu's rāga* for something like sex is counter-productive to the attainment of *mokṣa*, and hence ought to be eliminated, likewise the ambitious entrepreneur's desire to sleep in every morning is counter-productive to the attainment of wealth, and hence ought to be eliminated. To eliminate some desires so that others will be more easily satisfied is perfectly ordinary.

As I explain below in my elaboration of Śaṅkhapāṇi's commentary on this passage, at this point Maṇḍana reverts to calling the endorsed motivating state *rāga*, even though he has just drawn a distinction between mere *icchā* and *rāga*, and claimed that mere *icchā*, not *rāga*, motivates the successful *mumukṣu*. As Śaṅkhapāṇi explains, at this point Maṇḍana argues as if his opponent either does not comprehend or does not accept the distinction.

[The *pūrvapakṣin* objects:] and with regard to that, how is there a prohibition on attachment (*abhiniveśa*) towards an object other than the desired (*samīhita*) [object]?

Here the opponent asks, why is there a prohibition of just certain desires, rather than all desires, in the case of the person pursuing worldly ends?

[Maṇḍana replies:] because [in this case] there would be the [unwanted] consequence of no action [at all] if all [desires] were prohibited. Likewise, [in the case of the *mumukṣu*], there is a cessation of [any "desire"] other than the "desire" (*rāga*) for the highest happiness, even though it [that is, the highest happiness] may already be present. Thus it is said [in *Manusmṛti* 2.2]: "Essential desirefulness is not praiseworthy, but never does desirelessness exist here."

Here Maṇḍana seems to concede the point that without *rāga* no action is possible. I put the word "desire" in quotation marks, however, because Maṇḍana has just explained that the motivational state he advocates is not *rāga*. This translation is further supported by Śaṅkhapāṇi's commentary immediately below.

Maṇḍana's view, then, is that there is a distinction between *rāga* (desire) and mere *icchā* (purpose). When a person does something, it follows that they have a purpose. It does not follow, however, that they have a desire. *Rāga* is characterized by a lack of tranquility, and is based on false beliefs about the nature of reality. A mere *icchā*, in contrast, is tranquil and based on knowledge.

Śaṅkhapāṇi's subcommentary (on the immediately preceding) [p. 12, line 1]: Or else, let that [*icchā* for the bliss of *mokṣa*] be *rāga*.

> According to Śaṅkhapāṇi, Maṇḍana assumes that the *pūsrvapakṣin* either fails to notice or refuses to accept the distinction between *rāga* and mere *icchā*. This helps to make sense of the fact that Maṇḍana both insists that the pursuit of the bliss of *mokṣa* does not entail *rāga* and that the *mumukṣu* does indeed have *rāga* for the bliss of *mokṣa*. The thought is: "if you refuse to acknowledge the linguistic distinction between *icchā* and *rāga*, then forget it. Part of the point can be made without this distinction."

Even then, that [so-called *rāga* for the bliss of *mokṣa*] is not prohibited by the *śruti* on equanimity [*Bṛhadāraṇyaka Upaniṣad* 4.4.23], and so on. Rather, the *icchā* for the happiness of a perishable object less than that and opposed to that [is prohibited].

> If you insist that whatever state motivates the *mumukṣu* is *rāga*, then this *rāga* is unlike most *rāga*, in that it is tranquil. Since it is tranquil, it is not inconsistent with the injunction to equanimity, and hence does not preclude the attainment of *mokṣa*.

Notes

Preface

1 There are earlier verses that imply that one should eliminate desire. Kṛṣṇa mentions those with the nature of desire (*kāmātmānaḥ*) at 2.43, and describes them as ignorant (*avipaścitaḥ*). He also enjoins Arjuna to abandon attachment (*saṅgam*) (2.48). In at least one previous verse, Kṛṣṇa uses the phrase 'all desires' (*kāmān-sarvān*): "When a person abandons all desires that enter the mind, O Arjuna, and is satisfied with the true self, in the true self alone, that person is called 'established in wisdom' " (*prajahāti yadā kāmān sarvān pārtha manogatān / ātmanyevātmānā tuṣṭaḥ sthitaprajñastaducyate //*) (2.55, Sadhale 1985a: 214, lines 2–3).

2 *vihāya kāmān yaḥ sarvān pumāṃścarati nissprhaḥ /*
nirmamo nirahaṅkāraḥ sa śāntimadhigacchati //
eṣā brāhmī sthitiḥ pārtha naināṃ prāpya vimuhyati /
stitvā 'syāmantakāle 'pi brahmanirvāṇamṛcchati //

3 I use the word 'entail' here and throughout rather loosely (see Chapter 1).

Introduction

1 For a study of desire in Early Buddhism, see Webster (2005). For a more in-depth analysis of the role of desire in action in Dharmakīrti, see Taber (forthcoming).

2 See, for example, *Bṛhadāraṇyaka Upaniṣad* 4.4.6, *Kaṭha Upaniṣad* 2.20 and 6.14, *Śvetāśvatara Upaniṣad* 3.20, *Muṇḍaka Upaniṣad* 3.2.1 and *Taittirīya Upaniṣad* 2.8 (Olivelle 1998).

3 *vihāya kāmān yaḥ sarvān pumāṃścarati nissprhaḥ /*
nirmamo nirahaṅkāraḥ sa śāntimadhigacchati //
eṣā brāhmī sthitiḥ pārtha naināṃ prāpya vimuhyati /
stitvā 'syāmantakāle 'pi brahmanirvāṇamṛcchati //

4 This phrase is never mentioned in the *Gītā* itself. Kṛṣṇa advises Arjuna to act without desire (*pumāṅścarati nissprhaḥ*) (2.71, Sadhale 1985a: 242, line 9), eliminate all desire (*prajahāti yadā kāmān sarvān*) (2.55, Sadhale 1985a: 214, line 2), and so on, but he never uses this famous phrase. Śaṇkara uses the term *niṣkāma* at *Gītābhāṣya* 2.45: "Let you, O Arjuna, be without the *guṇas*. Let you be desireless" (*tvaṃ tu nistraiguṇyo bhava arjuna niṣkāmo bhavet*) (Sadhale 1985a: 184, lines 2–3).

1 Four interpretations of desireless action

1 I use the word 'entailment' somewhat loosely here. Taken strictly, entailment is a relationship between propositions. The entailment might be redescribed as the entailment between the claim 'X acts' and the claim 'X has some desire', but this seems unnecessary.

2 See, for example, S. Radhakrishnan (1911, see p. 8), A. Chakrabarti (1988: 329), A. Rambachan (1993: 5), D. Killingley (1997: 74), and Tara Chatterjea (2002: 128). M. M. Agrawal argues: "if human life is action-based, and actions have their source, fundamentally in desires, then, *prima facie*, a plea for non-attachment appears to be a recommendation for inaction" (Agrawal 1982: 39). R. C. Zaehner: "Now [Arjuna] is asked to give up 'desire' though this is inseparable from the human condition itself" (Zaehner 1969: 150).

3 *kāmātmatā na praśāstā na caivehāstyakāmatā/kāmyo hi vedādhigamaḥ karmayogaśca vaidikaḥ //* See Appendix i. This verse seems to allude to *Gītā* 2.43: "Those [who have] the nature of desire (*kāmātmānaḥ*), whose highest goal is heaven" (*kāmātmānaḥ svargaparā janmakarmaphalapradām / kriyāviśeṣabahulāṃ bhogaiśvaryagatiṃ prati //*) (Sadhale 1985a: 177, lines 33–34).

4 In his commentary to *Gītā* 2.48 and 2.55, Śaṅkara cites this objection (see Chapter 2, this volume). Additionally, both the Vedāntin opponent in the *Nyāyasūtra* (see Appendix iii) and Maṇḍana's opponent in the *Brahmasiddhi* (see n. 7 below) cite this objection.

5 The Brahmo Samaj (the Society of Brahman) was a Hindu reform movement, founded by Ram Mohan Roy in 1828. It emphasized devotion to the *Upaniṣadic* conception of God, and denied the importance of a wide range of Hindu customs, like "image worship, pilgrimage, festivals, and the rules of caste" (Kingsley 1993: 22).

6 Mikel Burley mentions the principle of charity, and cites Quine, in the introduction to his book *Classical Sāṃkhya and Yoga: An Indian Metaphysics of Experience* (Burley 2007: 7–8), but does not relate it to *lakṣanā* in the Indian traditions.

7 *mukhyāsaṃbhave gauṇamaśrīyate /* See also Chapter 6 and Appendix ii, this volume. Maṇḍanamiśra considers an objection of this kind to the claim that the *Upaniṣads* are authoritative: "Others think that since, when there is a grasping of the [literal] meaning of what is heard (*śruta*), there is a contradiction of the *vidhis* (injunctions) [of *śāstra*], and since there is a contradiction with perception, and so on, they are [to be taken] in [their] secondary (*upacaritārtha*) meaning only" (*anye tu karmavidhivirodhāt pratyakṣa – ādivirodhācca śrutārthaparigrahe upacaritārthānmanyante*) (Vacaspati and Sastri 1984: 1, lines 10–11; see Appendix iii, this volume).

8 The rules governing the application of this principle are complex. Nonetheless, Prasad's interpretation seems to violate it quite explicitly. See my paper, "The Use of *Lakṣanā* in Indian Exegesis" (Framarin 2008d).

9 Cf. "This ideal of disinterested action is misconceived when it is confused with motiveless action. A rational being cannot act without motives" (Radhakrishnan 1914: 175).

10 The thought seems to be that there is no justification for adopting an intentional explanation when a causal explanation is adequate. See Dennett (1998: 3–23).

11 The phenomenon of phototropism is explained by unequal growth in the plant. The side of the plant that is exposed to light grows less quickly.

12 See *Gītā*, chapters 13 and 14 in particular.

13 There is an important difference between intentions and predictions. Anscombe points out that

> [t]he distinction between an expression of intention and a prediction is generally appealed to as something intuitively clear. 'I am going to be sick' is usually a prediction; 'I am going to take a walk' usually an expression of intention.
>
> (Anscombe 1976: 2)

One can make a prediction without expressing an intention, and one can express an intention without expressing a prediction. I intend to be home by seven, but I predict that I will be late.

14 Just as the claim that all desires should be eliminated can be understood non-literally as the claim that only some desires should be eliminated (see pp. 14–15), likewise the claim that all purposes should be eliminated can be understood to mean that only some purposes – and not necessarily selfish purposes – should be eliminated. As I argued in the last section, the principle of charity seems to require that we not read the *Gītā* to say that action should be done without a purpose.

15 *prakṛteḥ kriyamāṇāni guṇaiḥ karmāṇi sarvaśaḥ / ahaṃkāravimūḍhātmā kartāham iti manyate // tattvavit tu mahābāho guṇakarmavibhāgayoḥ / guṇā guṇesu vartanta iti matvā na sajjate //* (Brodbeck's transliteration).

16 Desire and attachment are not necessarily equivalent, but Brodbeck, like many others, seems to take both words as roughly synonymous.

17 Alternatively, the verse might mean that when one eliminates the false belief, one eliminates attachment. That is, the two are distinct, but closely related.

18 *yadi sarvo janturātmanaḥ prakṛtisadṛśameva ceṣṭate na ca prakṛtiśūnyaḥ kaścidasti tataḥ puruṣakārasya viṣayānupapatteḥ śāstrānarthakyaprāptauvidaṃ ucyate . . .*

19 *tāveva jñānayogāya yatamānaṃ niyamitasarvendriyaṃ svavaśe kṛtvā prasahya svakāryeṣu niyojayataḥ /*

20 *Gītā* 13.6, for example, reads, "desire (*icchā*), aversion, pleasure, pain, the whole [empirical self], [*buddhi's*] consciousness, determination, this, in brief, is the field with its modifications described." *icchā dveṣaḥ sukhaṃ duḥkhaṃ saṅghātaścetanā dhṛtiḥ / etat kṣetraṃ samāsena savikāramudāhṛtam //* (Sadhale 1985c: 34, lines 1–2).

21 It is also false that "[t]he principle of intentionality resides within what the *Sāṃkhya-Kārikā* calls *puruṣa*." *Puruṣa* is characterized as an inactive witness. It neither does nor intends to do anything.

22 See n. 21 above.

23 Herbert Fingarette mentions both the *guṇas* and *karma* as causes of action. He then points out that

> [o]n the other hand, the existence of some genuine initiative on Arjuna's part is strongly suggested by the fact that the central dramatic point of the Gita narrative is for Krishna to persuade Arjuna to change his purpose and his conduct.
>
> (Fingarette 2004: 94)

He takes this to imply that the *Gītā* cannot be understood as entirely deterministic. I strongly recommend this paper. Fingarette's analysis of the apparent free will problem in the *Gītā* is insightful.

Mathur also mentions the tension between determinism and free will:

> [T]he Gita blurs the distinction between reflex and instinctive behavioral *reaction* on the one hand, and a willed intentional *action* on the other . . . [The] intentionality of an active self are undermined . . . [Yet Kṛṣṇa] attempts to reason out Arjuna from the mood of despondency and despair, and rouse him to manly *action*.
>
> (Mathur 1974: 43)

24 Even if Brodbeck is correct, and the moral injunctions of the *Gītā* are a red herring, it is still worthwhile to consider the theory of motivation that the *Gītā* feigns to endorse!

25 Radhakrishnan, for example, says, "[a] rational life is not a life of no desire, but a life of regulated desire" (Radhakrishnan 1914: 171). Lash argues that the *Gītā* advocates the "purification" of desire, rather than its elimination (Lash 1997).

26 See chapters 2 and 7 (this volume) for a summary and analysis of Hume's position.
27 I consider this debate in its contemporary form in some detail in Chapter 7.
28 This is not to say that *Gītā's* position is like Kant's, as Radhakrishnan and others argue. One big difference is that there is no suggestion in the *Gītā* that the right action can be determined by reason alone.
29 Desire is not analytically entailed by action unless, of course, one takes 'desire' and 'purpose' as synonyms. See pp. 17–18.
30 One way that analytic truth is often explained, at least at an introductory level, is to say that a truth's analyticity is not determined by means of empirical investigation. I do not need to interview 1000 bachelors to know that they are all unmarried men. Some analytic truths, however, do require investigation. That Hesperus is Phosphorus, for example, is an analytic truth, but also the result of empirical investigation. It is an a posteriori analytic truth (see Kripke 1980). These kinds of analytic truths are not obvious in the way that would require an interpreter to assume from the outset that a text is consistent with them.
31 For a further analysis of the distinction between these two senses of desire, see Chapter 5, where I clarify the distinction between a desire and an intention.
32 See "A second justification for the Some Desires Interpretation", pp. 21–22.
33 Henceforth, I use the word 'desire' to refer to desires proper.
34 In his commentary to 2.55, Śaṅkara explains that the phrase *kāmān sarvān* (all desires) means the "complete abandonment" (*prakareṇa jahāti*) of "all various desires" (*samastān kāmānicchābhedān*) (Sadhale 1985a: 214, lines 8–9). Rāmānuja also uses the word *sarva* to elaborate this verse (see Chapter 3, this volume).
35 *saṅkalpaprabhavān kāmāṃstyaktvā sarvānaśeṣataḥ* /.
36 *yogaścittavṛttinirodhaḥ* //.
37 *sarvaśabdāgrahaṇāt saṃprajñāto 'pi yoga ityā 'khyāyate* . . .
38 These two words are not synonyms in the *Gītā*. The *Gītā* explains in verse 2.62 that *saṅga* precedes, and typically produces *kāma*. "For a person [who] meditates on sense objects, *saṅga* towards [those objects] arises. From *saṅga, kāma* arises. From *kāma, krodha* (anger). (*dhyāyato viṣayān puṃsaḥ saṅgasteṣūpajāyate* / *saṅgātsañjāyate kāmaḥ kāmātkrodho 'bhijāyate* //)" (Sadhale 1985a: 226, lines 38–39). In a recent conversation, Arindam Chakrabarti suggested that the word *saṅga* be translated as something like "repeated contact." I remember a friend of mine in college who did not smoke, but who, after three or four months of hanging around with us smokers, eventually picked up the habit. The *saṅga* over the course of these months undoubtedly produced *kāma*.
39 It is not always clear from the *Gītā* itself how these words relate to *kāma*. The words *rāga* and *dveṣa* are typically paired (2.64, 3.34, 18.23, 18.51), and tend to refer to desires to attain and desires to avoid, respectively (see Chapter 2). They are often translated as 'desire' and 'aversion'. *Icchā* and *dveṣa* are also paired (7.27), which suggests that *icchā* and *rāga* are synonymous. *Spṛha* means intense desire or longing, and so probably refers to only a subset of *kāma*.
40 It is worth noting that the Indian tradition draws a distinction between desire (*cikīrṣā*) and purpose (*pravṛtti* – the "will to do") as well. The *Manusmṛti* draws the same distinction in terms of *kāma* or *icchā* and *adhyavasāya* (see Chapter 5, this volume). Hence the apparent equivocation by Teschner and others is problematic in this framework as well.
41 I recently asked Mohanty about the source of this model. He said that it comes from an old, well-known Sanskrit phrase, which no one seems able to trace to its origin.
42 Although see *Gītā* 18.18.

2 Desireless action in the *Yogasūtra*

1 When I say that a desire must play a necessary role in motivating action, I mean to say that there is some role that must be played by some desire or other, and that a certain desire plays that necessary role. I do not mean to say that some specific desire is necessary. It might be, for example, that in order to go to the café, some desire must play a necessary role in motivating my action, and that the desire to have a coffee might play this necessary role. It does not follow, however, that my desire to have a coffee is a necessary condition of my going to the café, just because some other desire – like the desire to visit my friend who works at the café – might play the necessary role.

2 My distinction between desires for a means and desires for an end, then, parallels T. Nagel's distinction between motivated and unmotivated desires (Nagel 1970: 29).

3 Although, even in this case, it may be that a person desires to avoid pain because it is counter-productive to some further end. A weightlifter, for example, might ordinarily be almost oblivious to the pain of their workout. When they get to the point at which further pain is detrimental, however, they may desire to avoid pain as a means to being better prepared to work out the following day.

4 A desire to do corresponds to what Alfred R. Mele calls 'action desires' (Mele 2003: 16).

5 *anena karmaṇedamiṣṭhaṃ phalaṃ sādhyata ityevaṃviṣayā buddhiḥ saṅkalpaḥ* /.

6 *cikīrṣā kṛtisādhyatvaprakārecchā ca yā bhavet / taddhetuḥ kṛtisādhyeṣṭasādhanatvamatir bhavet //*.

7 The primary difference is that Viśvanātha Nyāya-Pañcānana claims that two distinct beliefs are required: the belief that an action of the agent is a means to the desired end, and the belief that the action itself is possible. Kullūkabhaṭṭa either counts these two beliefs as a single belief, or denies – like the Mīmāṃsakas – that a belief in the possibility of the action is an additional requirement.

8 In Chapter 5 I consider the possibility that no desires for ends are permissible. In Chapter 6 I consider the possibility that no desires for ends or means are permissible.

9 S. S. Raghavachar, for example, attributes this view to Rāmānuja (Raghavachar 1998: 16–17). S. Tattvabhushan says, "we find Krishna appealing at first to Arjuna's lower motives in trying to induce him to fight. He appeals successively to his pupil's (1) desire for heaven, (2) desire for power, and (3) desire for fame" (Tattvabhushan 1912: 294). R. Minor also makes this point (1982: 33).

10 This analysis seems supported by the common distinction between *preyas* – that which is desired – and *śreyas* – that which is valuable. *Kathopaniṣad* 2.1–2, for example, reads:

> The good is one thing, the gratifying is quite another;
> their goals are different, both bind a man.
> Good things await him who picks the good;
> by choosing the gratifying, one misses one's goal.
>
> Both the good and the gratifying
> present themselves to a man;
> The wise assess them, not their difference;
> and choose the good over the gratifying;
> But the fool chooses the gratifying
> rather than what is beneficial.
>
> (Olivelle 1998: 69)

This passage implies, however, that even the pursuit of what is valuable might bind the agent to *saṃsāra*.

11 See Chapter 3 for a further analysis of the value of desires for means, and so on.
12 Smith uses the phrase 'fully rational' to describe a person who (1) has no false beliefs, (2) has all relevant true beliefs, and (3) deliberates correctly (Smith 1994: 156).
13 Citing D. Parfit (1984), Smith points out that there are counter-examples to this analysis of value (Smith 1994: 149). It might be, for example, that it is valuable that I act spontaneously, but that my desire to act spontaneously is an obstacle to doing so. Since these kinds of counter-examples are obscure, and since in the end I do not adopt this analysis of value without qualification, I ignore this objection in what follows.
14 See n. 13 above.
15 The words *rāga* and *dveṣa* are typically translated as 'desire' and 'aversion' respectively.
16 *sukhānuśayī rāgaḥ* //.
17 *duḥkhānuśayī dveṣaḥ* //.
18 *sukhābhijñasya sukhānusmṛtipūrvaḥ sukhe tatsādhane vā yo gardhastṛṣṇā lobhaḥ sa rāga iti* //.
19 *duḥkhābhijñasya duḥkhānusmṛtipūrvo duḥkhe tatsādhane vā yaḥ pratigho manyur-jighāṃsā krodhaḥ sa dveṣa iti* //.
20 This analysis of *rāga* and *dveṣa* is widely accepted throughout the Indian traditions. As I argue in Chapter 6, the distinction between *rāga* and *dveṣa* is central to the debate between the Naiyāyikas and Vedāntins over which types of desires are permissible. In the *Brahmasiddhi*, Maṇḍanamiśra's explanation of the genesis of *rāga* closely parallels Vyāsa's (see Chapter 6 and Appendix iii).
21 *avidyā 'smitārāgadveṣābhiniveśāḥ pañca kleśāḥ* /.
22 *kleśā iti / pañcaviparyyayā ityarthaḥ te syandamānā guṇādhikāraṃ draḍhayanti pariṇāmamavasthāppayanti kāryyakāraṇastrota unnamayanti parasparānugraha-tantrībhṣya karmvipākaṃ cābhinirharanti iti* //.
23 See, for example, *Yogasūtra* 4.34 and *Yogasūtrabhāṣya* 1.16. The latter is cited below.
24 *avidyā kṣetramuttareṣāṃ*.
25 *evāmī kleśā avidyābhedāḥ kasmāt? sarveṣvavidyaivābhiplavate yadavidyā vastvākā-ryyate tadevānuśerate kleśāḥ, viparyyāsapratyayakāle upalabhyante, kṣīyamāṇāṃ cāvidyāmanu kṣīyanta iti* //.
26 Maṇḍanamiśra also claims that *rāga*, which is counter-productive to the attainment of *mokṣa*, is that based on false beliefs (see Chapter 6 and Appendix iii).
27 *dṛṣṭānuśravikaviṣayavitṛṣṇasya vaśīkārasaṃjñā vairāgyam* //.
28 *tat paraṃ puruṣakhyāterguṇavaitṛṣṇyām* //.
29 J. H. Woods translates *anābhoga* as "the absence of non-experience" (Woods 2003: 36). The word can also mean "non-enjoyment," however.
30 *striyo 'nnapānamaiśvaryamitidṛṣṭaviṣayavitṛṣṇasya svargavaidehyaprakṛtilayatva – prāptāvānuśravikaviṣaye vitṛṣṇasya divyādivyaviṣayasaṃprayoge 'pi cittasya viṣaya-doṣadarśinaḥ prasaṅnkhyānabalād anābhogātmikā heyopādeyaśūnyā vaśīkārasañjñā vairāgyam* //.
31 Cf. *Gītā* 2.52: "When your discrimination will pass completely across the heap of confusion, then you will go to impartiality with the heard and the to-be-heard" (*yadā te mohakalilaṃ buddhirvyatitariṣyati / tadā gantāsi nirvedaṃ śrotavyasya śrutasya ca* //) (Sadhale 1985a: 207, lines 2–3).
32 A. Sharma makes this point in the context of the *Gītā*.

> Let us consider, for instance, the prospect of going to heaven held out by Kṛṣṇa to Arjuna should Arjuna fall in battle fighting his enemies. From a Vedāntin point of view, which advocates liberation from the cycle of *saṃsāra*,

this can hardly be considered a worthwhile goal as it keeps one bound to the cycle of *saṃsāra*.

(Sharma 1985: 190)

33 *dṛṣṭānuśravikaviṣayadoṣadarśī viraktaḥ puruṣadarśanābhyāsāttatchuddhipra – vivekāpyāyitabuddhirguṇebhyo vyaktāvyaktadharmakebhyo virakta iti tad dvayaṃ vairāgyaṃ tatra yaduttara tajjñānaprasādamātraṃ yasyodaye pratyuditakhyātirevammanyate prāptaṃ prāpaṇīyaṃ kṣīṇāḥ kṣetavyāḥ kleśāḥ chinnaḥ śliṣṭaparvā bhavasaṃkramo yasya – avicchedājjanitvā mriyate mṛtvā ca jāyate iti jñānasyaiva parā kāṣṭā vairāgyam etasyaiva hi nāntarīyakaṃ kaivalyamiti //.*

34 *kleśakarmavipākāśayairaparāmṛṣṭaḥ puruṣaviśeṣa īśvaraḥ //.*

35 *tatra niratiśayaṃ sarvajñabījam //.*

36 *pūrveṣāmapi guruḥ kālenānavacchedāt //.*

37 *tasyātmānugrahābhāve 'pi bhūtānugrahaḥ prayojanaṃ jñānadharmopadeśena kalpapralayamahāpralayeṣu saṃsāriṇah puruṣānuddhariṣyāmīti tathā coktam ādividvān nirmāṇacittamadhiṣṭhāya kāruṇyādbhagavān paramarṣirāsuraye jijñāsamānāya tantraṃ provāca iti //.*

38 An alternative interpretation is that Vyāsa purposefully uses the word *prayojana* rather than *rāga* or some other word that is normally translated as 'desire' in order to draw a distinction between desire and some other mental state that is capable of motivating action (see Chapter 6).

3 The desire for *Mokṣa*

1 *atha kena prayukto 'yaṃ pāpaṃ carati pūruṣaḥ /.*

2 *kāma eṣa krodha eṣa rajoguṇasamudbhavaḥ / mahāśano mahāpāpmā viddhyenamiha vāiriṇam // dhūmenā 'vriyate vahniryathā 'darśo malena ca / yatholbenāvṛto garbhas tathā tenedam āvṛtam // āvṛtaṃ jñānam etena jñānino nityavairiṇā / kāmarūpeṇa kāunteya duṣpūrelānalena ca //.*

3 *tatra niratiśayaṃ sarvajñabījam //.*

4 *na me pārthāsti kartavyaṃ triṣu lokeṣu kiñcana / nānavāptamavāptavyaṃ varta eva ca karmaṇi // yadi hyahaṃ na varteya jātu karmaṇyatandritaḥ / mama vartmānuvartante manuṣyāḥ pārtha sarvaśaḥ //.*

5 *utsīdeyurime lokā na kuryāṃ karma cedaham / saṅkarasya ca kartā syāmupahanyāmimāḥ prajāḥ //.*

6 *saktāḥ karmaṇyavidvāṃso yathā kurvanti bhārata / kuryād vidvāṃstathā 'saktaścikīrṣurlokasaṅgraham // . . . lokasaḍgrahamev / āpi saṃpaśyankartumarhasi //.*

7 *traiguṇyaviṣayā vedā nistraiguṇyo bhavārjuna /.*

8 *nirdvandvo nityasattvastho niryogakṣema ātmavān //.*

9 It at least seems that if a person attains either God or the true self, they attain *mokṣa* as well, and vice versa.

10 *bāhyasparśeṣvasaktātmā vindatyātmani yatsukham / sa brahmayogayuktātmā sukhamakṣayamaśnute // yo 'ntaḥsukho 'ntarārāmastathā 'ntarjyotireva yaḥ / sa yogī brahmanirvāṇaṃ brahmabhūto 'dhigacchati //.*

11 *prajahāti yadā kāmān sarvān pārtha manogatān / ātmanyevātmanā tuṣṭaḥ sthitaprajñastadocyate //.*

12 Here we can see the same basic idea that is still current – if an agent has no desire, intentional action is impossible.

13 *yadi karmaphalaprayuktena na kartavyaṃ karma kathaṃ tarhi kartavyaṃ /.* Again, the objection implies that desireless action is a contradiction.

14 *karmāṇi kevalaṃ īśvarārthaṃ tatrāpi īśvaro me tuṣyatu iti saṅgaṃ tyaktvā dhanañjaya /.*

15 *ātmanyevātmanā manasā ātmaikāvalambanena tuṣṭastena toṣeṇa tadvyatiriktān sarvānmanogatān kāmān yadā prakarṣeṇa jahāti tadā 'yaṃ sthitaprajña ityucyate /.*

16 *Gītā* 7.14 seems to make this point in a more straightforward way. It reads, "this *māyā* of mine, produced by the *guṇas*, is indeed divine" (*daivī hyeṣā guṇamayī mama māyā* . . .) (Sadhale 1985b: 28, line 9).
17 Nelson repeats the claim in his paper on Advaita: "It is the self (*ātman*) that is important, not nature" (Nelson 2000: 140).
18 *api cedasi pāpebhyaḥ sarvebhyaḥ pāpakṛttamaḥ / sarvaṃ jñānaplavenāiva vṛjinaṃ santariṣyasi //.*
19 *śraddhāvaṃ labhate jñānaṃ tatparaḥ saṃyatendriyaḥ / jñānaṃ labdhvā parāṃ śāntimacireṇādhigacchati //.*
20 *sannyāsaḥ karmayogaśca niśśreyasakarāvubhau / tayostu karmasannyāsāt karmayogo viśiṣyate //.*
21 *dharmyāddhi yuddhācchreyo 'anyat kṣatriyasya na vidyate //.*
22 Even if one were to press this point, and insist that according to Advaita nothing in the world relates in any way to whether or not one attains *mokṣa* – this kind of view is implicit in the second quotation from Basant K. Lal below – this is certainly not the case for Rāmānuja and others.
23 This is also D. C. Mathur's view.

> The ideal of lokasamgraha is held in high esteem and Krishna appeals to Arjuna to act in its name. (III.20). Its doctrine of Niskama-Karma or disinterested action can be understood only in the light of the *ultimate* end which is conceived as Moksa.
>
> (Mathur 1974: 34)

24 To be fair, Nelson titles a section of his paper "The Denial of Intrinsic Worth," which leaves open the possibility that states of affairs other than *mokṣa* have instrumental value on his view. Nelson never says this explicitly, however, and characterizes all earthly matters as one-sidedly negative and to be avoided. He makes no case for the instrumental value of anything.
25 In the same chapter, Chatterjea clarifies that "[a]ltruistic trends . . . are not intrinsically valuable" (Chatterjea 2002: 147).
26 *niryogakṣemaḥ ātmasvarū patatprāptyupāyabahirbhū tānāmarthānāṃ yogaṃ paripālanaṃ prāptānāṃ ca kṣemaṃ parityajya ātmavān bhava.*
27 See n. 34 below.
28 See Framarin (unpublished).
29 See Lal (1986), for example. Roy W. Perrett cites this as a standard interpretation and rejects it (Perrett 1993: 92–96).
30 This seems to be the sense behind the common claim that the *Gītā* considers the liberated person to be "beyond good and evil." See, for example, Nelson (2000: 144–145).
31 This objection parallels Socrates' objection in the *Euthyphro*.
32 Although see my "The Value of Animals in Hinduism" (unpublished) for a careful analysis of this position.
33 Perrett also argues that a rights-based argument can be extracted from the Indian traditions, according to which any being that is a subject-of-a-life – in the sense that Tom Regan outlines (1983) – is inherently valuable (Perrett 1993: 91).
34 I argue that it must be that something other than *mokṣa* is intrinsically valuable. From this it does not follow that the states of affairs that lead to *mokṣa* are themselves intrinsically valuable, as I assume above. It may also be that the value of these states of affairs is derived from the intrinsic value of some other state of affairs besides *mokṣa*. The problem with this alternative is that there is no obvious candidate for what the additional state of affairs might be. Even if the value of these states of affairs were derived from the intrinsic value of some state of affairs other than *mokṣa*, desires for that intrinsically valuable state of affairs might be permissible.

35 See, for example, Fort and Mumme (1998) and Framarin (forthcoming).
36 Feinberg argues that the first premise of this argument – that when a person gets what they want, they feel pleasure – is dubious. Maṇḍana also considers this claim and rejects it (see Appendix iii).

4 Unselfish desires

1 S. Radhakrishnan (1914: 174), Ian Whicher (1998: 97 and 104) and D. C. Mathur (1974: 43) accept this view. M. M. Agrawal says, "the *Gītā* is prohibiting . . . the 'motive of self' " (Agrawal 1982: 24).
2 Another point worth noting here is that throughout this chapter I talk about self-interest, whereas Williams defines a selfish desire in terms of "I content." The merit of Williams' criteria is that they allow for cases in which an agent acts selfishly even though she knows it is not in her self-interest (as when someone smokes). As a matter of convenience I use 'self-interest' in what follows, but not because I have failed to see these kinds of counter-examples.
3 – or the liberation seeker.
4 *vihāya kāmān yaḥ sarvān pumāṃścarati nisspṛhaḥ / nirmamo nirahaṅkāraḥ sa śāntimadhigachati //.*
5 *mayi sarvāṇī karmāṇī sannyasyādhyātmacetasā / nirāśīrnirmamo bhūtvā yudhhyasva vigatajvaraḥ //.*
6 *nirmamaḥ* and *nirahaṅkāraḥ* are in the nominative case. *Nirmama* and *nirahaṅkāra* are without case endings.
7 According to Rāmānuja, one cannot be one without the other. See pp. 65–66.
8 *anātmani dehe ātābhimānarahitaḥ.*
9 *nirmamaḥ sarveṣvanātmīyeṣvātmīyabuddhirahitaḥ* . . . The natural assumption that *nirahaṅkāra* is epistemological, and that *nirmama* is practical, then, is not right.
10 *ahaṅkāro nāma anahamarthe prakṛtavahamityabhimānaḥ.*
11 *nirgatāhampratyayaḥ /.*
12 *nirahaṅkāraḥ vidyāvatvādinimittātmasambhāvanārahita /.*
13 *dehajīvanamātre 'pi nirgatamamabhāvo nirmamo.*
14 Another issue here is whether it is a mistake for the sage to identify with a particular *ātman* or *puruṣa*. This is the view of the Advaita Vedāntins (like Śaṅkara), but not most others. In this chapter this further complication is avoided, and unselfishness has to do with self-interest or excessive self-interest where 'self' refers to the empirical self.
15 *sa ātmānaṃ dṛṣṭvā śāntimadhigacchati //.*
16 *mama idaṃ iti abhiniveśavarjitaḥ.*
17 These kinds of counter-factual considerations allow us to make sense of selfishness and unselfishness in solitude.
18 Of all the systems, the one that seems to come closest to saying this sort of thing is the Advaita Vedāntins, according to whom the empirical self is entirely illusory. One might conclude from this that the empirical self is entirely without value, and that therefore no self-interest is justified (in the sense of the interest of the empirical self). This cannot be right, however, because the empirical selves of others are entirely illusory as well, yet they are not entirely without value. That the Advaita Vedāntins deny the more extreme of the two views under consideration is well supported by Śaṇkara's commentary to *Gītā* 2.71. There he says that the saint does not cling to (that is, does not excessively desire) the preservation of his body and life, and that any efforts that have to do with himself aim at basic sustenance (see p. 69).
19 *nātyaśnatastu yogo 'sti na cāikāntamanaśnataḥ / na cātisvapnaśīlasya jāgrato nāiva cārjuna // yuktāhāravihārasya yuktaceṣṭasya karmasu / yuktasvapnāvabodhasya yogo bhavati duḥkhahā //.*

20 It may be possible to get around some of these problems by saying that there is something valuable about the state of affairs in which an unliberated agent helps the liberated, or the liberated helps the unliberated, even if neither life is valuable in itself. I think the most difficult example to account for, however, is the one in which one liberated person helps another liberated person. If the life of the endangered liberated person is not valuable enough for that liberated person to save themselves, and the second liberated person is already liberated anyway, what could be the merit in saving them? Yet the expectation is that the saint does not turn away from the person in need on recognizing them as a liberated person. Again, all of this is avoided on my view, and the avoidance of this complexity is another reason to prefer it.
21 *mamedaṃ ityabhiniveśavarjitaḥ*.
22 *bhūmirāpo 'nalo vāyuḥ khaṃ mano buddhireva ca / ahaṅkāra itīyaṃ me bhinnā prakṛtiraṣṭadhā //*.
23 *abhimāno 'haṅkaras tasmād dvividhaḥ pravartate sargaḥ / ekādaśakaś ca gaṇas tanmātraḥ pañcakaścai'va //* (Larson's transliteration).
24 *dambhamānamadānvitāḥ*.
25 *karṣayantaḥ śarīrasthaṃ bhūtagrāmamacetasaḥ / māṃ caivāntaśśarīrasthaṃ tānviddhyāsuraniścayān //*.
26 See pp. 70–75 for a consideration of the view that the advice to eliminate selfishness is the advice to eliminate excessive self-interest, but that the advice to eliminate selfish desires amounts to the advice to eliminate all self-interested desires.
27 See chapters 5 and 6, for example.

5 Desireless action in the *Manusmṛti*

1 It should be kept in mind that the *Manusmṛti* is first and foremost a law text, not a philosophical text. Nonetheless, the *Manusmṛti's* commentators – especially Medhātithi – are strongly influenced by more straightforwardly philosophical literature, and deal with interpretive problems by utilizing a familiar philosophical methodology. Additionally, later texts and commentators – like Maṇḍana – cite the *Manusmṛti* itself when elaborating their own position. This suggests that the *Manusmṛti* is taken by classical Indian philosophers to be part of the broader philosophical tradition, if not exclusively so.
2 The word 'intention', like the word 'purpose', can refer either to the agent's end or means. If I choose to drink water and eat a salad rather than have a milk shake, as a means to losing weight, the word 'intention' might refer to that which I hope to achieve – losing weight – or that which I intend to do – drink water and eat a salad. Likewise, if I am asked my purpose, I might say "to lose weight" or "to eat a salad."
3 It might be, for example, that I have the intention to have a milk shake, but I still must reason about what further intentions to adopt as a means to this end. In this case, my intention to have a milk shake is an input into deliberation and some other intention – like the intention to go to the ice-cream shop – is an output. Likewise, I might reason from desires to further desires.
4 Alfred R. Mele says, "to intend to A is, at least in part, to be settled (but not necessarily irrevocably) on A-ing" (Mele 2003: 135). See my "Motivation-encompassing attitudes" for an argument against desires having this feature (Framarin 2008b).
5 It is reasonable to assume that Doniger and Smith have this commonsense conception of intention in mind, rather than some technical sense that diverges from this one, given their wide audience. B. K. Matilal, referring to *Manu* 2.2–2.5 in particular, translates *saṅkalpa* as 'determination' (Matilal 2002: 132), and this supports reading Doniger and Smith's 'intention' as consistent with

Bratman's analysis. Patrick Olivelle also translates *saṅkalpa* as 'intention' (Olivelle 2005: 94).

6 Olivelle also notes this (Olivelle 2005: 243).

7 Another alternative is that Manu uses *mūla* as a masculine noun. As Olivelle points out, however, it "is used throughout by Manu as a neuter noun" (ibid.). My thanks to an anonymous reviewer at *Journal of Indian Philosophy* for pointing this out.

8 This question and response is from an opponent, but Medhātithi does not reject the analysis.

9 *atha ko ayaṃ saṅkalpo nāma yaḥ sarvakriyāmūlam ucyate / yaccetaḥsandarśanaṃ nāma yadanantaraṃ prārthanādhyavasāyau krameṇa bhavataḥ / ete hi mānasā vyāpārāḥ sarvakriyāpravṛttiṣu mūlatāṃ pratipadyante / na hi bhautikā vyāpārāstamantareṇa sambhavanti / tathāhi – prathamaṃ padārthasvarūpanirūpaṇam ayaṃ padārtha imāmarthakriyāṃ sādhayatīti yajñānaṃ sa iha saṅkalpo 'bhipretaḥ /.*

10 Compare Hume: "It can never in the least concern us to know, that such objects are causes, and such others effects, if both the causes and effects be indifferent to us" (Hume 1992: 414).

11 *anena karmaṇedamiṣṭam phalaṃ sādhyata ityevaṃviṣayā buddhiḥ saṅkalpaḥ /.*

12 *tathāhi bubhukṣita ādau bhujikriyāṃ paśyati tata icchati buhñjīyeti tato 'dhyavasyati / vyāpārāntarebhyo vinivṛttya bhojanaṃ karomīti tataḥ karmakaraṇasthānādhikāriṇa āha sajjīkuruta saravatīṃ sañcārayateti /.*

13 Typically, in the context of performing ritual acts, the word *saṅkalpa* does refer to the agent's intention. Often, *saṅkalpa* refers to the explict utterance of the agent's intention to perform a certain ritual (Monier-Williams 1998: 1126). It may even be that this is the sense of the word in the original *Manusmṛti* verse. Nonetheless, it is clear that at least in this passage, both Medhātithi and Kullūkabhaṭṭa understand *saṅkalpa* differently. If anything, they claim that the agent's *adhyavasāya* sets their goal of performing a certain action. It should be kept in mind, then, that I do not mean to recommend the translation of *saṅkalpa* as 'belief' wherever it occurs in the *Manusmṛti* and its commentaries.

14 *akāmasya kriyā kācid dṛśyate neha karhicit / yadyaddhi kurute kiñcittattatkāmasya ceṣṭitaṃ //.*

15 *neha loke kahicitkadācidapi jāgradavasthāyāṃ kriyā kācidanuṣṭheyatvenānicchataḥ sambhavati /.*

16 *nityeṣu phalābhilāṣalakṣaṇaḥ /.*

17 *kāmātmatā na praśastā na caivehāstyakāmatā / kāmyo hi vedādhigamaḥ karmayogaśca vaidikaḥ /.*

18 *phalābhilāṣaḥ karmapravṛtterheturyasya sa kāmātmā tadbhāvaḥ kāmātmatā /.*

19 *sarvameva kriyānuṣṭānaṃ phalasiddhyarthaṃ na svarūpaniṣpattaye /.*

20 *taditamāpatitam na kiṃcitkenacitkartavyaṃ sarvaistūṣṇīṃbhūtaiḥ sthātavyam /.*

21 *vidvadbhiḥ sevitaḥ sadbhirnityamadveṣarāgibhiḥ / hṛtidayenābhyanujñāto yo darmastaṃ nibodhata //.*

22 The *pūrvapakṣin* offers these objections in the reverse order. For these and the *pūrvapakṣin's* third objection, see Appendix i.

23 See p. 141 for Medhātithi's own assessment of the view of the *Gītā*.

24 Medhātithi attributes the more austere view to the Advaitins in his commentary to *Manusmṛti* 2.5 (see p. 141).

25 *yattāvaduktaṃ kāmyeṣu sauryādiṣu niṣedhaprasaṅga iti tatra vakṣyati yathāsaṅkalpitāṃśceha sarvān kāmān samaśnuta iti / niṣedhe hi kutaḥ saṅkalpaḥ kutaśca kāmāvāptiḥ /.*

26 Verse 2.5 reads:

> The person living rightly with regard to these [desires] goes to the state of being in the immortal world. Additionally they attain all desires in this world

as they are thought [of] (*saṅkalpitāṃ*) (*teṣu samyata vartamāno gacchatyamaralokatām / yathā saṅkalpitāṃśceha sarvānkāmānsamaśnute //*).

(Dave 1972–1985: 159, lines 29–30)

27 It might be that while the *Manusmṛti* does not prohibit the desires that motivate *kāmyakarmas*, it nonetheless discourages them.
28 *nityeṣu phalaṃ nābhisandhayam aśrutatvāt / . . . na hyabhisandhimātrātpramāṇato 'navagate phalasādhanatve phalamutpadyate /.*
29 Hence Medhātithi rejects the Mīmāmsa claim that when *phala* is not mentioned, the *phala* of heaven should be inferred (see Appendix i).
30 "Then which [desire] is prohibited? In the case of *nityakarmas*, a desire characterized by *phala* [is prohibited]." *kiṃ tarhi nityeṣu phalābhilāṣalakṣaṇaḥ /.*
31 *sādhanasampattistu kāmyaiva /.*
32 It must be remembered that a desire to do is a desire to perform a specific action, not a more generic desire to do something or other.
33 As I mentioned above, *adhyavasāya* (purpose) is also a necessary condition of action. My point here is that the belief that motivates the desire to do and the desire to do itself are the only beliefs and desires that are necessary conditions of action.
34 Even Kant should admit that the properly motivated agent tells the truth rather than lies, because it is in accord with the moral law. That is, their reason for telling the truth is that telling the truth is in accord with the moral law.
35 *tatra nityānāṃ pratyavāyānutpattirvidhyarthasampattirvā prayojanam /.*
36 A note of warning: there is little evidence in the *Manusmṛti* itself to suggest that *prayojana/hetu* is a distinct state. It may be, for example, that the agent has a *prayojana/hetu* simply in virtue of their pursuing some state of affairs. A number of philosophers (e.g., Nagel, Schueler, Vadas, and others) have pointed out that action entails that the agent has some reason or purpose, but that it does not entail that the agent has some mental state called their purpose.
37 The Agnihotra sacrifice is a daily morning sacrifice. For a description, see Dumont (1964).
38 *aphalākāṅkṣibhiryajño vidhidṛṣṭo ya ijyate / yaṣṭavyameveti manaḥ samādhyāya sa sāttvikaḥ // abhisandhāya tu phalaṃ dambhārthamapi caiva yat / ijyate bharataśreṣtha taṃ yajñaṃ viddhi rājasam //.*
39 *yaḥ śāstravidhimutsṛjya vartate kāmakārataḥ / na sa siddhimavāpnoti na sukhaṃ na parāṃ gatim // tasmācchāstraṃ pramāṇam te kāryākaryavyavasthitau / jñātvā śāstravidhānoktaṃ karma kartumihārhasi //.*
40 Even the passages above can be interpreted to refer to all actions, since Kṛṣṇa advises Arjuna to make all actions an offering to him. "That which you do, that which you eat, that which you offer [in sacrifice], that which you give, that austerity which you perform, O Arjuna, do that as an offering to me!" (*yatkaroṣi yadaśnāsi yajjuhoṣi dadāsi yat / yattapasyasi kaunteya tat kuruṣva madarpaṇam*) // (9.27, Sadhale 1985b: 182, lines 12–13). If all actions are a sacrifice to Kṛṣṇa, then all actions should be done without desire for *phala*.
41 *karmaṇyevādhikāraste mā phaleṣu kadācana / mā karmaphalaheturbhṣrmā te saṅgo 'stvakarmaṇi //.*
42 *buddhau śaraṇamanviccha kṛpaṇāḥ phalahetavaḥ // karmajaṃ buddhiyuktā hi phalaṃ tyaktvā manīṣiṇaḥ / janmabandhavinirmuktāḥ padaṃ gacchantyanāmayam //.*
43 A *naimittikakarma* is an occasional *karma* – performed at a certain time of year, for example – for which no *phala* is mentioned.
44 *yāmimāṃ puṣpitāṃ vācaṃ pravadantyavipaścitaḥ / vedavādaratāḥ pārtha nānyadastīti vādinaḥ // kāmātmānaḥ svargaparā janmakarmaphalapradām / kriyāviśeṣabahumāṃ bhogaiśvaryagatiṃ prati // bhogaiśvaryaprasaktānāṃ tayā 'pahṛtacetasām / vyavasāyātmikā buddhiḥ samādhau na vidhīyate //.*

45 *brahmavādinastu sauryādīnāṃ niṣedhārthaṃ kāmātmateti manyante / phalārthitayā kriyamāṇā bandhātmakā bhavanti /.*

46 Monier-Williams says that Kṛṣṇadvaipāyana refers to Vyāsa, author of the *Mahābhārata* and the Purāṇas (Monier-Williams 1998: 307).

47 *taduktaṃ bhagavatā kṛṣṇadvaipāyanena mā karmaphalaheturbhūḥ / tathā sādhanānāmakṛtsnatvānmaurkhyātkarmakṛtastathā / phalasya cābhisandhānāda-pavitro vidhiḥ smṛtaḥ iti /.* I could not find the source of the second quotation in the *Gītā*. It might be a paraphrase. Dave offers the first citation (Dave 1972–1985: 160, line 23).

48 Presumably an action fails in this context when it produces *karma.*

49 *tasmādasaktaḥ satataṃ kāryaṃ karma samācara / asakto hyācaran karma paramāpnoti pūruṣaḥ //.*

50 *pravṛttiṃ ca nivṛttiṃ ca kāryākārye bhayābhaye / bandhaṃ mokṣaṃ ca yā vetti buddhiḥ sā pārtha sātvikī //.*

51 *saktāḥ karmaṇyavidvāṃso yathā kurvanti bhārata / kuryādvidvāṃstathāsaktaścikīrṣur – lokasaṃgraham //.*

52 N. Lash (1997: 6) and D. Killingley (1997: 73) emphasize this point in their analyses of desireless action in the *Gītā.*

53 See also Radhakrishnan (1911: 465, 473 and 1914: 177), Tattvabhushan (1912: 292), Upadhyaya (1969: 163), and Sharma (1985: 191).

54 D. C. Mathur says, "the Gita's doctrine of ethics is deontological since it exhorts us to do our duties because they are our duties without regard to any consequences they lead to" (Mathur 1974: 36).

6 Desireless action in the *Nyāyasūtra* and *Brahmasiddhi*

1 R. Minor summarizes the passages in the *Gītā* that seem to characterize *mokṣa* both positively and negatively (Minor 1982: 77).

2 *nityaṃ sukhamātmano mahattvavat tattu mokṣe abhivyajyate tenābhivyaktenā 'tyantaṃ vimuktaḥ sukhī bhavatīti kecit manyante /.*

3 *ihāyaṃ lokaḥ pravartamāna iṣṭādhigamārthaṃ pravartate / pravartante ca mokṣamāṇāḥ / teṣāmapīṣṭādhigamārthayā pravṛttyā bhavitavyam seyaṃ pravṛttirnityasukhe 'rthavatī nānyatheti /.*

4 It only follows that the *mumukṣu* must believe that *mokṣa* is pleasurable, not that *mokṣa* really is pleasurable. These philosophers were willing to grant that the *mumukṣus* were not wrong about this. As A. Chakrabarti points out, the argument assumes that "if *mokṣa* consists of permanent pleasure it would be known to do so by the *mumukṣu*" (Chakrabarti 1983: 172).

5 *yadi punarayaṃ sañcakṣāṇako mokṣe nityaṃ sukhamiti sukharāgeṇa pravartate na mucyeta / kasmāt rāgasya bandhanasamājñānāt /.*

6 *atra kecit ānandātma katve brahmaṇaḥ ānandarāgānmumukṣupravṛttiḥ syāt rāganibandhanā ca pravṛttiḥ saṃsārabījamiti na muktaye syāt.*

7 *na pravṛttidvaitadarśanāt / dve pravṛttī loke dṛṣṭe iṣṭādhigamārthāniṣṭādihānārthā ca /.*

8 *yadyapi dveṣāt pravartate duḥkhaṃ hāsyāmīti tathāpi na mucyeta dveṣasya bandhanasamājñānāditi rāgadvaiṣau hi bandhanamiti /.*

9 *na apratikūlatvāt / apratikūlaṃ duḥkhahānaṃ bhavati / na punarayaṃ duḥkhaṃ dveṣṭi / adviṣaṃścāya pravartamāno 'pratikūlaṃ duḥkhahānamadhigacchatīti //.*

10 It is clearer in Vacaspati's commentary that this line of reasoning is meant as an argument. Since *dveṣa*, like *rāga*, precludes the attainment of *mokṣa*, and since the *mumukṣu's* avoidance of pain does not preclude the attainment of *mokṣa*, it cannot be that the *mumukṣu* is motivated by *dveṣa*. "Since pursuing eternal bliss is counter-productive, [because it is motivated] by attachment, which is counter-productive to [the attainment of] *mokṣa*, [therefore] the complete elimination of

duḥkha is not attended by *dveṣa*" (*na apratikūlatvāt / yathā nityasukhopādānaṃ mokṣam apratikūlayā saktyā apratikūlaṃ naivamātyantikaduḥkhahānaṃ duḥkhad-veṣānuṣaktam /*) (Thakur 1967: 459, lines 24–25). Of course, a parallel response seems open to the Vedāntin (see pp. 150–151).

11 Compare *Yogasūtra* 2.8.

12 *dveṣaḥ krodho manyurityanarthāntaram / jvalanātmako hi sa bhavati / naivaṃ vai-rāgyam /.*

13 *na ca rāganibandhanā tatra pravṛttiḥ / na hīcchāmātraṃ rāgaḥ / . . . cetasaḥ prasādo 'bhirucirabhīcchā na rāgapakṣe vayvasthāpyate.*

14 One problem with Balasubramanian's interpretation is that he understands *icchā* and *rāga* as mutually exclusive. It is clear from both Maṇḍana and Saṅkhapāṇi, however, that *rāga* is a subset of *icchā* (see p. 169, and Appendix iii).

15 See p. 101 for a more thorough analysis of Chakrabarti's position. In the end I suspect his position is closer to mine than these quotations suggest.

16 *śāntasya dāntasya cātmani darśanamucyate na cānandarāgāti pravartamānaḥ śānto bhavati /.*

17 Śaṅkhapāṇi makes this explicit: "*prasāda, abhiruci,* [and] *abhīcchā* – this is an indication of synonymy" (*prasādo 'abhirucirabhīccheti paryāyanirdeśaḥ*) (Vacaspati and Sastri 1984: 11, lines 23–24).

18 The *śruti* cited is *Bṛhadāraṇyaka Upaniṣad* 4.4.23.

19 *adhunā bhavatu sā rāgaḥ tathāpi na sā śāntatādiśrutyā niṣidhyate.*

20 *āpūryamāṇamacalapratiṣṭaṃ samudramāpaḥ praviśanti yadvat / tadvatkāmā yaṃ praviśanti sarve sa śāntimāpnoti na kāmakāmī /.*

21 I mean for this to be a rather loose way of talking about the relationship between desires and desire sensations. Perhaps certain desires are in part constituted by sensations rather than accompanied by them. Nothing I say depends on getting this relationship exactly right.

22 *muktasaṅgo 'nahaṃvādī dhṛtyutsāhasamanvitaḥ / siddhyasiddhyornirvikāraḥ kartā sāttvika ucyate //.*

23 The words *na dveṣṭi* are the same as those that Uddyotakara uses to characterize the properly motivated *mumukṣu* above.

24 *yaḥ sarvatrānabhisnehastattat prāpya śubhāśubham / nābhinandati na dveṣṭi tasya prajñā pratiṣṭitā //.*

25 *atha kena prayukto 'yaṃ pāpaṃ carati pūruṣaḥ /.*

26 *kāma eṣa krodha eṣa.*

27 *sa eṣa kāmaḥ pratihataḥ kenacitkrodhatvena pariṇamate /* Rāmānuja understands the verse in this way as well.

28 *kāmātkrodho 'bhijāyate //.*

29 Note that this does not mean that all desires in fact produce these sensations. I might manage to satisfy a desire without feeling joy. The point here is that under different circumstances, the desire might produce joy (or disappointment).

30 One day a friend of mine told me that he did not care whether Barack Obama or Hillary Clinton won the Democratic nomination for President. A few weeks later, he said, "I didn't think I had a preference, but I noticed that when Hillary lost, I felt disappointed. So I guess I want Hillary to get the nomination."

31 *na punaricchāmātramanena niṣidhyate tadāha na caivehāstyakāmateti / yato vedas-vīkaraṇaṃ vaidikasakaladharmasaṃbandhaścecchāviṣaya eva /.*

32 One might object that a purpose, like a desire, disposes the agent to joy or disappointment, depending on whether the purpose is fulfilled or not. See Conclusion.

33 See Framarin (2006b: 607–608).

34 Of course, the Humean might insist that the person could not have adopted the purpose without perceiving it as a means to the satisfaction of some desire of their own. Even if this is correct, however, it does not follow that the purpose itself

disposes the agent to joy or disappointment. It could just as well be the desire from which the purpose is derived that disposes them.

35 *alaṃ pratyayo hi sa.*

36 Remember that Śaṅkara characterizes *rāga* in terms of *abhiniveśa* as well (see Chapter 4).

37 *tattvadarśanavaimalyāttu tattve cetasaḥ prasādo 'bhirucirabhīcchā na rāgapakṣe vyavasthāpyate yathā saṃsārāsāratātattvadarśananiṣpanno nodvegastato dveṣa-pakṣe.*

38 Alternatively, (BS1) could be diagrammed so that *icchā* produces both *kāma* and *karma* directly. If mere *icchā* can motivate action without *kāma*, then perhaps *kāma* arises without playing any role in motivating the action.

39 *neṣṭamaniṣṭenānanubaddhaṃ sambhavatīti aniṣṭānubandhāt iṣṭamapyaniṣṭaṃ sam-padyate aniṣṭahānāya ca ghaṭamāna iṣṭamapi jahāti vivekahānasyāśakyatvāditi* /.

40 This does not entail that Maṇḍana accepts that action might be motivated by *udvega* or *dveṣa*. It is noteworthy, however, that unlike the Vedāntin *pūrvapakṣin* of the *Nyāyasūtra*, nothing that Maṇḍana says implies its denial.

41 It is not clear that Maṇḍana admits that *udvega* might motivate action without the help of *dveṣa*.

42 *na hi tapasvī tapāṃsīcchan rāgītyucyate loka iti bhāvaḥ* /.

7 A defense of desireless action

1 As I stipulated in Chapter 1, my distinction between desires for means and desires for ends corresponds to Nagel's distinction between motivated and unmotivated desires.

2 Smith's use of the word 'seems' is merely stylistic here. Smith's position is that motivating reasons are indeed psychological states.

3 This way of analyzing Anscombe's distinction comes from Mark Platts (1979: 257).

4 For a consideration of the objection that Smith's use of perception to define belief is circular, see David Sobel and David Copp (2001: 46–48).

5 Nick Zangwill (1998) and others point out that these are not functions that beliefs and desires tend to perform, but functions that beliefs and desires ought to perform. Smith seems to drop the normative aspect from these functions, even though they are central in both Anscombe's and Platts' (whom Smith also cites extensively) analyzes. In Smith's defense, he does cite rationality as a condition of normative beliefs causing corresponding desires (Smith 1994: 180), which implies that normative beliefs should, but might not, perform the function of causing corresponding desires. See pp. 117–118 for the relevant passage from Smith.

6 Hence the argument is not obviously different from the argument that Pettit and Smith offer in an earlier paper:

> P1: Having a reason to ϕ, specifically a motivating reason to ϕ, is having a goal: say the goal that p.
>
> P2: Having such a goal is being disposed, given appropriate beliefs, to act so that p.
>
> P3: And being so disposed is desiring that p.
>
> C: Hence having a reason to ϕ, specifically a motivating reason to ϕ, is desiring that p.
>
> (Pettit and Smith 1990: 573)

I point this out because I make the case for the claim that talk of directions of fit is finally a red herring (see p. 117).

7 Following Hume, Bricke draws the distinction between desire and aversion.

> Someone with a reason *not* to act in a certain way is in a similar goal-directed, practical state . . . The individual has a con-attitude with respect to acting in the way in question. For simplicity's sake we may take a con-attitude to be a pro-attitude with respect to not acting in a certain way. What could such a pro-attitude be but a desire with negative content, a desire not to act in a certain way?
>
> (Bricke 1996: 16, italics in original)

These two claims mirror the two objections offered by the Naiyāyikas and Vedāntins. If an agent is motivated to pursue some positive end, then they are motivated by a desire. If an agent is motivated to pursue some negative end, then they are motivated by an aversion, which may also be characterized as a desire. Combined, the two claims seem to contradict the advice to act without desire – at least if it is taken literally.

8 Two distinctions are important here. First, a desire for an end is a desire that the agent does not have for a reason. Hence this claim does not apply to desires for ends. Second, I assume that a desire for a means is rationally arrived at, where 'rational' means that the agent reasons – with or without cogency, and with or without being fully aware that they are reasoning – to their desire for a means. As I pointed out in Chapter 2, my distinction between desires for means and desires for ends parallels Nagel's distinction between motivated and unmotivated desires.

9 It is worth noting that Pettit and Smith take the preceding argument to be convincing in their paper "Backgrounding Desire" (Pettit and Smith 1999).

10 Smith mentions that McDowell (1978) and McNaughton (1988) make this point.

11 Mele offers a nice example of this basic intuition, which he calls 'the problem of listlessness' (Mele 2003: 113).

12 Smith's argument is only superficially dissimilar from the argument that Pettit and Price call the 'bare functional argument':

> Let Bx be the total set of beliefs held by an agent X, and suppose that X performs action A. Could A be explained by Bx alone? The [anti-Humean] seems bound to think that it could . . . But surely this can't be right, for isn't it perfectly conceivable that another agent might be in the same belief state Bx and not do A?
>
> (Pettit and Price 1989: 163)

For additional objections to this argument, see Pettit and Price 1989.

13 I take this term from William Kneale (1949). My thanks to John Baker for referring me to Kneale.

14 Another possibility is that it is the perception itself that eliminates the belief. This cannot be right, however, because sometimes an agent weighs their belief against the evidence of a perception and chooses to retain the belief. Surely neither the perception nor the belief perform this function.

15 In Smith's defense, this latter function of desires is much less important to Smith's overall point. It may be that he ignores it in the passage under discussion for this reason. Still, it is hard to imagine that Smith did not at least consider how he would make the latter function fully explicit.

16 Smith and others have argued that the term 'desire' might be taken broadly, to include any mental state with world-to-mind direction of fit.

> [I]f 'desire' is not a suitably broad category of mental state to encompass all of those states with the appropriate direction of fit, then the Humean may simply define the term 'pro-attitude' to mean 'psychological state

> with which the world must fit', and then claim that motivating reasons are constituted, inter alia, by pro-attitudes.
>
> (Smith 1994: 117)

If this broader category is adopted, however, then at least some normative beliefs are desires!

Conclusion

1 I say 'so-called *rāga*' in order to reflect Maṇḍana's claim that the motivating state he endorses "does not fall on the side of *rāga*." (see Chapter 6 and Appendix iii).
2 *tathottamasukharāgāditarasmādupanatādapi nivṛttiḥ* /.
3 *evaṃ tāvattatvabhūtanityaniratiśayānandecchā na rāgo bhavatītyuktam* /.
4 *tatparipanthitadalpakṣayiviṣayasukhecchā.*
5 *aniṣṭoparamārtho mokṣopadeśaḥ pravṛttiśca mumukṣūṇāmiti* /.

Appendix i

1 All references to Medhātithi's *Manubhāṣya* refer to Dave (1972–1985).
2 To complicate matters even further, there are also cases in which no *phala* is mentioned, and the words 'as long as life' are absent, but for which no *phala* can be assumed. My thanks to Arindam Chakrabarti for pointing this out.
3 Monier-Williams says that Kṛṣṇadvaipāyana refers to Vyāsa, author of the *Mahābhārata* and the Purāṇas (Monier-Williams 1998: 307).

Appendix ii

1 All references to Vātsyāyana's *Nyāyadarśanabhāṣya*, Uddyotakara's *Nyāyabhāṣyavārttika* and Vācaspatimiśra *Nyāyavārttikatātparyaṭīkā* refer to Thakur (1967).
2 Chakrabarti mentions that some Kashmīrī Naiyāyikas reject this position, and accept a view more like the Vedāntins' (Chakrabarti 1983: 171).
3 The sense capacities are distinct from the physical organs that they inhabit. The capacity of sight, for example, is not identical with the eye, since a person may have an eye but be unable to see. So the sense capacities mentioned here are not simply parts of the body.

Appendix iii

1 All references to Maṇḍana's *Brahmasiddhi* and Śaṅkhapāṇi's *Brahmasiddhivyākhyā* refer to Vacaspati and Sastri (1984). One oddity of the edited volume is that the authors paginate Śaṅkhapāṇi's *Brahmasiddhivyākhyā* beginning with the number one, even though it follows the *Brahmasiddhi* within the same volume. This should be kept in mind when referencing these texts.

References

Primary Sanskrit texts

Bhagavadgītā, in Sadhale (1985a–c).
Bhagavadgītābhāṣya. Rāmānuja, in Sadhale (1985a–c).
Bhagavadgītābhāṣya. Śaṅkara, in Sadhale (1985a–c).
Bhāṣāpariccheda. Nyāya-Pañcānana, Viśvanātha, in Mādhavānanda (1954).
Brahmasiddhi. Maṇḍanamiśra, in Vacaspati and Sastri (1984).
Brahmasiddhivyākhyā. Śaṅkapāṇi, in Vacaspati and Sastri (1984).
Manvartha Muktāvalī. Kullūkabhaṭṭa, in Dave (1972–1985).
Manusmṛtibhāṣya. Medhātithi, in Dave (1972–1985).
Nyayāyadarśanabhāṣya. Vātsyāyana, in Thakur (1967).
Nyāyabhāṣyavārttika. Uddyotakara, in Thakur (1967).
Nyāyavārttikatātparyaṭīkā. Vācaspati, in Thakur (1967).
Sāṃkhyakārika. Īśvarakṛṣṇa, in Larson (1979).
Yogasūtra. Patañjali, in Sārvabhauma and Nyāyaratna (1970).
Yogasūtrabhāṣya. Vyāsa, in Sārvabhauma and Nyāyaratna (1970).

Edited volumes of Sanskrit texts

Dave, J. H. (ed.) (1972–1985) *Manusmṛtiḥ: Medhātithi – Sarvajñanārāyaṇa – Kullūka – Rāghvānanda – Nandana – Rāmacandra – Manirāma – Govindarāja – Bhāruci iti vyākhyānavakena samalaṅkṛta*, Mumbai: Bharatiya Vidya Bhavanam.

Larson, G. J. (ed.) (1979) *Classical Sāṃkhya: An Interpretation of its History and Meaning* (2nd edn), Delhi: Motilal Banarsidass.

Mādhavānanda (ed.) (1954) *Bhāsā-Pariccheda with Siddhānta-Muktāvalī*, Calcutta: Avaita Ashrama.

Sadhale, S. G. S. (ed.) (1985a) The Bhagavad-Gītā *with Eleven Commentaries*, vol. 1, Delhi: Parimal Publications.

Sadhale, S. G. S. (ed.) (1985b) The Bhagavad-Gītā *with Eleven Commentaries*, vol. 2, Delhi: Parimal Publications.

Sadhale, S. G. S. (ed.) (1985c) The Bhagavad-Gītā *with Eleven Commentaries*, vol. 3, Delhi: Parimal Publications.

Sārvabhauma, D. and Nyāyaratna, S. T. (eds) (1970) *Sāṅga Yogadarśana or Yoga Darśana of Patañjali with the Scholium of Vyāsa and the Commentaries – Tattva Vaiśārdi, Pātañjala Rahasya Yogavārttika and Bhāsvati of Vācaspati Miśra,*

Rabhavānanda Sarasvatī, Vijñāna Bhikṣu and Hariharānanda Āraṇya, Varanasi: Chaukhambha Sanskrit Bhawan.

Thakur, A. (ed.) (1967) *Nyāyadarśana of Gautama with Bhāṣya of Vātsyāyana, Vārttika of Uddyotakara, Tātparyaṭīkā of Vācaspati, and the Pariśuddhi of Udayana*, Varanasi: Mithila Institute.

Vacaspati, M. V. and Sastri, S. K. (eds) (1984) *Brahmasiddhi by Acharya Maṇḍanamiśra with Commentary by Śaṅkhapāṇi*, Delhi: Satguru Publications.

Translations of Sanskrit texts

Doniger, W. and Smith, B. K. (1991) *The Laws of Manu*, London: Penguin.

Olivelle, P. (1998) *Upaniṣads*, Oxford: Oxford University Press.

Olivelle, P. (2005) *Manu's Code of Law: A Critical Edition and Translation of the Mānava-Dharmaśāstra*, Oxford: Oxford University Press.

Texts in English

Agrawal, M. M. (1982) *The Philosophy of Non-attachment (The Way to Spiritual Freedom in Indian Thought)*, Delhi: Motilal Banarsidass.

Anscombe, G. E. M. (1976) *Intention*, Ithaca, NY: Cornell University Press.

Balasubramanian, R. (1976) *Advaita Vedanta*, Madras, India: Centre for Advanced Study in Philosophy, University of Madras.

Bratman, M. (1987) *Intention, Plans, and Practical Reason*, Cambridge, MA: Harvard University Press.

Bricke, J. (1996) *Mind and Morality: An Examination of Hume's Moral Psychology*, Oxford: Oxford University Press.

Brodbeck, S. (2004) 'Calling Kṛṣṇa's bluff: Non-attached action in the *Bhagavadgītā*', *Journal of Indian Philosophy*, vol. 32, 81–103.

Burley, M. (2007) *Classical Sāṃkhya and Yoga: An Indian Metaphysics of Experience*, New York: Routledge.

Chakrabarti, A. (1988) 'The end of life: A Nyāya-Kantian approach to the *Bhagavadgītā*', *Journal of Indian Philosophy*, vol. 16, 327–334.

Chakrabarti, A. (1983) 'Is liberation (*mokṣa*) pleasant?', *Philosophy East and West*, vol. 33, 167–182.

Chatterjea, T. (2002) *Knowledge and Freedom in Indian Philosophy*, Lanham, MD: Lexington Books.

Davidson, D. (1963) 'Actions, reasons, and causes', *Journal of Philosophy*, vol. 60, 685–686.

Dennett, D. C. (1998) *Brainstorms: Philosophical Essays on Mind and Psychology*, Cambridge, MA: MIT Press.

Dumont, P. (1964) 'The Agnihotra (or Fire-God oblation) in the *Taittirīya-Brāhmaṇa*', *American Philosophical Society*, vol. 108, 337–353.

Feinberg, J. (2005) 'Psychological egoism', in *Reason and Responsibility* (12th edn), ed. J. Feinberg and R. Shafer-Landau, Belmont, CA: Wadsworth/Thomson.

Fingarette, H. (2004) *Mapping Responsibility: Explorations in Mind, Law, Myth, and Culture*, Chicago, IL: Open Court Press.

Fort, A. O. and Mumme, P. Y. (1998) *Living Liberation in Hindu Thought*, Albany, NY: SUNY Press.

Framarin, C. G. (2006a) 'Motivation in the *Manusmṛti*', *Journal of Indian Philosophy*, vol. 34, 397–413.
Framarin, C. G. (2006b) 'The desire you are required to get rid of: A functionalist analysis of desire in the *Bhagavadgītā*', *Philosophy East and West*, vol. 56, 604–617.
Framarin, C. G. (2007) 'Good and bad desires: Implications of the dialogue between Kṛṣṇa and Arjuna', *International Journal of Hindu Studies*, vol. 11, 147–170.
Framarin, C. G. (2008a) 'Motivation in the *Nyāyasūtra* and *Brahmasiddhi*', *Religious Studies*, vol. 44, 43–61.
Framarin, C. G. (2008b) 'Motivation-encompassing attitudes', *Philosophical Explorations*, vol. 11, 121–30.
Framarin, C. G. (2008c) 'Unselfishness', *International Philosophical Quarterly*, vol. 48, 69–83.
Framarin, C. G. (2008d) 'The Use of *Lakṣanā* in Indian Exegesis', Paper Presentation, American Academy of Religions, Chicago, IL.
Framarin, C. G. (forthcoming) 'The problem with pretending: Rāmānujuna's arguments against *Jīvanmukti*', *Journal of Indian Philosophy*.
Framarin, C. G. (unpublished) 'The value of animals in Hinduism'.
Halbfass, W. (1991) *Tradition and Reflection: Explorations in Indian Thought*, Albany, NY: SUNY Press.
Hubin, D. C. (1999) 'What's special about Humeanism', *Nous*, vol. 33, 30–45.
Hume, D. (1951) *Enquiries Concerning the Human Understanding and Concerning the Principles of Morals* (2nd edn), Oxford: Clarendon Press.
Hume, D. (1992) *A Treatise of Human Nature* (2nd edn), Oxford: Clarendon Press.
Hursthouse, R. (1991) 'Arational actions', *The Journal of Philosophy*, vol. 88, 57–68.
Kant, I. (1995) *Foundations of the Metaphysics of Morals*, Upper Saddle River, NJ: Prentice Hall.
Kierkegaard, S. (1992) *Concluding Unscientific Postscript*, trans. Howard V. Hong and Edna H. Hong, Princeton, NJ: Princeton University Press.
Killingley, D. (1997) 'Enjoying the world: Desire (*kāma*) and the *Bhagavadgītā*', in *The Fruits of Our Desiring*, ed. Julius Lipner, Calgary, AB: Bayeux Arts.
Kim, J. (1997) *Philosophy of Mind*, Boulder, CO: Westview Press.
Kingsley, D. R. (1993) *Hinduism: A Cultural Perspective* (2nd edn), Upper Saddle River, NJ: Prentice Hall.
Kneale, W. (1949) *Probability and Induction*, Oxford: Clarendon Press.
Kripke, S. A. (1980) *Naming and Necessity*, Lanham, MD: Blackwell.
Krishna, D. (2007) 'The myth of the ethics of the *Puruṣārtha* or humanity's life-goals', in *Indian Ethics: Classical Traditions and Contemporary Challenges, Volume I*, ed. P. Bilimoria, J. Prabhu, and R. Sharma, Burlington, VT: Ashgate.
Lal, B. K. (1986) 'Hindu perspectives on the use of animals in science', in *Animal Sacrifice: Religious Perspectives on the Use of Animals in Science*, ed. T. Regan, Philadelphia, PA: Temple University Press.
Larson, G. (1969) *Classical Sāṃkhya: An Interpretation of its History and Meaning*, Delhi: Motilal Banarsidass.
Lash, N. (1997) 'The purification of desire', in *The Fruits of Our Desiring*, ed. Julius Lipner, Calgary, AB: Bayeux Arts.
Lenman, J. (1996) 'Belief, desire and motivation: An essay in quasi-hydraulics', *American Philosophical Quarterly*, vol. 33, 291–301.
McDowell, J. (1978) 'Are moral requirements hypothetical imperatives?' *Proceedings of the Aristotelian Society*, Supplementary Volume, 13–29.

McNaughton, D. (1988) *Moral Vision*, Malden, MA: Blackwell.
Mathur, D. C. (1974) 'The concept of action in the Bhagavad-Gita', *Philosophy and Phenomenological Research*, vol. 35, 34–45.
Matilal, B. K. (2002) *The Collected Essays of Bimal Krishna Matilal, Volume 2: Ethics and Epics*, Oxford: Oxford University Press.
Mele, A. R. (2003) *Motivation and Agency*, Oxford: Oxford University Press.
Minor, R. N. (1982) Bhagavad-Gītā: *An Exegetical Commentary*, Columbia, MO: South Asia Books.
Minor, R. N. (1986) *Modern Interpreters of the Bhagavadgita*, Albany, NY: SUNY.
Mohanty, J. N. (1997) 'The Idea of the Good in Indian Thought', in *A Companion to World Philosophies*, ed. E. Deutsch and R. Bontekoe, Oxford: Blackwell.
Mohanty, J. N. (2007) '*Dharma*, imperatives, and tradition: toward an Indian theory of moral action', in *Indian Ethics: Classical Traditions and Contemporary Challenges, Volume I*, ed. P. Bilimoria, J. Prabhu, and R. Sharma, Burlington, VT: Ashgate.
Monier-Williams, M. (1998) *A Sanskrit–English Dictionary*, Oxford: Oxford University Press.
Moore, G. E. (1903) *Principia Ethica*, Cambridge: Cambridge University Press.
Nagel, T. (1970) *The Possibility of Altruism*, Princeton, NJ: Princeton University Press.
Nelson, L. (1998) 'The dualism of non-dualism: Advaita Vedānta and the irrelevance of nature', in *Purifying the Earthly Body of God: Religion and Ecology in Hindu India*, ed. L. Nelson, Albany, NY: SUNY Press.
Nelson, L. (2000) 'Reading the *Bhagavadgītā* from an ecological perspective', in *Hinduism and Ecology*, ed. C. K. Chapple and M. E. Tucker, Cambridge, MA: Harvard University Press.
Pal, J. (2004) *Karma, Dharma, and Moksha: Conceptual Essays on Indian Ethics*, Delhi: Abhijeet Publications.
Parfit, D. (1984) *Reasons and Persons*, Oxford: Oxford University Press.
Perrett, R. W. (1993) 'Moral vegetarianism and the Indian tradition', in *Ethical and Political Dilemmas of Modern India*, ed. Ninian Smart and Shivesh Thakur, New York: St. Martin's Press.
Perrett, R. W. (1998) *Hindu Ethics: A Philosophical Study*, Honolulu: University of Hawaii Press.
Pettit, P. and Price, H. (1989) 'Bare functional desire', *Analysis*, vol. 49, 162–169.
Pettit, P. and Smith, M. (1990) 'Backgrounding desire' *Philosophical Review*, vol. 99, 565–592.
Plato (1987) *Euthyphro, Apology, Crito*, trans. F. J. Church, Upper Saddle River, NJ: Prentice Hall.
Platts, M. (1979) *Ways of Meaning*, London: Routledge & Kegan Paul.
Prasad, R. (1999) Varṇadharma, Niṣkāma Karma *and Practical Morality: A Critical Essay on Applied Ethics*, New Delhi: D. K. Printworld.
Quine, W. V. O. (1960) *Word and Object*, Cambridge, MA: MIT Press.
Radhakrishnan, S. (1911) 'The ethics of the Bhagavadgita and Kant', *International Journal of Ethics*, vol. 21, 465–475.
Radhakrishnan, S. (1914) 'The Ethics of the Vedanta', *International Journal of Ethics*, vol. 24, 168–183.
Raghavachar, S. S. (1998) *Rāmānuja on the Gītā*, Delhi: Advaita Ashram.
Railton, P. (1986) 'Moral realism', *The Philosophical Review*, vol. 95, 163–207.

Rambachan, A. (1993) *Gitamṛtam: The Essential Teachings of the Bhagavadgita*, Delhi: Motilal Banarsidass.

Regan, T. (1983) *The Case for Animal Rights*, Berkeley: University of California Press.

Rosati, C. (1995) 'Persons, perspectives, and full information accounts of the good', *Ethics*, vol. 105, 296–325.

Schueler, G. F. (1995) *Desire: Its Role in Practical Reasoning and Explanation of Action*, Cambridge, MA: MIT Press.

Shafer-Landau, R. (2003) *Moral Realism*, Oxford: Clarendon Press.

Sharma, A. (1985) 'The *Bhagavadgītā*: A Mīmāṃsic Approach' in *The Contemporary Essays on the Bhagavad Gītā* ed. Braj M. Sinha, New Delhi: Siddharth Publications.

Sharma, A. (2005) *Classical Hindu Thought: An Introduction*, New Delhi: Oxford University Press.

Smith, M. (1994) *The Moral Problem*, Lanham, MD: Blackwell.

Sobel, D. and Copp, D. (2001) 'Against direction of fit accounts of belief and desire', *Analysis*, vol. 61, 44–53.

Taber, J. (forthcoming) 'Did Dharmakīrti think the Buddha had desires?', in *Proceedings of the IVth International Dharmakīrti Conference*.

Tattvabhushan, S. (1912) 'Ethical science among the Hindus', *International Journal of Ethics*, vol. 22, 287–298.

Teschner, G. (1992) 'Anxiety, anger and the concept of agency and action in the *Bhagavadgītā*', *Asian Philosophy*, vol. 2, 61–77.

Upadhyaya, K. N. (1969) 'The *Bhagavad Gita* on war and peace', *Philosophy East and West*, vol. 19, 159–169.

Vadas, M. (1984) 'Affective and non-affective desire', *Philosophy and Phenomenological Research*, vol. 45, 273–279.

Webster, D. (2005) *The Philosophy of Desire in the Buddhist Pali Canon*, New York: Routledge/Curzon.

Whicher, I. (1998) *The Integrity of the Yoga Darśana: A Reconsideration of Classical Yoga*, Albany, NY: SUNY Press.

Williams, B. (1973) *Problems of the Self*, Cambridge: Cambridge University Press.

Woods, J. H. (2003) *Yoga System of Patanjali*, Delhi: Motilal Banarsidass.

Zaehner, R. C. (1969) The Bhagavad-Gītā, *with a Comentary Based on Original Sources*, Oxford: Clarendon Press.

Zangwill, N. (1998) 'Direction of fit and normative functionalism', *Philosophical Studies*, vol. 91, 173–203.

Index

abhilāṣa: 1, 83, 85, 127, 129, 133–4, 140

Bhagavadgītā/*Gītā*: x, xii, xv, 1–2, 4–5, 7–14, 16–19, 21–3, 29, 34, 40–8, 52, 57, 60–5, 68–71, 73–4, 77, 88–91, 93–4, 99–101, 108–12, 122–3, 141, 156–7,
Brahmasiddhi: x, xiv, 4, 93–112, 122–3, 155, 157, 173, 177, 184, 188–91
Brodbeck, S.: iii, xiv, 8–14, 40, 174, 190

Chakrabarti, A.: xii, xiv, 91, 98, 101, 173, 175, 184, 185, 188, 190
Chatterjea, T.: 21, 50, 61, 71, 91, 173, 179

desire(s)
- for ends: 23–4, 27–8, 30, 86, 90, 93–4, 103–4, 176, 187
- for means: 23, 27–8, 30, 51, 55, 57, 91, 94, 103–4, 110–11, 186–7
- for *mokṣa*: ix, 2, 15, 20, 41–59, 72, 98, 102, 109, 124, 178
- permissible/impermissible: ix, 2, 4–5, 23, 24, 29–30, 34–5, 39, 41–4, 58, 60–2, 72, 74, 97, 99–100, 123–4
- phenomenologically salient/non-salient: 2, 42, 93, 97–101, 109, 124, 154
- selfish/unselfish: ix–x, 2, 43, 60–76, 91, 109, 124, 180–1
- two senses of: xii, 4–5, 175

Doniger, W: 76–9, 181

hetu: 83, 86–7, 92, 103–4, 127, 132–3, 183
Hume, D./Humean/anti-Humean: x, xii–xiii, 16–18, 25–8, 76–7, 80–3, 87, 102, 110–18, 122, 175, 182, 185–7
Hursthouse, R.: 72

icchā: 1, 19, 27–8, 97–100, 103–8, 125, 127, 133–6, 138–9, 167–71, 174–5, 185–6, 189
intention: xiii, 6–7, 9–11, 13, 18, 69, 76–80, 87, 92, 137–8, 173–5, 181–2
intentional/non-intentional action: xii, 3–4, 6–13, 18, 136, 174, 178

kāma: 1, 18–19, 42–3, 46, 79–80, 83, 86–7, 92, 99, 101, 105, 128–9, 133–7, 139, 157, 164–6, 172, 175, 186
Kant, I.: xii, 16, 175, 183
Kullūkabhaṭṭa: 27, 79, 103–4, 176, 182

Lal, B. K.: 50, 179, 191

Maṇḍana: 95, 97–100, 102–3, 105–7, 109, 124–5, 155–64, 166–71, 173, 177, 180, 186, 188–9
Manusmṛti/Manu: x, xiv, 4, 6, 27, 76–93, 103–6, 110–12, 122, 127–9, 131–5, 137–8, 140, 170, 175, 177–8, 181–3, 188–91
Matilal, B. K.: 21, 61, 70, 89, 181, 192
Medhātithi: 79–81, 83–7, 90, 93, 103, 127–38, 140–1, 181–3
Mohanty, J. N.: 21, 91, 175, 192
mokṣa: ix, 2, 14–15, 20, 41–60, 65, 68, 72, 90, 93–9, 102–3, 106, 108–9, 124–6, 128, 136, 142–53, 157–8, 167–71, 177–9, 184

Nagel, T.: 67, 172, 176, 186–7
Nelson, L. 48–50, 179, 192
Nyāyasūtra: x, xiv, 2, 8, 72, 93–5, 98–112, 122–6, 142, 173, 184, 186

Olivelle, P.: 45, 172, 176, 182

Pal, J.: 6, 8, 17–8
Patañjali: 35–6, 38, 43, 109, 169
Perrett, R. 21–2, 53, 91, 179, 192
prakṛti: 12–14, 36–8, 40, 43–4, 46, 48, 65, 69
Prasad, R.: 6–8, 17, 173, 192
prayojana: 38, 86–7, 92–3, 103–5, 178, 183
purpose: 1, 4, 9, 10, 11–14, 18–21, 26–7, 33, 48, 51, 55, 59, 62, 77, 79–80, 83, 85–8, 91–3, 103–9, 112, 122–30, 132–3, 136–40, 143, 146–7, 149, 156–7, 167–9, 171, 174–5, 178, 181, 183, 185–6
puruṣa: 13, 20, 36–8, 40, 44, 64–5, 92, 174, 180

Railton, P.: 32–3
Rāmānuja: 8, 12–13, 46, 48, 52, 55, 65–6, 175–6, 179–80, 185, 189, 192
Rosati, C.: 32

Sāṃkhya: 10, 13, 69, 173–4
Sāṃkhyakārika: 13, 69, 189
saṅkalpa: 27, 75, 78–80, 85–7, 92, 131, 136–7, 181–2
Saṅkara: 8, 12–13, 46, 48, 65, 101, 156, 172–3, 175, 180, 186, 189
Śaṅkhapāṇi: 99, 102–3, 108, 125, 155, 167–71, 185
Schueler, G. F.: 4, 17, 18, 183, 193
Smith, M.: 32–3, 116–21, 177, 188
Smith, B. K.: 76–9, 181

Taber, J.: 172, 193
Teschner, G.: 8–14, 19–20, 40, 175, 193

Uddyotakara: 94–7, 142, 148–52, 154, 158, 168, 185

Vācaspatimiśra: 8, 98, 100–1, 105, 108, 125, 151–4, 158, 168, 184
Vātsyāyana: 94, 106, 125, 142, 144–52, 157–8
Vyāsa (commentator on *Yogasūtra*): 19, 35–9, 42–5, 57, 65, 84, 89, 92, 100–1, 109–12, 122–3, 168, 177–8

Whicher, I.: 39, 180
Williams, B.: 63, 104, 180

Yogasūtra: ix–x, 2, 19, 23–43, 169, 176–7, 185
Yogasūtrabhāṣya: 35–6, 39, 84, 89, 161, 165, 168, 177

Routledge

CPSIA information can be obtained
at www.ICGtesting.com
Printed in the USA
BVHW04s2243190718
521993BV00002B/44/P

9 780415 627573